STUDIES IN LAW, POLITICS, AND SOCIETY

STUDIES IN LAW, POLITICS, AND SOCIETY

Series Editors: Austin Sarat and Patricia Ewick

Volumes 1–2:	Edited by Rita J. Simon
Volume 3:	Edited by Steven Spitzer
Volumes 4–9:	Edited by Steven Spitzer and Andrew S. Scull
Volumes 10–16:	Edited by Susan S. Sibey and Austin Sarat
Volumes 17–27:	Edited by Austin Sarat and Patricia Ewick

STUDIES IN LAW, POLITICS, AND SOCIETY VOLUME 28

STUDIES IN LAW, POLITICS, AND SOCIETY

EDITED BY

AUSTIN SARAT

Department of Law, Jurisprudence & Social Thought and Political Science, Amherst College, USA

PATRICIA EWICK

Department of Sociology, Clark University, USA

Emerald

United Kingdom – North America – Japan
India – Malaysia – China

Emerald Group Publishing Limited
Howard House, Wagon Lane, Bingley BD16 1WA, UK

Reprints and permission service
Contact: booksandseries@emeraldinsight.com

British Library Cataloguing in Publication Data
A catalogue record for this book is available from the British Library

ISBN: 978-0-7623-1015-9
ISSN: 1059-4337 (Series)

CONTENTS

PART III. THE CHALLENGES OF (AND TO) RIGHTS

LIST OF CONTRIBUTORS

Yasmin A. Dawood	Political Science, University of Chicago, USA
Jonathan Goldberg-Hiller	Political Science, University of Hawaii, Manoa, USA
Patrick Hanafin	Law, Birkbeck College, USA
Thomas M. Hawley	Political Science, University of Hawaii, Manoa, USA
Matthew J. Moore	Political Science, Johns Hopkins University, USA
Ellen S. Podgor	Law, Georgia State University, USA

EDITORIAL BOARD

PART I.
ISSUES IN CONSTITUTIONAL INTERPRETATION

REVISITING CONSTITUTIONAL INTERPRETATION: A COMPARATIVE PERSPECTIVE ON THE AMERICAN DEBATES

Matthew J. Moore

ABSTRACT

The author argues that the familiar distinction between interpretive and non-interpretive theories of constitutional interpretation obscures another important distinction: that between hermeneutically open and hermeneutically closed theories. Closed theories seek resolution to constitutional conflict by employing methods of interpretation that are intuitively persuasive. Open theories deny that such methods are always available, and seek resolution of conflict through a combination of legal, political, and social means. The author argues that closed theories have failed to live up to their implicit promise of self-justification, and examines the practice of constitutional interpretation in Canada and Australia to support this view.

INTRODUCTION

Although the question of the proper methodology of constitutional interpretation is a perennial issue in American legal scholarship, in the late 1980s the conversation reached what seems to have been an historic peak of both volume and intensity.

Studies in Law, Politics, and Society
Studies in Law, Politics, and Society, Volume 28, 3–31

ISSN: 1059-4337/PII: S1059433702280011

Just over ten years later, the debates have cooled considerably, but not because the issues have been satisfactorily resolved.[1] Instead, a kind of stalemate has been reached, in which the various positions and criticisms are well known to all, and no new developments have arisen to tip the balance in favor of any particular methodology. In this essay, I propose that there are two ways of understanding the current stalemate. From one perspective, it is a failure, an inability to arrive at a consensus that is crucial to the success of democratic constitutionalism (I refer to theories taking this position as *hermeneutically closed*). From another perspective, the stalemate is to be expected in a diverse polity, and needn't necessarily stand in the way of our most basic political and legal commitments (I refer to such theories as *hermeneutically open*).[2]

To make sense of these two perspectives, I return to the interpretation debates from both a theoretical angle and a comparative angle. On the theoretical side, I propose a way of grouping the various positions – and thus what is at stake between them – that is different from the most common organizing schema. On the empirical side, I look at constitutional interpretation in Canada and Australia to suggest that one side of the interpretation debates (the closed theories) has not lived up to its implicit claim of being *self-justifying*. Finally, I return to theoretical analysis to examine more closely the promise and problems of open theories.

OPEN AND CLOSED APPROACHES TO INTERPRETATION

What is at issue in the interpretation debates is part of a more general concern: Profound and persistent disagreements over substantive policies and methods of arriving at them pose a problem for democracy. A democratic polity is only legitimate, according to the standard implicit in the idea of democracy itself, if its citizens feel represented by it. To the extent that the normal functioning of a democratic society results in the creation or maintenance of a body of citizens who feel merely caught in its institutions, rather than represented by them, that society is persistently failing to live up to its self-conception.[3] This raises the danger that a polity in this situation may be unable to perpetuate or foster institutional, social, and cultural frameworks necessary to support democracy. In other words, it is not clear whether democracy is possible when a polity is deeply divided not only over questions of policy, but, more importantly, over questions of how to resolve those substantive conflicts.[4]

Ironically, constitutionalism adds to the problem. One of the main purposes of adopting an entrenched constitution is to provide a standard for distinguishing between the normal give and take of politics (*someone* is likely to be unhappy about any major policy decision) and situations that violate the basic commitments of democracy (when, for example, some groups are persistently unable to pursue their important life aims). However, the creation of a standard immediately raises the questions of who will decide whether it has been violated, and of how they will go about doing so.

Because of our particular legal and political tradition, in the United States we generally discuss this problem in terms of the legitimacy and methodology of judicial review.[5] Although the question of the legitimacy of judicial review is still debated, the main focus of the debates of the 1980s was the methodology of interpretation. To address the problem of democratic legitimacy, a judicial interpretation of the constitution has to meet two criteria. First, it must resolve the substantive conflict in the case at hand, in a manner consistent with the polity's legal and political traditions. Second, the interpretation cannot itself become a new avenue for the controversy to continue.

There are a number of different schema in the literature for identifying and comparing general approaches to interpretation.[6] One of the most influential has been the distinction, in John Hart Ely's terms, between interpretive and non-interpretive approaches. Interpretive theories call for judges to "confine themselves to enforcing norms that are stated or clearly implicit in the written Constitution," while non-interpretive theories call for judges to "go beyond that set of references and enforce norms that cannot be discovered within the four corners of the document" (Ely, 1980, p. 1). One reason for this distinction's influence has been, I believe, that it points to two apparently intuitive approaches to justification: Use a method that is logically unassailable (what could be more obvious than to look at the text itself?); or, Refer to an authoritative source of extra-textual norms (isn't the point of the Constitution to entrench certain values?). Thus, on the interpretive side, we have theories that emphasize *procedure*, such as Judge Bork's emphasis on uncovering original intent (see e.g. Bork, 1985), Justice Scalia's emphasis on discovering original meaning (see e.g. Scalia, 1997), or even Ely's emphasis on the representation-reinforcing ethos of the Constitution. On the non-interpretive side we have theories that emphasize *norms*, such as Justice Brennan's vision of the Constitution as a living, adaptable document (see e.g. Brennan, 1986), or Ronald Dworkin's ideal of preserving the "integrity" of the legal tradition (see e.g. Dworkin, 1986).

What the interpretive/non-interpretive distinction obscures, or, rather, assumes, is that all of these theories are seeking what I call *hermeneutic closure*. That is, both procedure-based and norms-based theories are premised on the idea that a definitive interpretation can and must be arrived at and justified *by the use of the correct method*. On this view, what makes a decision definitive is that it is legitimate, and what makes it legitimate is that it was arrived at by using the correct method. Implicit in these theories is the idea that the correct method of interpretation is self-justifying. To prevent the interpretation from itself becoming the site of further controversy, the method has to be such that there could be no reasonable disagreement with it. Otherwise, the method becomes in some way contingent, a product of a particular history or tradition, which may itself be contested. To avoid the potential crisis in democracy threatened by profound differences of values, both interpretive and non-interpretive theories seek methods of interpreting the constitution that can achieve principled finality.

Much of the debate of the 1980s involved proponents of various interpretive and non-interpretive methodologies identifying flaws and weaknesses in the opposing view. Without reproducing those arguments in any detail, I would like to identify two general lines of criticism. The first is the argument that interpretive theories cannot work, because they inevitably invite an infinite regress of interpretation.[7] If we are to look only at the text, then how shall we interpret vague or general clauses? If we are to look at the original intent behind the constitution, then whose intent shall we look at, and how shall we determine it? If we are to look at the original meaning of the words of the constitution, then whose understanding of those meanings are relevant, and how do we plan to discover them? More generally, what assurance do we have that our understandings are accurate? More to the point, how can such methods put to rest these skeptical questions, so as to achieve hermeneutic closure?

The other general line of criticism challenges non-interpretive theories to justify their employment of non-textual norms.[8] The main argument is simple and powerful: If we expect the constitution to act as a restraint on the actions of government, including judges, we must avoid allowing values not "clearly implicit" in the constitution to influence interpretation, at the peril of making the constitution so porous as to be no restraint at all. No matter how valuable or authoritative the extra-textual norms may be, it is difficult to justify their use when the constitution makes no mention of them. A secondary line of argument repeats the main criticism of interpretivism: Even assuming that we could agree on a set of extra-textual norms to use in interpretation, how will we show that any particular decision is the uniquely correct implementation of them in the case at hand?

What these two lines of criticism together amount to is an argument against hermeneutic closure. They suggest that, while there may be many good reasons to adopt various methods of constitutional interpretation, none of them is capable of the kind of self-justification that seems to be necessary to avoid the crisis of democratic legitimacy. By assuming hermeneutic closure as the goal of interpretation, the division of theories into interpretive and non-interpretive makes it harder to see other possible solutions to the problem of democracy. However, there are a number of theorists who argue for a different understanding of the goal of interpretation. They generally hold that, while hermeneutic closure either cannot be had, or cannot be had by reference to a theory of interpretation, constitutional controversies can still be resolved in ways consistent with democracy.[9] In this broad camp, which I am calling *hermeneutically open*, we find thinkers such as Stanley Fish, Dennis Patterson, Owen Fiss, Philip Bobbitt, and Joseph Singer, among others.[10]

Although I will put off consideration of their positions for the moment, I want to identify two problems that hermeneutically open theories face. The first is the problem of indeterminacy. If we think that no theory of interpretation can be arrived at that will legitimate a single correct reading of the constitution, how will we ever arrive at interpretations in particular cases? Thus, it is not clear how open theories will satisfy the requirement that an adequate approach to interpretation make possible the resolution of the controversies that arise. The second problem is the same one faced by closed theories: avoiding the crisis of democratic legitimacy. Theorists of closed approaches have the advantage of providing an intuitively obvious set of solutions to this problem – employing logically persuasive procedures, or referring to a set of authoritative values. If theorists of open approaches deny that these approaches are possible (or that they are always available), the burden falls on them to show what other strategies of justification are available.

A COMPARATIVE PERSPECTIVE: CONSTITUTIONAL INTERPRETATION IN CANADA AND AUSTRALIA

Theories of interpretation have both a normative aspect and a quasi-empirical aspect. On the normative side, theories of interpretation are injunctions, commands to interpret in one way and not others. As I argued above, the point of these injunctions is to avoid the potential crisis of democratic legitimacy. But theories of interpretation also have a quasi-empirical side, in that they must not only be capable in principle of avoiding the crisis of legitimacy, they must actually do so. If and when a theory of interpretation itself becomes the object of inquiry or controversy, it must be possible to demonstrate its legitimacy.

Closed theorists assume an additional burden because the legitimacy of their theories rests on their intuitive plausibility and persuasiveness. Thus, for example, an open theory that holds that interpretations are justified if they are consistent with the existing traditions of interpretation in the polity,[11] relies not on the intuitive appeal of the methods, but rather on a concrete history of interpretation and debate about interpretation.[12] Closed theories intentionally avoid such explanations because they threaten the contingency that definitive interpretation is trying to forestall. Rather, closed theories have to rely for their justification either on the intuitive persuasiveness of their procedure, or on the intuitive authoritativeness of their norms.

Now if closed theories are correct in their assertion of their own intuitive persuasiveness, we would expect them to be both self-justifying and self-universalizing.

In other words, we would expect thoughtful people of goodwill who have looked into the matter to endorse only closed theories of interpretation. This, I believe, is a quasi-empirical hypothesis implicit in the search for hermeneutic closure.

It is not immediately obvious how one might go about testing this hypothesis. Clearly, it is not disprovable, because counter-evidence could always be attributed to a lack of understanding or good faith on the part of adherents of other views. However, I would like to suggest, if closed theories fail to live up to their implicit promise of self-justification, that gives us a reason or a motivation to look at them more critically, and to examine possible alternatives. My contention is that a combination of theoretical criticism and empirical counter-evidence would combine to give us good reasons to view hermeneutically closed theories skeptically, and to examine hermeneutically open theories carefully.

I believe a comparative empirical perspective is especially interesting, for two reasons. First, it forces us to make explicit the assumptions and presuppositions that underlie the familiar ideas and debates, and thus makes them available for critical assessment. Second, it allows us to see how familiar issues are debated in unfamiliar settings, and thus perhaps helps us to see them with fresh eyes.[13] I have chosen to look at constitutional interpretation in Canada and Australia because of the historical and structural similarities between those countries and the United States, in particular the shared common-law tradition, the presence of entrenched constitutions, and the relatively long traditions of judicial review. If closed theories developed in America are capable of propagation, I would expect to find them most prominently in legal systems similar to that of the United States.

To preview my tentative empirical conclusions, I suggest that we find two things of note. First, there does not seem to be convergence in practice on any one method of construction, either interpretive or non-interpretive. None of the extant theories has shown itself to be so superior to the others as to be the obvious winner, at least among courts in the U.S., Canada and Australia. Second, Canada and Australia have distinctive cultures of constitutional interpretation that differ from one another, and from that of the United States. This suggests, not surprisingly but contrary to the implicit assumptions of much of the debate, that the appeal of various interpretive theories is influenced by cultural and historical factors, in addition to their innate soundness.

Constitutional Interpretation in Canada: A Brief Overview

The Canadian Constitution[14] is built around the Constitution Act, 1867 (formerly known as the British North America Act), which established the basic framework of Canadian government. Under that act, the British Privy Council remained the court of last appeal for Canadian cases, and only the Imperial Parliament in London had the power of amendment. The Statute of Westminster (1931) limited the Imperial Parliament's power to legislate with regard to Canada to passing acts requested by the Canadian Parliament. However, the Privy Council remained the court of last appeal until 1949, when the Canadian Supreme Court took over that role. In that same year, the Canadian Parliament received the authority to amend the Constitution, so long as the changes did not infringe on provincial power. The Constitution was fully patriated by the Canada Act, 1982, through which the Canadian Parliament gained authority to amend the Constitution on all matters.[15] As part of the same act, the Canadian Charter of Rights and Freedoms was enacted as an entrenched bill of rights.[16]

As in the United States, there is a large Canadian literature about constitutional interpretation.[17] Interestingly, there seems to be little disagreement about how the Canadian Supreme Court actually interprets the Charter,[18] though there is some disagreement about whether the Court's method is justifiable.[19] There seems to be consensus, both on the Court itself and among commentators, that the Supreme Court interprets using a "purposive approach," and that this approach was developed over the course of a handful of seminal Charter cases.[20]

The first clear articulation came in *Hunter v. Southam* (1984). Lawson Hunter, the Director of Investigations and Research of the Combines Investigation Branch, authorized several of his investigative agents to search the offices of Southam, Inc. and remove documents relating to an investigation into unfair trade practices. As required by the Combines Investigation Act, Hunter's authorization of the search was certified by a member of the Restrictive Trade Practices Commission. Southam sought summary judgment on the grounds that the act was inconsistent with Section 8 of the Charter, which reads: "Everyone has the right to be secure against unreasonable search or seizure." A lower court found for Southam, and Hunter appealed to the Supreme Court.

Justice Dickson wrote for a Court that held unanimously for Southam: "[W]here it is feasible to obtain prior authorization, I would hold that such authorization is a precondition for a valid search and seizure" (Hunter, p. 161). "For such an authorization procedure to be meaningful it is necessary for the person authorizing the search to be able to assess the evidence . . . in an entirely neutral and impartial manner . . . The person performing this function need not be a judge, but he must at a minimum be capable of acting judicially" (Hunter, p. 162). Because the Restrictive Trade Practices Commission member was not impartial as regards an investigation of illicit business practices, and because the Combines Investigation Act did not specify standards for the authorization of searches, those sections of the act were found to be inconsistent with the Charter.

Justice Dickson's explanation of the Court's approach to interpreting the vague terms of Section 8 began to lay out the concept of purposive analysis:

> The *Canadian Charter of Rights and Freedoms* is a purposive document. Its purpose is to guarantee and to protect, within the limits of reason, the enjoyment of the rights and freedoms it enshrines. It is intended to constrain governmental action inconsistent with those rights and freedoms... Since the proper approach to the interpretation of the *Charter of Rights and Freedoms* is a purposive one, before it is possible to assess the reasonableness or unreasonableness of the impact of a search or of a statute authorizing a search, it is first necessary to specify the purpose underlying Section 8: in other words, to delineate the nature of the interests it is meant to protect (Hunter, pp. 156–157).

The details of purposive analysis began to take shape in *Regina v. Big M Drug Mart Ltd.* (1985). Big M Drug Mart was charged with selling goods on a Sunday, in violation of the Lord's Day Act. The trial court held for Big M, and the government appealed. In response, Big M argued that the Lord's Day Act was a violation of the Charter's guarantee of freedom of religion, contained in Section 2, which reads in part: "Everyone has the following fundamental freedoms: (a) freedom of conscience and religion..." Big M also argued that Section 27 was relevant: "This Charter shall be interpreted in a manner consistent with the preservation and enhancement of the multicultural heritage of Canadians."

The majority held for Big M, on the grounds that the purpose of the impugned act was to compel sectarian religious observance in violation of the Charter. The outcome of the case turned on the question of the purpose of the protection of religious freedom in the Charter, and the Court discussed this question at some length. It is worth reproducing part of Justice Dickson's majority opinion:

> This Court has already, in some measure, set out the basic approach to be taken in interpreting the *Charter*. In *Hunter v. Southam Inc.*... this Court expressed the view that the proper approach to the definition of the rights and freedoms guaranteed by the *Charter* was a purposive one. The meaning of a right or freedom guaranteed by the *Charter* was to be ascertained by an analysis of the purpose of such a guarantee; it was to be understood, in other words, in the light of the interests it was meant to protect. In my view this analysis is to be undertaken, and the purpose of the right or freedom in question is to be sought by reference to the character and the larger objects of the *Charter* itself, to the language chosen to articulate the specific right or freedom, to the historical origins of the concepts enshrined, and where applicable, to the meaning and purpose of the other specific rights and freedoms with which it is associated within the text of the *Charter*. The interpretation should be, as the judgment in *Southam* emphasizes, a generous rather than a legalistic one, aimed at fulfilling the purpose of the guarantee and securing for individuals the full benefit of the *Charter*'s protection (Big M, p. 344).

This explanation of purposive analysis nicely captures its central features. The purpose of a Charter protection is to be determined by looking at a broad range of factors – the text of the Charter, the larger goals of the Charter, the historical origins of the rights protected, and the context in which a particular protection is granted. One element that seems to be missing (at least to those socialized by the American debates) is the legislative history of the Charter. That question is addressed in a subsequent case: *Re B. C.* Motor Vehicle Act (1985).

Section 94(2) of the Motor Vehicle Act (British Columbia) made driving under a suspended or revoked license an "absolute liability offense." Thus, guilt was established by the proof of driving without a valid license, regardless of whether the driver knew of the suspension or revocation. The provincial government asked the Court of Appeal to issue an advisory opinion on the constitutionality of the act. That court found that the act violated Section 7 of the Charter: "Everyone has the right to life, liberty and security of the person and the right not to be deprived thereof except in accordance with the principles of fundamental justice." The provincial government appealed to the Supreme Court.

A majority found that the act did indeed violate the principles of fundamental justice. The immediate question of interpretation was whether "fundamental justice" was equivalent to "natural justice," itself a term of art whose meaning in Canadian legal discourse is synonymous with procedural due process (Motor Vehicle Reference, pp. 503–504). The argument for reading fundamental justice as equivalent to natural justice was based in part on testimony contained in the *Minutes of the Proceedings and Evidence of the Special Joint Committee of the Senate and of the House of Commons on the Constitution.* Some of that testimony clearly indicates that a number of the people involved in drafting and passing the Charter thought that fundamental justice would be interpreted as equivalent to natural justice.

The Court decided to permit this evidence about the intentions of the framers to be taken into consideration, but then qualified it as follows:

> [T]he simple fact remains that the *Charter* is not the product of a few individual public servants, however distinguished, but of a multiplicity of individuals who played roles in the negotiating, drafting and adoption of the *Charter*. How can one say with any confidence that within this enormous multiplicity of actors, without forgetting the role of the provinces, the comments of a few federal civil servants can in any way be definitive? . . . In view of the indeterminate weight of the data, it would in my view be erroneous to give these materials anything but minimal weight (Motor Vehicle Reference, pp. 508–509).

Then the majority goes further, citing not merely the indeterminacy of the historical materials, but also the undesirability of tying interpretation of the Charter to its historical origins. It is worth quoting the opinion at some length:

> Another danger with casting the interpretation of Section 7 in terms of the comments made by those heard at the Special Joint Committee Proceedings is that, in so doing, the rights, freedoms and values embodied in the *Charter* in effect become frozen in time to the moment of adoption with little or no possibility of growth, development and adjustment to changing societal needs. . . . If the newly planted 'living tree' which is the *Charter* is to have the possibility

> of growth and adjustment over time, care must be taken to ensure that historical materials, such as the Minutes of Proceedings and Evidence of the Special Joint Committee, do not stunt its growth (Motor Vehicle Reference, p. 509).

The crux of the Court's decision is thus: "Whether any given principle may be said to be a principle of fundamental justice within the meaning of Section 7 will rest upon an analysis of the nature, sources, *rationale* and essential role of that principle within the judicial process and in our legal system, as it evolves" (Motor Vehicle Reference, p. 513).

The last case I want to discuss is *Regina v. Oakes* (1986), which illustrates the open and somewhat philosophical character of purposive analysis. Mr. Oakes was found guilty in trial court of possession of narcotics. Under Section 4(2) of the Narcotics Control Act, a person found guilty of possession of narcotics must also be convicted of the separate offense of possession for the purpose of trafficking unless the defendant can prove that he or she had no intent to traffic. Oakes appealed this second conviction, and the Supreme Court found that it constituted a "reverse onus," in violation of Section 11(d) of the Charter, which reads: "Any person charged with an offence has the right . . . (d) to be presumed innocent until proven guilty according to law in a fair and public hearing by an independent and impartial tribunal."

Having determined that the act violated a Charter right, the Court had to decide whether the violation was justifiable under Section 1, which states that Charter rights are bound by ". . . such reasonable limits prescribed by law as can be demonstrably justified in a free and democratic society." Here for the first time the Court articulated a standard for analyzing abridgements under Section 1. First, Charter rights can only be infringed for an objective that relates "to concerns which are pressing and substantial in a free and democratic society" (Oakes, p. 138). Second, the infringement must be proportionate to the importance of the objective: "There are, in my view, three important components of a proportionality test. First, the measures adopted must be carefully designed to achieve the objective in question . . . Second, the means, even if rationally connected to the objective in this first sense, should impair 'as little as possible' the right or freedom in question . . . Third, there must be a proportionality between the effects of the measures which are responsible for limiting the *Charter* right or freedom, and the objective which has been identified as of 'sufficient importance' " (Oakes, p. 139).

In terms of the Court's emerging doctrine of Charter interpretation, *Oakes* continued the development of purposive analysis. The majority wrote:

> A second contextual element of interpretation of Section 1 is provided by the words 'free and democratic society.' Inclusion of these words as the final standard of justification for limits on rights and freedoms refers the Court to the very purpose for which the *Charter* was originally entrenched in the Constitution: Canadian society is to be free and democratic. The Court must

> be guided by the values and principles essential to a free and democratic society which I believe embody, to name but a few, respect for the inherent dignity of the human person, commitment to social justice and equality, accommodation of a wide variety of beliefs, respect for cultural and group identity, and faith in social and political institutions which enhance the participation of individuals and groups in society (Oakes, p. 136).

What can the Canadian Supreme Court's method of constitutional construction tell us about the American interpretation debates? The first question to ask is how the Court's "purposive approach" relates to the division between interpretive and non-interpretive methods, and also to my proposed division between hermeneutically open and closed methods. I follow Canadian constitutional scholar Peter Hogg in thinking that the purposive approach is not well described as either interpretive or non-interpretive (Hogg, 1987, esp. pp. 99–103). It seems plain that the Court is not committed to a simple textualism. It is explicitly opposed to any version of originalism, as is made clear in the *Motor Vehicle Reference*. Yet the Court's discussion of the animating values of the Charter, particularly in *Oakes*, suggests a philosophy that is ambiguously situated between interpretivism and non-interpretivism. We might read the Court's emphasis on the Charter's injunction to respect the values of a free and democratic society as providing a textual basis for a general, guiding principle of the Charter as a whole, much as Ely reads the Fourteenth Amendment (Ely, 1980). Alternately, we might read it as explicitly calling upon future justices to apply contemporary Canadian values to the new cases and situations that arise in that country's future, as Justice Brennan might suggest (Brennan, 1986). Or we might read it as simply a continuation of Canada's particular legal and political traditions (for example, the long refusal of British and Canadian courts to refer to legislative history[21]), as Bobbitt (discussed below) might (Bobbitt, 1982, 1991). In my view, the Court's practice, and the debate surrounding it, suggest that the quasi-empirical hypothesis implicit in hermeneutically closed theories of interpretation (that they are self-justifying and self-universalizing) is not borne out in Canadian jurisprudence.

Constitutional Interpretation in Australia: A Brief Overview

As with the Canadian Constitution, the story of the Australian Constitution's development is the tale of that country's separation from Britain and emergence as a fully sovereign power.[22] This process began with the Imperial Parliament's passage of the Australian Constitution as the Commonwealth of Australia Constitution Act in 1900. The next major stage was, as in Canada, the passage of the Statute of Westminster by the Imperial Parliament in 1931. However, Australia did not pass the necessary implementing legislation until 1942 (the Statute of Westminster

Adoption Act). The final stage was the passage of the Australia Act in 1986, which made both the federal and state governments of Australia independent of imperial control.

The interpretive practices of the High Court of Australia are the object of much controversy and debate. There appears to be universal agreement that a 1920 case, *The Amalgamated Society of Engineers v. The Adelaide Steamship Company Ltd.*, established the theory of constitutional interpretation that governed the High Court's activity for roughly the next 70 years.[23] This approach, a variant of interpretivism called both *legalism* and *literalism*, was largely abandoned in several major cases during the 1990s. However, the Court's adoption of a more non-interpretive approach was itself subsequently set aside, in favor of a partial return to legalism. At present, there seems to be widespread agreement, both on the Court and in the scholarly literature, that literalism as it was practiced historically is dead, but also that the Court has yet to arrive at a clear and persuasive alternative.[24]

The *Engineers' Case* concerned an industrial dispute between the engineers' union and several hundred employers around Australia, including several state governments that operated industrial enterprises. The union submitted this dispute to the Commonwealth Court of Conciliation and Arbitration. That Court requested a ruling from the High Court as to whether there existed an industrial dispute extending beyond the limits of one state. If this question were answered affirmatively, that would bring the dispute into federal jurisdiction under Section 51(xxxv) of the Constitution: "The Parliament shall, subject to this Constitution, have power to make laws for the peace, order, and good government of the Commonwealth with respect to: . . . (xxxv) Conciliation and arbitration for the prevention and settlement of industrial disputes extending beyond the limits of any one State."

The states involved argued that the constitutional provision was not intended to apply to the states themselves as parties to industrial disputes, and thus that the case could not come under federal jurisdiction in any case. This argument was based on a doctrine of "implied prohibition" allegedly found as an implication of the express terms of the Constitution by earlier decisions. Implied prohibition was similar to what American scholars call "dual federalism": the argument that since the states could not bind the federal government in areas of power granted to it by the Constitution, then reciprocally the federal government could not bind the states except in areas in which federal supremacy was explicitly granted.

The Court, vexed by this argument and the state of the relevant precedents, decided to clarify both the law and the appropriate method of constitutional interpretation. Chief Justice Isaacs and Justices Rich and Starke wrote: "The question presented is of the highest importance to the people of Australia . . . and it has necessitated a survey . . . of many of the decisions of this Court . . . The more the decisions are examined, and compared with each other and with the Constitution, the more evident it becomes that no clear principle can account for them" (Engineers' Case, p. 141). "[The states' case relies on] an interpretation of the Constitution depending on an implication which is formed on a vague, individual conception of the spirit of the compact.... This method of interpretation cannot, we think, provide any secure foundation for Commonwealth or State action..." (Engineers' Case, p. 145).

Most importantly, the three justices articulated the correct method of constitutional construction: "The one clear line of judicial inquiry as to the meaning of the Constitution must be to read it naturally in the light of the circumstances in which it was made, with knowledge of the combined fabric of the common law, and the statute law which preceded it, and then *lucet ipsa per se*" (Engineers' Case, p. 152). On this reading, the states' argument must fail: "The doctrine of 'implied prohibition' finds no place where the ordinary principles of construction are applied so as to discover in the actual terms of the instrument their expressed or necessarily implied meaning" (Engineers' Case, p. 155).

In the early 1990s the Court issued a series of opinions that marked a significant departure from the *Engineers*' approach. It is convenient to group these cases into two sets. The first three cases – *Nationwide News Pty. Ltd. v. Wills* (*Nationwide News*), *Australian Capital Television Pty. Ltd. and Others and the State of New South Wales v. The Commonwealth of Australia and Another* (*ACTV*), and *Theophanous v. The Herald and Weekly Times Limited and Another* (*Theophanous*) (collectively called the Speech Cases) – all found a freedom of political communication implied in the structure of the Constitution, despite the lack of an entrenched bill of rights.[25] The two final cases – *James Andrew McGinty and Others v. The State of Western Australia* (*McGinty*) and *David Russell Lange v. Australian Broadcasting Corporation* (*Lange*) – represent, respectively, a refusal to extend the logic of the Speech Cases to find other implied rights, and an attempt to scale back the impact of the speech cases and the style of interpretation they depend on. These five cases illustrate very clearly a move on the part of one High Court away from legalism, and then an attempt by a somewhat different Court to return closer to the Court's historical practice. In the interest of brevity, I will discuss only *Nationwide News*, *Theophanous*, and *Lange*.

In 1989 the newspaper *The Australian* published an article entitled "Advance Australia Fascist," which was sharply critical of the Australian Industrial Relations Committee. Subsequently, the paper's parent company, Nationwide News Pty. Ltd., was charged with violating Section 299(1)(d) of the Industrial Relations Act 1988, which, among other things, prohibited using speech or writing "to bring a member of the Commission or the Commission into disrepute."

Nationwide News, in defense, argued that the Australian Constitution contains an implicit guarantee of freedom of speech to discuss and criticize government, and that therefore the relevant portion of the act was invalid. The Court was divided as to this argument, as is represented in the variety of reasoning in the six opinions from the seven justices (the High Court generally writes seriatim opinions, so the large number is not unusual). All seven justices agreed that the impugned section of the act was invalid. Three (Mason, Dawson & McHugh) based their decisions on the argument that, while the federal Parliament did have a constitutional right to protect the Commission from interference with its work, the impugned section was too far removed from that legitimate purpose to be upheld as an implied power. A majority of four justices (Brennan, Deane and Toohey (writing together), and Gaudron), however, accepted Nationwide News' argument that the Constitution contained a structural implication of freedom of speech regarding political matters.

Although there are some differences among the majority opinions, there is general agreement on the idea that that Australian Constitution creates a representative government, and that some unenumerated protections may be so essential to the creation and maintenance of that form of government as to be necessarily implied constitutional rights. Thus, Justice Brennan writes: "[W]here a representative democracy is constitutionally entrenched, it carries with it those legal incidents which are essential to the effective maintenance of that form of government. Once it is recognized that a representative democracy is constitutionally prescribed, the freedom of discussion which is essential to sustain it is as firmly entrenched in the Constitution as the system of government which the Constitution expressly ordains" (Nationwide News, pp. 48–49). Justices Deane and Toohey come to essentially the same conclusion: "It follows from what has been said above that there is to be discerned in the doctrine of representative government which the Constitution incorporates an implication of freedom of communication of information and opinions about matters relating to the government of the Commonwealth" (Nationwide News, pp. 72–73).

In *Theophanous*, the Court expanded the doctrine of implied speech rights, and divisions within the Court became more clear. In 1992 The Herald and Weekly Times Ltd. published in its paper *The Sunday Herald Sun* a letter written by Mr. Bruce Ruxton. Mr. Ruxton's letter was sharply critical of Member of Parliament Dr. Andrew Theophanous. Dr. Theophanous sued both the paper and Mr. Ruxton for defamation. The defendants claimed several defenses, in particular the common law defenses of fair comment and qualified privilege, and the constitutional defense that their speech was protected under the implied freedom of political communication found by the Court in *Nationwide News*.

There seems to have been general agreement on the Court that the common law defenses were not available to the defendants, and thus that the outcome of the case turned on the constitutional issue. As Justices Mason, Toohey and Gaudron, writing together, explained: "The common law defences of fair comment and qualified privilege are not always available. Fair comment is available only for the expression of opinion and, then, only if the comment is based on facts which are notorious or truly stated. Qualified privilege depends on the absence of malice and on the person who makes the communication having an interest or duty in its making and on the recipient having a corresponding interest or duty in receiving it. The requirement for reciprocity of interest has the effect that common law qualified privilege is usually not available where the information has been disseminated to the public generally ..." (Theophanous, p. 133).

On the constitutional issue, the Court was deeply divided. In essence, four justices found that the implied constitutional right to freedom of political communication extends both to shaping the common law and to affecting state laws (Mason, Toohey, Gaudron & Deane). The other three justices, while continuing to recognize that the Constitution does indeed confer some limited speech rights relating to government, refused to extend those rights beyond what is directly implied by the text (Brennan, Dawson & McHugh).

A bare majority then articulated a new standard for determining whether a publication will be actionable for defamation: "[I]f a defendant publishes false and defamatory matter about a plaintiff, the defendant should be liable in damages unless it can establish that it was unaware of the falsity, that it did not publish recklessly (i.e. not caring whether the matter was true or false), and that the publication was reasonable in the sense described. These requirements will redress the balance and give the publisher protection, consistently with the implied freedom, whether or not the material is accurate" (Theophanous, p. 137). Although Justice Deane did not fully agree with this standard, he endorsed it to make a majority, because he agreed with the outcome, and otherwise no new standard would emerge from the decision (see Theophanous, pp. 187–188).

The dissenters in *Theophanous* continued roughly the same arguments they had put forward in the *ACTV* case (decided after *Nationwide News*), though with a bit more vehemence. Justice Dawson's overview is especially interesting in comparison with the practice of the Canadian Supreme Court: "If a constitutional guarantee of freedom of speech or of communication is to be implied, the implication must be drawn from outside the Constitution by reference to some such concept as 'the nature of our society' ... That is not an implication which can be drawn consistently with established principles of interpretation" (Theophanous, p. 193).

Justice McHugh continued in the same line: "With great respect, it seems to me that those judgments in Australian Capital Television and Nationwide News Pty. Ltd. v. Wills ... that hold that the institution of representative democracy is part of the Constitution independently of the terms of certain sections of the Constitution unintentionally depart from the method of constitutional interpretation that has existed in this country since the time of the Engineers' Case" (Theophanous, p. 202).

The interpretive tide began to turn two years later, in the *McGinty* case. The Court began to move away from the implied protections doctrine, and back towards something like legalism. This comes across very clearly in the *Lange* case, which is largely a revisiting of the issues in *Theophanous*. Mr. Lange, the former Prime Minister of New Zealand, brought a defamation action against the Australian Broadcasting Corporation (ABC) for broadcasts made while he was in office. ABC responded by claiming the defense set out in *Theophanous*. Mr. Lange claimed, in response, both that *Theophanous* (and a related case, *Stephens v. West Australian Newspapers Ltd.*) was bad in law, and that, in any case, it did not apply to discussion of political matters outside of Australia, and thus was not applicable.

A unanimous Court (including, significantly, Justices Toohey and Gaudron, who had been in the *Theophanous* majority) decided to partially revise *Theophanous* (and *Stephens*). The Court arrived at a substantively very similar outcome as in the previous cases, though through quite different reasoning. "[*T*]*heophanous* and *Stephens* should be accepted as deciding that in Australia the common law rules of defamation must conform to the requirements of the Constitution . . . [However, t]he full argument we heard in the present case and the illumination and insights gained from . . . [other] cases . . . now satisfy us . . . that some of the expressions and reasoning in the various judgments in *Theophanous* and *Stephens* should be further considered in order to settle both constitutional doctrine and the contemporary common law of Australia governing the defence of qualified privilege in actions of libel and slander" (Lange, p. 103).

The Court decided, in effect, to limit (though not overturn) the implied freedom of speech, and to resolve the libel question through a reinterpretation of the common law. "Accordingly, this Court should now declare that each member of the Australian community has an interest in disseminating and receiving information, opinions and arguments concerning government and political matters that affect the people of Australia. The duty to disseminate such information is simply the correlative of the interest in receiving it . . . The interest that each member of the Australian community has in such a discussion extends the categories of qualified privilege. Consequently, those categories now must be recognised as protecting a communication made to the public on a government or political matter" (Lange, p. 115).

One element that makes Australia a particularly interesting comparison case is that the High Court's changing opinions about interpretation have been made explicit through its decisions. What kind of approach does the Court employ? Legalism was clearly a kind of interpretivism. The approach adopted in *Nationwide*

News and *Theophanous* was some version of non-interpretivism, in which the Court was willing not only to draw implications from the text,[26] but apparently also to draw them from the general concept of representative government.[27] Although the Court subsequently returned to something like legalism, it is not clear that it is the same approach established by the *Engineers*' case.[28]

The Court's willingness to find important unenumerated rights, as well as its willingness to take into account political and social changes that affect the scope and impact of the Constitution, both affirmed in *Lange*, suggest that the High Court's interpretive methodology, like the Canadian purposive approach, falls somewhere between interpretivism and non-interpretivism. At the same time, the Court's shifts back and forth between legalism and a willingness to discover broad implied rights and protections suggest that neither approach has been wholly satisfactory. However, the Australian case lends less support than the Canadian to my proposed division between hermeneutically open and closed methods, since the Australian Court appears to have employed only closed methods.

Overall, I believe that these comparative investigations offer little support to the quasi-empirical hypothesis that hermeneutically closed theories will be self-justifying and self-universalizing. The Australian case seems to support closed theories generally, but no specific methodology in particular. The Canadian case seems to support open theories slightly more strongly than its supports closed. As predicted, empirical investigation has not provided clear proof or disproof of the self-justification hypothesis. However, it has suggested that closed theories have yet to live up to their implicit promise. While this is not sufficient evidence to conclude that they will not or cannot, it does suggest that closed theories are not now providing an accurate predictor of interpretive practices. More generally, I believe that the combination of theoretical criticism and empirical counter-evidence provides an incentive for us to examine open theories.

HERMENEUTICALLY OPEN THEORIES OF INTERPRETATION

Within the broad camp of thinkers I am calling hermeneutically open, there are several different theories about how constitutional controversies are resolved. What holds these theories together as a group is precisely that none of them relies on interpretive methodology as the route to definitive resolution. Here I discuss five general non-hermeneutic approaches.[29] Owen Fiss argues that interpretation can be constrained by what he calls "disciplining rules" – hierarchies of institutions that both socialize members of the legal profession and supervise their work. Stanley Fish and Dennis Patterson, despite their (ostensible) differences, argue that the meaning of most legal texts is non-controversial in the first place, since meaning inheres in the practices (or grammar) of linguistic communities. Philip Bobbitt argues that the methods of constitutional interpretation are determined historically (essentially through the normal functioning of the institutions that make up Fiss' disciplining rules), and that the legitimacy of their application is determined, ultimately, by moral judgment. Joseph Singer (and Dennis Patterson, in another mood) argues that the legal system may not be able to produce definitive interpretations of all laws or aspects of the constitution, but that if in finding its limits it uncovers significant social disagreements, that may be the first step towards a process of consensus building. Finally, Joel Bakan argues that there are no good justifications of constitutional interpretation, and that the various inadequate justifications are merely elaborate pleas for the polity to repose its faith in the legal system as a form of social organization.

As I suggested above, open theories face two general problems: the problem of indeterminacy (that accepting an open theory threatens the possibility that some – or perhaps all – interpretive disputes cannot be resolved by the normal operation of the legal system); and the problem of democratic legitimacy. On my reading, the various open theories circle around these problems without fully resolving them. After discussing several theories in more depth, I will conclude by sketching a way of combining them to respond to these problems more fully.

Fiss: Disciplining Rules

By his own account, Owen Fiss is trying to find a middle ground between what he calls "mechanistic" approaches to interpretation (by which he means interpretivism) and theories that seem to leave judges wholly free to choose among interpretations (1985, p. 183). He argues that "mechanistic" theories have a flawed understanding of how interpretation works. He writes: "I take issue with the Ely-Perry conception of interpretation because it is excessively mechanistic. As I argued in [*Objectivity and Interpretation* (Fiss, 1982)], such a conception confuses interpretation with execution.... Interpretation is not reducible to either textual determinism or originalism, but, instead, contemplates a dynamic interaction between text and reader..." (1985, p. 180).

He also argues against theories that seem to suggest that legal texts are indeterminate, claiming that they fail to understand the social and contextual nature of interpretation. Fiss endorses a conventionalist approach to knowledge: "Conventionalism is a viewpoint, most closely associated with the later writings of Wittgenstein, that emphasizes practice and context. It holds, for example, that we understand a concept not when we grasp some fact, but when we can successfully use that concept within a language game or a defined context, and that truth is a function of the agreement of those participating within a practice rather than the other way around" (1985, p. 177). In the case of legal interpretation, Fiss argues, there are many practices and institutions – which he groups under the term "disciplining rules" – that both constitute and constrain the meanings that members of the legal interpretive community can find and act upon. He writes: "It should be remembered, however, that in the law there are procedures for resolving these disputes – for example, pronouncements by the highest court and perhaps even legislation and constitutional amendment. The presence of such procedures and a hierarchy of authority for resolving disputes . . . is one of the distinctive features of legal interpretation" (1982, p. 747). Thus, while mechanistic theories fail to take into account the role of the reader in constructing meaning, so-called "nihilistic" theories fail to take into account the role of context and social institutions.

Fiss has brought our attention to a very important consideration. Legal interpretation is different from literary interpretation precisely because it: (a) has to result in a single interpretation – a plurality of readings is a bad outcome; and (b) it can be and is reviewed by other institutions empowered to modify or reject it. Fiss argues that this explanation is still compatible with disagreement. There can be disagreement that is internal to the interpretive community: "From the internal perspective, the standards of evaluation are the disciplining rules themselves, and the authority of the interpretive community is fully acknowledged. The criticism, say, of *Plessy v. Ferguson* might be that the judges did not correctly understand the authoritative rules, or may have misapplied them . . ." (1982, p. 748). Disagreement can also question the disciplining rules themselves: "Someone who stands outside of the interpretive community and thus disputes the authority of that community and its rules may provide another viewpoint. A criticism from this so-called external perspective might protest *Plessy* on the basis of some religious or ethical principle" (1982, p. 749).

It seems to me that there are two problems with Fiss' theory. The first one – that there may not be enough agreement to arrive at or enforce disciplining rules – he recognizes: "The image I have in mind is that of a judge moving toward judgment along a spiral of norms that increasingly constrain. At any point in the spiral there might be a disagreement over the meaning of a rule . . .. To resolve this dispute, the disciplining rules must be interpreted, and the process of interpreting those rules must itself be constrained by other norms further along or higher up the spiral. Of course, if the dispute about any norm is so pervasive as to return one to the previous level of constraint, then we have made no progress" (1985, p. 185). However, Fiss does not think that this is a significant threat: "Some may insist that my account of constraint collapses because the disputes about the meaning or the application of the disciplining rules . . . are more pervasive than I was originally willing to allow . . . Maybe the judge has no guidance besides the spacious words of the equal protection clause. I don't think so . . ." (1985, p. 186).

The second problem is one that Fiss seems to me to acknowledge, but not take seriously enough: the problem of democratic legitimacy. Fiss leaves room for "external" criticism of interpretations/decisions, but by separating the internal perspective of the legal community from the external perspective of the rest of the polity, he abandons the idea that the one might help to form and cohere the other. What happens when there are competing disciplining rules, or multiple possible answers provided by the same disciplining rules?

Bobbitt: Moral Judgment

Philip Bobbitt's theory of interpretation makes a distinction similar to Fiss' split between the internal and external perspectives. In *Constitutional Fate*, Bobbitt argues that we should distinguish between the *legitimacy* of a court decision and the *justification* of that decision. According to his view, decisions are legitimate when they employ a method of interpretation that is widely accepted within the legal culture. In the case of the United States, Bobbitt identifies six such "modalities": historical, textual, doctrinal, prudential, structural, and ethical (1982). Any decision that is cast in these terms (and is not obviously merely pretending to abide by the traditions and practices they represent) is legitimate. In essence, this is a narrower version of Fiss' idea of disciplining rules.

The question of the justification of a decision – whether it is a good decision on moral or political grounds – is determined separately. In *Constitutional Interpretation*, Bobbitt acknowledged that he had largely failed to address this issue in the earlier work: "Accepting (if only provisionally) that the analysis in *Constitutional Fate* resolves the problem of judicial review, let us turn to the problems that resolution poses. If legitimacy is maintained by the modalities, what if the modalities conflict? . . . . If a legitimate system does not ensure justice, how can it be justified?" (1991, p. 10). In the end, Bobbitt argues, we can assess the justification of a decision – and a legal system – only by making a moral judgment: "How do we decide that a decision is just? We measure it against our values" (1991, p. 166). And that assessment is not itself further analyzable: "There are no grounds independent of the sensibility that is judging those grounds. We can say only: these are the sensibilities we have" (1991, p. 168).

As with Fiss, it seems to me that Bobbitt does an admirable job of showing how it is that the behavior of the legal community can be constrained by internal norms and practices. However, also as with Fiss, it seems to me that he has underplayed the importance of the possibility of conflict. When Bobbitt says that we evaluate the justice of a decision by comparing it to our values, the obvious retort is: Whose values? To the extent that constitutional interpretation is supposed to resolve conflict within the broader polity and not just within the legal community, Bobbitt's theory seems to leave us no better off than we were before. It is still not at all clear that constitutional law can perform that important task.

Grammar and Practices: Patterson and Fish

Although they have been very critical of each other, I believe that Dennis Patterson and Stanley Fish hold nearly identical views about interpretation (see Fish, 1993; Patterson, 1993a, b, 1996).[30] Coming at the issue of interpretation from two different starting points – Patterson from Wittgenstein, Fish from literary criticism – they converge on the view that meaning inheres in the practices and understandings of a linguistic community. Thus, Patterson writes "The most salient aspect of Wittgenstein's argument is that insistence on linguistic essence as a ground for meaning leads one to dismiss as irrelevant the general forms of language that provide the public basis of meaning.... Wittgenstein's account of meaning demonstrates that discourse rests upon shared linguistic practices..." (1984, p. 688). Fish's argument is very similar: "In the course of this book, I say very little about its title, *Doing What Comes Naturally*. I intend it to refer to the unreflective actions that follow from being embedded in a context of practice. This kind of action – and in my argument there is no other – is anything but natural in the sense of proceeding independently of historical and social formations; but once those formations are in place (and they always are), what you think to do will not be calculated in relation to a higher law or an overarching theory but will issue from you as naturally as breathing" (1989, p. ix).

Their theories diverge, I believe, in the way that Patterson and Fish try to respond to the problem of conflicting interpretations that I have argued limits the effectiveness of Fiss' and Bobbitt's approaches. Fish emphasizes social and political solutions: "How are these conflicts to be settled? The answer to this question is that they are always in the process of being settled, and that no transcendent or algorithmic method of interpretation is required to settle them. The means of settling them are political, social, and institutional, in a mix that is itself subject to modification and change" (1989, p. 130).

Patterson seems to think that these conflicts can be resolved through some kind of interpretation, though what he means by that is not clear. He writes: "Interpretation is one of a number of reflective practices we engage in when conventional meanings are called into question. In the activity of interpretation, participants advance proposals for taking our conventional meanings one way rather than another....

Throughout all of this, the point of the activity is to advance interpretations in the hope of reaching agreement about how to go on with our practices (legal and otherwise)" (1993a, pp. 54–55). But here Patterson's argument seems obscure. In essence, Patterson has recreated the general problem of interpretation: How are we to decide which of the competing perspectives to choose, and how are we to justify that decision (especially to those who lose by it)?[31]

Singer and Bakan. Conflict as Therapy and Interpretation as Faith

I find two other hermeneutically open approaches to constitutional interpretation in the literature. One is represented by Joseph Singer, who argues that the point of interpretation debates is not to resolve conflicts, but to attempt to ameliorate them. ". . . [C]onsensus, if it exists, is not something that just happens to be there, that we could describe accurately. It must be *created*, and the work of creating it is the work and play of daily life, of living, contending, sharing, and being with other people. Like law, consensus must be made, not found . . .. Legal theory can help create communal ties and shared views by freeing us from the sense that current practices and doctrines are natural and necessary and by suggesting new forms of expression to replace outworn ones" (1984, p. 64). This position echoes a point that Patterson sometimes makes (following Wittgenstein): that studying interpretation is more likely to help us see that our anxieties are ill-placed, than to show us how to solve them. Patterson writes: ". . . [I]nterpretation is best seen as a therapeutic activity; one for reaching understanding, not explaining it" (1993a, p. 55).

The final open approach that I have identified is one taken by Joel Bakan. Bakan's argument – which I should clarify is cast as a criticism of theories of interpretation, and not as itself a positive theory – is that interpretations are just sophisticated requests for the polity to repose its faith in the institutions of judicial review. He writes: "Notwithstanding the pretensions of intellectual rigour and analytical depth, constitutional arguments are really just appeals for faith in the institution of judicial review and, correspondingly, obedience to the outcomes of that institution. They do not provide good reasons for the authority of judicial power" (1989, p. 193). I want to suggest that we might usefully take this insight as itself an open theory of interpretation. In this light, we could read Bakan to be saying that when there is controversy over a constitutional interpretation, it will not be possible to resolve it hermeneutically – by identifying a method of construction or an authoritative source of values in the light of which further debate would be foreclosed. Rather, at some point a decision will be rendered, and the losers will be asked to accept the outcome, despite their potential disagreement with its substance.

An Open Synthesis?

I draw two general conclusions from this brief look at hermeneutically open theories of interpretation. First, the problem of democratic legitimacy seems inevitable within a heterogeneous polity. Unless we can find some basis for interpretation that cannot be gainsaid – and I think that the theoretical critiques of interpretivism and non-interpretivism suggest that we cannot – then it will always be possible that there will be citizens who lose by some decision, and who cannot be convinced that their loss is both reasonable and legitimate. This is the cost of forming a single social system among people who have differing views of the world, given that we seem unable to identify neutral, meta-level principles or methods that everyone can or must agree on. Second, there are a variety of ways to limit and constrain the interpretations that are produced, and also a number of ways to limit the impact and destructiveness of the failures of democratic legitimacy.

Hermeneutically closed theories seek a basis for democratic consensus in principle, by identifying either a method of interpreting the constitution that cannot be objected to, or by identifying an extra-constitutional but consensual source of values or norms that can help elucidate the constitutional text. Hermeneutically open theories seek a basis for democratic consensus in a combination of principle, institutions, practices, inter-personal relationships, and faith. They start from the view that agreement in principle may be impossible due to the apparently irreducible heterogeneity of beliefs and value commitments that coexist within pluralistic democratic societies. But they do not view this as a reason to despair. Rather, they point out that democratic consensus can emerge *despite* the failures of legitimacy that inevitably arise when someone cannot accept the justification of one decision or another. Their point is that more holds together a democratic polity than shared principles, and that the inevitable disagreements about principle can be overcome if there is sufficient cohesion around the other elements of collective life (an idea that I call "layered pluralism").

From this perspective, I think that we can read the various open theories synthetically. Patterson and Fish point out that the vast majority of legal decisions will be unproblematically determinate and legitimate, since they will flow without controversy from the context of socialization and institutional activity that makes them possible. Bobbitt and Fiss point out that that very context of socialization and institutions gives rise to settled habits and ways of "doing law" that can be mobilized to constrain the activities of mavericks within the system. Nevertheless, there will apparently always be some portion of decisions that remain irremediably controversial. In those cases, Singer and Bakan remind us (despite himself, in the case of Bakan) that we may be able to call on other resources to cohere the polity despite the on-going conflicts. Singer's view is progressive, in the sense that he sees conflicts as opportunities to try to build more consensus. Bakan's concern is that relying on the polity's faith in the legal system might lead to acceptance of injustice through inertia. There is no perfect answer to this last pair of concerns – conflict as opportunity, resolution as acquiescence – other than to echo Bobbitt's point that: "We are incapable of making something that will obviate (rather than suppress) the requirement for moral decision" (1991, p. 186). In the end, this hermeneutically open synthesis suggests, we cannot rely on the legal system mechanistically producing acceptable results in every case, but must instead continuously reevaluate and decide again for ourselves whether the existing system, with all its inevitable compromises and injustices, is worth it. Can we ask for more?

NOTES

1. Some more recent work that continues to look at questions of interpretation includes (Fish, 1999; Marmor, 1995; Patterson, 1996, 2001; Whittington, 1999).
2. For an interesting discussion of the history of the use of the term "hermeneutic" in legal discourse, as well as of some of the problems with this terminology, see Leyh (1992).
3. It is difficult to specify the difference between losses that are inevitable in politics and losses that result in a breach of the democratic promise, though I believe the distinction is sound. Although I do not agree with his entire analysis, John Rawls provides one of the most thorough investigations of this question (Rawls, 1993, esp. pp. xv–xxxii and 35–43).
4. Alexander Bickel's well-known "countermajoritarian difficulty" (the apparent contradiction of permitting unelected judges to overturn the decisions of elected legislators) is an aspect of this broader problem of democratic legitimacy (Bickel, 1962).
5. Walter Murphy provides a concise overview of the many contemporary methods of constitutional review (Murphy, 1993).
6. For example: Ely's interpretive/non-interpretive split (Ely, 1980); Bobbitt's six modalities (historical; textual; doctrinal; prudential; structural; and ethical) (Bobbitt, 1982, 1991); Dworkin's distinction between semantic and interpretive understandings of law (Dworkin, 1986); and the ambiguous distinction between judicial activism and judicial restraint.
7. Many of these criticisms are made in Fish (1989), Fiss (1982), and Bobbitt (1982, 1991).
8. Ely makes this argument, and provides a concise summary of many of the main non-interpretivist arguments (Ely, 1980, esp. pp. 43–72).
9. This recent round of arguments in many ways echoes earlier arguments made by pragmatists and legal realists. A helpful summary history can be found in Williams (1987).
10. A number of other thinkers might also plausibly be included in this broad tendency, including Sanford Levinson, John Dewey and later pragmatists, and many others. I mention only Fish, Patterson, Fiss, Bobbitt, and Singer because they are the thinkers whose work I discuss explicitly (along with Joel Bakan, but see the text for an important clarification about his position). I do not intend to suggest that they are the only members of the non-hermeneutic camp.
11. See Bobbitt (1982, 1991).

12. An historical theory like the one in my example has to establish its legitimacy on two levels. On an abstract level, the theory has to be persuasive as an explanation of how interpretations have actually been assessed and justified. On a more concrete level, the theory must also accurately identify the specific interpretive traditions of the polity. However, neither level rests on the intuitive persuasiveness of the polity's particular approaches to interpretation. Instead, both rest on the accumulation of historical evidence to show that interpretations based on the existing traditions are usually seen as legitimate, and then to show what those particular traditions consist in.

13. Kommers suggests some more general reasons for the value of comparative constitutional law (Kommers, 1976).

14. The Constitution of Canada consists of at least 31 documents, though many of them are of minor importance. I say that the Constitution consists of *at least* 31 documents, because the clause of the Constitution Act, 1982 that defines the constitution reads "The Constitution of Canada *includes* [the 31 documents mentioned]" (52(2); emphasis added), and in at least one case the Supreme Court has interpreted that language to allow for the inclusion of additional elements. (The case was *New Brunswick Broadcasting Co. v. Nova Scotia*, and the decision is discussed by Hogg (1997, p. 9).)

15. The Constitution Act of 1867 did not contain any amendment clause. The British North America Act, 1949 added subsection (1) to Article 91, allowing the Canadian Parliament to amend the Constitution, with certain limitations, chief among them the requirement not to infringe on the enumerated powers of the provinces. Subsection (1) was repealed and replaced by Part V of the Constitution Act, 1982, which permits amendment by resolution of the Senate and House of Commons, accompanied by resolutions by at least two-thirds of the provinces, so long as those provinces contain at least 50% of the population of all of the provinces.

16. This section draws on Hogg (1997, Ch. 1).

17. Bakan (1989) provides an extremely helpful, if now somewhat dated, historical survey of the main arguments in Canadian constitutional interpretation.

18. Compare both with the intense debates about how the United States Supreme Court interprets, and with Griffin's (1996) and Bobbitt's (1982) argument that the Court uses a variety of methods.

19. Thus, Hogg (1987, 1990, 1997) argues that the Court's "purposive approach" is unproblematically legitimate, while Manfredi (1993a, b) and Morton (1993) worry that the approach is undertheorized, and Bakan (1989) argues that the Court's method is not legitimate, since no method is.

20. The key cases are (*Hunter*, 1984; *Motor Vehicle Reference*, 1985; *Big M*, 1985; *Oakes*, 1986).

21. See Hogg (1987, pp. 97–99).

22. This account draws on Hanks (1996, Ch. 1).

23. See Hanks (1996), Thomson (1997), Mason (1996), and Rich (1993).

24. See Rich (1993), Mason (1996), Kirby (2000), and Sampford and Preston (1996).

25. For a recent comparative perspective on these cases, and their relationship to American free speech jurisprudence see Rosenberg and Williams (1997).

26. Former Chief Justice Anthony Mason has argued that legalism was not generally understood as a narrow textual literalism: "Not all the statements in the *Engineers'* case can be taken at face value. The recognition in later cases that implications could be drawn . . . amounted to a specific and fundamental qualification of what had been said in the *Engineers'* case. Dixon and Evatt JJ were at pains to point out that the *Engineers'* case did

not decide that no implications could be drawn from the Constitution. And Dixon J subsequently said that we should not be fearful about making implications" (Mason, 1996, p. 24).

27. The willingness of some justices to look to the general concept of representative democracy comes across most clearly in the minority opinions in the *McGinty* case. Justices Toohey and Gaudron would have had the Court hold that a one-vote-one-value system of equal representation between electoral districts is a necessary implication in a system of democratic representative government (McGinty).

28. Galligan writes: "Making the Constitution meet national needs for a nation growing in unity and national awareness may have been the real guiding principle of High Court judges . . . Overall, the High Court has been highly effective but for much of the post-war period, its true role was disguised by the public rhetoric of legalism. Abandoning legalism and admitting to a more active role as shaper and developer of the Constitution requires the High Court to develop a defensible methodology and constitutional jurisprudence. *Engineers* no longer suffices because it assumes a literalist method of interpreting the Commonwealth's enumerated heads of power irrespective of the broader federal architecture of the Constitution. Having served the purposes of nation building for three-quarters of a century, the *Engineers* methodology is now obsolete. The High Court needs to develop an interpretive methodology appropriate for a federal constitution for the next century of federation" (Galligan, 1996, pp. 201–202).

29. There are certainly other authors whose work might be included in this group (see note 9 above). However, I believe that the five authors I discuss represent the main strategies of hermeneutically open justification in the literature.

30. Fish agrees (see Fish, 1993), while Patterson sees substantial differences (see Patterson, 1993a, b).

31. See Patterson (2001, p. 358), where Patterson acknowledges that interpretation is sometimes inevitable, and then criticizes several theories of interpretation, but does not propose an alternative.

ACKNOWLEDGMENTS

Many people helped me in thinking about and writing this article. I would especially like to thank Joel Grossman of the Johns Hopkins University and Peter Quint of the University of Maryland School of Law, for whose Comparative Constitutional Law class this article began as a paper. Many thanks are due to Erin Ackerman and Jennifer Culbert, who listened to several iterations of these ideas. I would also like to thank the two anonymous reviewers, whose helpful comments made this a much better article. Finally, I would like to thank Grant Huscroft, whom I have never met in person, who very generously read two versions of this article via email and gave me much helpful feedback. All the remaining flaws are, of course, my own.

An earlier version of this article was presented at the 2002 Annual Meeting of the Law and Society Association, in Vancouver, B. C. I thank Kim Lane Scheppele and Christian Boulanger for their very helpful comments and suggestions on that occasion.

REFERENCES

Australia Act, (1986) (Australia).

Bakan, J. (1989). Constitutional arguments: Interpretation and legitimacy in Canadian constitutional thought. *Osgoode Hall Law Journal*, *27*(1), 123–193.

Bickel, A. (1962). *The least dangerous branch*. Indianapolis: Bobbs-Merrill.

Bobbitt, P. (1982). *Constitutional fate: Theory of the constitution*. New York and Oxford: Oxford University Press.

Bobbitt, P. (1991). *Constitutional interpretation*. Oxford and Cambridge, MA: Blackwell.

Bork, R. (1985). The constitution, original intent, and economic rights. *San Diego Law Review*, *23*, 823.

Brennan, W. J. (1986). The constitution of the United States: Contemporary ratification. *South Texas Law Review*, *27*, 433.

Canada Act, 1982 c.11 (1982) (UK).

Combines Investigation Act, 1970 R. S. C. c.C-23 (1970) (Canada).

Commonwealth of Australia Constitution Act, 63 & 64 Victoria c. 12, (1900) (UK).

Constitution Act, 30 & 31 Victoria c.11 (1867) (UK).

Constitution Act, 1982 c.11 (1982) (UK).

David Russell Lange v. Australian Broadcasting Corporation, 145 A. L. R. 96 (High Court of Australia 1997).

Dworkin, R. (1986). *Law's empire*. Cambridge, MA: Harvard University Press.

Ely, J. H. (1980). *Democracy and distrust: A theory of judicial review*. Cambridge and London: Harvard University Press.

Fish, S. (1989). *Doing what comes naturally: Change, rhetoric, and the practice of theory in literary and legal studies*. Durham and London: Duke University Press.

Fish, S. (1993). How come you do me like you do? A response to Dennis Patterson. *Texas Law Review*, *72*, 57–65.

Fish, S. (1999). *The trouble with principle*. Cambridge, MA and London: Harvard University Press.

Fiss, O. (1982). Objectivity and interpretation. *Stanford Law Review*, *34*, 739–763.

Fiss, O. (1985). Conventionalism. *Southern California Law Review*, *58*, 177–197.

Galligan, B. (1996). The Australian High Court's role in institutional maintenance and development. In: C. Sampford & K. Preston (Eds), *Interpreting Constitutions: Theories, Principles and Institutions*. Sydney: The Federation Press.

Griffin, S. M. (1996). *American constitutionalism: From theory to politics*. Princeton: Princeton University Press.

Hanks, P. (1996). *Constitutional law in Australia* (2nd ed.). Sydney: Butterworths.

Hogg, P. W. (1987). The Charter of Rights and American theories of interpretation. *Osgoode Hall Law Journal*, *25*(1), 87–113.

Hogg, P. W. (1990). Interpreting the Charter of Rights: Generosity and justification. *Osgoode Hall Law Journal*, *28*(4), 817–838.

Hogg, P. W. (1997). *Constitutional law of Canada* (4th ed.). Scarborough, Ont.: Carswell Thomson Professional Publishing.

Hunter v. Southam Inc., 2 S. C. R. 145 (Supreme Court of Canada 1984).

James Andrew McGinty and Others v. The State of Western Australia, 186 C. L. R. 140 (High Court of Australia 1996).

Kirby, M. (2000). Constitutional interpretation and original intent: A form of ancestor worship? *Melbourne University Law Review*, *24*, 1.

Kommers, D. P. (1976). The value of comparative constitutional law. *John Marshall Journal of Practice and Procedure, 9*, 685.

Leyh, G. (Ed.). (1992). *Legal hermeneutics: History, theory and practice*. Berkeley: University of California Press.

Lord's Day Act, 1970 R. S. C. c.L-13 (1970) (Canada).

Manfredi, C. (1993a). Inalienable rights and reasonable limits: The U.S. Bill of Rights and the Charter of Rights and Freedoms. In: D. Thomas (Ed.), *Canada and the United States: Differences that Count*. Peterborough, Ont.: Broadview Press.

Manfredi, C. (1993b). *Judicial power and the charter: Canada and the paradox of liberal constitutionalism*. Norman, Okla.: University of Oklahoma Press.

Marmor, A. (Ed.). (1995). *Law and interpretation: Essays in legal philosophy*. Oxford: Oxford University Press.

Mason, A. (1996). The interpretation of a constitution in a modern liberal democracy. In: C. Sampford & K. Preston (Eds), *Interpreting Constitutions: Theories, Principles and Institutions*. Sydney: The Federation Press.

Minutes of the Proceedings and Evidence of the Special Joint Committee of the Senate and of the House of Commons on the Constitution (Canada).

Morton, F. L. (1993). The politics of rights: What Canadians should know about the American Bill of Rights. In: M. C. McKenna (Ed.), *The Canadian and American Constitutions in Comparative Perspective*. Calgary: University of Calgary Press.

Motor Vehicle Act, 1979 R. S. B. C. c.288 (1979) (B. C.).

Murphy, W. F. (1993). Constitutions, Constitutionalism, and Democracy. In: D. Greenberg, S. Katz, M. B. Oliviero & S. C. Wheatley (Eds), *Constitutionalism and Democracy: Transitions in the Contemporary World* (pp. 3–25). New York: Oxford University Press.

Narcotics Control Act, 1970 R. S. C. c.N-1 (1970) (Canada).

Nationwide News Pty. Ltd. v. Wills, 177 C. L. R. 1 (High Court of Australia 1992).

New Brunswick Broadcasting Co. v. Nova Scotia, 1 S. C. R. 319 (Supreme Court of Canada 1993).

Patterson, D. (1984). Interpretation in law: Toward a reconstruction of the current debate. *Villanova Law Review, 29*, 671.

Patterson, D. (1993a). The poverty of interpretive universalism: Toward a reconstruction of legal theory. *Texas Law Review, 72*, 1–56.

Patterson, D. (1993b). You made me do it: My reply to Stanley Fish. *Texas Law Review, 72*, 67–77.

Patterson, D. (1996). *Law and truth*. New York and Oxford: Oxford University Press.

Patterson, D. (2001). Normativity and objectivity in law. *William and Mary Law Review, 43*, 325–363.

Rawls, J. (1993). *Political liberalism*. New York: Columbia University Press.

Re B. C. Motor Vehicle Act, 2 S. C. R. 486 (Supreme Court of Canada 1985).

Regina v. Big M Drug Mart, 1 S. C. R. 295 (Supreme Court of Canada 1985).

Regina v. Oakes, 1 S. C. R. 103 (Supreme Court of Canada 1986).

Rich, W. (1993). Approaches to constitutional interpretation in Australia: An American perspective. *University of Tasmania Law Review, 12*(2), 150–181.

Rosenberg, G. N., & Williams, J. M. (1997). Do not go gently into that good right: The first amendment in the High Court of Australia. *Supreme Court Review*, 439.

Sampford, C., & Preston, K. (Eds). (1996). *Interpreting constitutions: Theories, principles and institutions*. Sydney: The Federation Press.

Scalia, A. (1997). *A matter of interpretation: Federal courts and the law*. Princeton: Princeton University Press.

Singer, J. W. (1984). The player and the cards: Nihilism and legal theory. *Yale Law Journal, 94*(1), 1–70.
Statute of Westminster Adoption Act, (1942) (Australia).
Statute of Westminster, 22 Geo. V c.4 (1931) (UK).
Stephens v. West Australian Newspapers Ltd., 182 C. L. R. 211 (High Court of Australia 1994).
The Amalgamated Society of Engineers v. The Adelaide Steamship Co. Ltd., 28 C. L. R. 129 (High Court of Australia 1928).
Theophanous v. The Herald and Weekly Times Ltd. and Another, 182 C. L. R. 104 (High Court of Australia 1994).
Thomson, J. A. (1997). American and Australian constitutions: Continuing adventures in comparative constitutional law. *John Marshall Law Review, 30*, 627–698.
Whittington, K. (1999). *Constitutional interpretation: Textual meaning, original intent, and judicial review*. Lawrence: University of Kansas Press.
Williams, J. (1987). Critical legal studies: The death of transcendence and the rise of the new langdells. *New York University Law Review, 62*(3), 429–496.

MINORITY REPRESENTATION, THE SUPREME COURT, AND THE POLITICS OF DEMOCRACY

Yasmin A. Dawood

ABSTRACT

This article develops an alternative theoretical approach to the Supreme Court's controversial electoral redistricting decisions in Shaw v. Reno (1993) and its progeny. Instead of relying on the traditional equal protection interpretation, this paper argues that controversies over electoral redistricting are at base disputes among competing visions of democracy. In the Court's recent redistricting cases, the majority and the dissent adopted fundamentally different visions of democracy – Individualist Democracy and Democracy as Power. In addition to elaborating these rival understandings of democracy, this article develops the concept of Symbolic Democracy to explain a central paradox in the Court majority's decision: its simultaneous denial and recognition of the relevance of racial groups in representation.

INTRODUCTION

Racial oppression in the United States has been historically tied to the exclusion of African Americans from the polity. The quest for democratic inclusion continues to this day, although the objective is no longer the attainment of the formal right to vote. In the contemporary period, racial oppression is fundamentally based on the

Studies in Law, Politics, and Society
Studies in Law, Politics, and Society, Volume 28, 33–72

ISSN: 1059-4337/PII: S1059433702280023

lack of political power. Although African Americans have the ballot, they enjoy scant legislative influence on the public policies that govern their everyday lives. These urgent issues – voting, representation, race, power and exclusion – are at the center of the Supreme Court's recent adjudication of minority representation.

In the 1990s, the Supreme Court ushered in its "new jurisprudence" on minority representation with its controversial rulings in *Shaw v. Reno* (1993) and its progeny.[1] The Court held in *Shaw v. Reno* (1993) that certain majority African-American electoral districts violated the equal protection clause of the Fourteenth Amendment. In *Shaw*, the Court considered the constitutionality of the Twelfth District, a majority-minority legislative district in North Carolina. What appeared to fuel the Court's hostility to the district was its unusual shape: it followed the I-85 corridor for almost 160 miles until, as the lower court described it, the district "gobble[d] in enough enclaves of black neighborhoods." In an ironic twist, white voters launched suit claiming that the state had created an unconstitutional racial gerrymander and had violated their constitutional right to participate in a color-blind electoral process. Adding to the controversy surrounding the *Shaw* case was the fact that, as a result of the Twelfth District, North Carolina sent its first African-American representatives to Congress since Reconstruction (*Shaw v. Reno* 509 U.S. 630; 1993).

The *Shaw* case represented a dramatic departure from the Court's prior position that race conscious districting would at times be required in order to protect the ability of racial minorities to elect a candidate of their choice.[2] In the next case, *Miller v. Johnson* (1995), the Court broadened the scope of *Shaw* by holding that a redistricting plan would be found invalid if "race was the predominant factor" motivating the legislature when it devised the plan (*Miller v. Johnson* 515 U.S. 900; 1995). The Supreme Court applied its new jurisprudence in *Bush v. Vera* (1996) and *Shaw v. Hunt* (1996) to overturn the constitutionality of the majority-minority districts at issue in those cases. In all four cases, the dissenting justices rigorously criticized the Court's new stance on minority representation.

What is at stake in the Supreme Court's recent adjudication of minority representation? For the most part, commentators characterize the disagreement between the Court majority and the dissent as a clash between a color-blind and a color-conscious approach to the equal protection clause of the Fourteenth Amendment. A central difficulty with the traditional interpretation, however, is that these recent redistricting decisions do *not* adhere rigidly to a color-blind/color-conscious dichotomy; indeed, the Court majority floated unhappily between permitting the use of "some" race as mandated by the Voting Rights Act, and forbidding the influence of "too much" race on the basis that it presumptively violated the Constitution.

In contrast to the traditional interpretation, I develop an alternative theoretical approach to the recent redistricting cases, one that applies the insights of democratic theory to the Supreme Court's adjudication of minority representation.[3] In general, I argue that controversies over electoral redistricting are at base disputes among competing visions of democracy. By crafting the rules and standards that govern electoral redistricting, the Court implicitly adopted certain theories of representation and embraced particular conceptions of democracy (see also Issacharoff et al., 1998).[4]

A primary objective of this article is to identify and analyze the competing visions of democracy in the Supreme Court's new jurisprudence on minority representation. While these (and other) conceptions of democracy animate the Court's voting rights jurisprudence as a whole, I focus specifically on the rival conceptions of democracy in *Shaw v. Reno* (1993) and its progeny.[5] In addition, I argue that these rival visions of democracy are often at the heart of the apparent incoherence that marks the Court's adjudication of minority representation. Tensions among competing visions of democracy explain not only the complexities of the majority opinion, but also help to explain the deep divide between the majority and the dissent over the constitutionality of majority-minority districts.[6] The Court's understanding of democracy, it will be shown, embodies a series of compromises among different visions of democracy, leading to a jurisprudence that is often contradictory, even incoherent, and at times paradoxical.

To uncover these rival understandings of democracy, I treat the Supreme Court's decisions as political texts in their own right. I distinguish between the "explicit" and the "implicit" visions of democracy in the Court's recent redistricting cases. By "explicit" visions of democracy, I am referring to what the Court itself *actually says* about democracy and representation in its decisions. I analyze the Court's articulation of these conceptions of democracy, and show how these understandings are relevant to the outcome of the cases. By "implicit" conceptions of democracy, I am referring to those theories of democracy and representation that are implied by the Court's decisions. That is, I examine how the Court's constitutional doctrines instantiate certain forms and understandings of democracy and representation.

In *Shaw v. Reno* (1993) and its progeny, the majority and dissenting opinions adopted fundamentally different visions of democracy. The *Shaw* majority adopted an explicit vision of democracy that I refer to as "Individualist Democracy." In the majority's vision, a system of government represents the interests of individuals, and not groups, in the political process. When describing its conception of democracy, the majority contended that race was not and should not be treated as politically salient in the structure of a representative system. By contrast, the dissenting opinion in *Shaw v. Reno* (1993) had an entirely different understanding of democracy. The dissent's explicit vision of democracy, which I refer to as

"Democracy as Power," stressed the imbalance in political power between the dominant (white) majority and a less powerful (black) minority. Rather than representing the interests of individuals, democracy was presented as involving the relative political power of groups within a society. I argue that the conflict between these explicit visions of democracy sheds light on the deeply held disagreements between the majority and dissenting opinions in the Supreme Court's new jurisprudence on minority representation.

At the same time, the explicit vision of Individualist Democracy does not fully explain the Court's position in these cases. I contend that the *Shaw* majority betrayed a curious vacillation on the use of race in redistricting – what I refer to as "the paradox of simultaneous group denial and group recognition." On the one hand, the Court sharply condemned the use of race in drawing districts lines, arguing that race is simply irrelevant in a system of representation. On the other hand, the Court acknowledged the problem of minority vote dilution, thereby implying that race *is* relevant in a system of representation. The *Shaw* majority's commitment to an Individualist Democracy is in keeping with its hostility to race-based redistricting, but it does not account for those parts of the decision in which the majority *does* recognize the political salience of race.

The paradox of simultaneous group denial and group recognition can be understood, I suggest, by a conception of democracy that is implicitly located in the Court's decisions. I develop the theory of "Symbolic Democracy" to take account of the Court's concern with the symbolic dimension of democracy. By Symbolic Democracy, I mean that the Court was concerned not only with the *actual* fairness of the democratic process (as encapsulated by the 'one person-one vote' rule), but also with the *appearance* of fairness. If the process *looks* illegitimate, then it *is* illegitimate. Given the majority's commitment to an Individualist Democracy, the appearance of the Twelfth District symbolized unfairness and illegitimacy because of the district's obvious racial composition. For this reason, the Court forbade the use of "too much" race in electoral redistricting.

Paradoxically, the Court's concern with Symbolic Democracy also animated its persistent reluctance to prohibit the use of race altogether in electoral redistricting. A democratic process that hardly ever results in the election of an African-American to office *appears* illegitimate and therefore requires the cleansing powers of the Voting Rights Act. Were the Court to completely ban the use of race in redistricting, it would in effect hold the Voting Rights Act unconstitutional. Given the historic disenfranchisement of African Americans, however, the Voting Rights Act symbolizes legitimacy in the democratic process because of its central role in ensuring the inclusion of blacks in voting and representation. For this reason, the majority had little choice but to allow the consideration of "some" race as mandated by the Voting Rights Act.

Before elaborating these visions of democracy, it may be helpful to discuss the general approach of this article. Thinking about judicial opinions is a "rhetorical and literary activity," one that requires close attention to the use of language, the choice of words, and the form of arguments (White, 1985, pp. x–xi). Legal reasoning is important not only for the set of rules it produces, but also for the *meanings* that are articulated in and through its principles, metaphors, analogies and narratives. In particular, I view legal discourse as a rich, and often overlooked, source of political philosophy. A central premise of the arguments presented here is that constitutional doctrines, and the legal reasoning that renders these doctrines intelligible, presuppose and enunciate different political theories. An interdisciplinary approach that attends to the intersection of constitutional law and political theory would enrich our understanding of the Supreme Court's jurisprudence. Indeed, the convergence of law and theory has not gone unnoticed by the Supreme Court. In his dissent from the Court's decision to review apportionment schemes in *Baker v. Carr* (1962), Justice Frankfurter observed that:

> One cannot speak of 'debasement' or 'dilution' of the value of the vote until there is first defined a standard of reference as to what a vote should be worth. What is actually asked of the Court in this case is to choose among competing bases of representation – ultimately, really, between competing theories of political philosophy – in order to establish an appropriate frame of government . . . for all the States of the Union (*Baker v. Carr* 369 U.S. 186; 1962).

For Frankfurter, the Court is choosing among "competing theories of political philosophy" when it selects a particular constitutional standard from among a range of options (see also Bybee, 1998, p. 42).[7] In a similar vein, Rogers Smith asserted that "different constitutional interpretations ultimately reveal conflicts between competing political visions, a view that American constitutional history confirms" (Smith, 1985, p. 228). By uncovering the theoretical underpinnings of the legal standards crafted by the Court, it is possible to address the larger philosophical questions that are raised by constitutional norms and arguments.

The theories and visions that are embodied in constitutional doctrines are relevant precisely because they have important political implications. By adjudicating the rules of electoral redistricting, the Court is playing a central role in the democratic system. In his celebrated defense of judicial review, John Hart Ely argued that the Court is "policing the process of representation" (Ely, 1980, p. 73). Rather than dictating any substantive results, the Court behaves like a referee, stepping in only when one side is unfairly disadvantaging the other.[8] By clearing the "stoppages" in the democratic process, the Court broadens access to representative government and thereby ensures participation on an equal footing. While the characterization of the Supreme Court as the guardian of democracy is widely accepted, I claim that it understates the Court's institutional role. In general, I suggest that the Supreme

Court, rather than clearing blockages in the democratic process, is actually *constructing democracy* itself.[9] The Court is not merely refereeing or policing a political process that is fixed and unchanging; instead, the Court also creates the very processes and institutions that constitute democracy. For this reason, Ely's assertion that the task of the Court is to "keep the machinery of democratic government running as it should" (Ely, 1980, p. 76) overlooks the Court's function in creating, shaping and altering the machinery of representative government. In order to understand the Court's construction of democracy, it is vitally important to consider how the Court envisions and conceptualizes representation and democracy.

Although the analysis of Supreme Court decisions may appear to be a puzzling choice in an exploration of the intersection of democratic thought and democratic practice, this article claims that Court opinions embody thought and action in ways that have wide-ranging implications for the politics of democracy. It is essential to consider how the justices have legally conceived of and defined representative government because their actions and opinions have literally constituted democracy itself. Judicial practices in the arena of minority representation are informed by certain structures of ideas, and justified by certain rationales, which, when taken together, have important consequences for what is meant by representation and democracy. To understand the strengths and weaknesses of our contemporary democratic system, it is important to consider the political theories and values that are at stake in constitutional doctrines. For this reason, we cannot afford to ignore the political philosophies enunciated in legal discourse.

This article is organized in three parts. In Part I, I discuss the Supreme Court's new jurisprudence on minority representation, and analyze the limitations of the conventional equal protection interpretation of these cases. I also explore the complexity of the Court majority's opinion in *Shaw v. Reno* (1993), focusing in particular on the paradox of simultaneous group denial and group recognition. Part II of the article is devoted to the Court's competing visions of democracy. I argue that the deep divide on the Court can be better understood by analyzing the explicit visions of democracy – Individualist Democracy and Democracy as Power – that were adopted by the majority and the dissent, respectively. Finally, in Part III, I develop the theory of Symbolic Democracy to explain the Court majority's vacillation on the place of race in a representative government.

I: MINORITY REPRESENTATION

In the 1990s, the Supreme Court ushered in its new jurisprudence for minority representation with its decision in *Shaw v. Reno* (1993). In a marked departure from its earlier redistricting decisions, the Supreme Court, in an opinion authored by Justice O'Connor, recognized a new constitutional claim against race-based redistricting. Specifically, the Court held in a 5 to 4 decision that the appellants had stated an "analytically distinct" claim under the equal protection clause by alleging that North Carolina had adopted a redistricting plan "so irrational on its face" that it "cannot be understood as anything other than an effort to segregate citizens into separate voting districts on the basis of race" (*Shaw v. Reno* 509 U.S. 630; 1993). In effect, the Court determined that certain majority African-American electoral districts violated the equal protection clause of the Fourteenth Amendment.[10]

The dissenting justices in *Shaw v. Reno* (1993) argued that the majority had established a completely new electoral redistricting claim under the Fourteenth Amendment, one that was invalid and unjustifiable because it was not based upon any cognizable injury such as vote dilution. Race-based redistricting, according to Justice White, implicated the Fourteenth Amendment only if there was an allegation of discriminatory purpose and effect. In the *Shaw* case, however, white voters could not allege discriminatory effect because they still constituted a voting majority in the newly drawn congressional districts that was proportional to their percentage of the state's population. In a similar vein, Justice Souter expressed the view that the Fourteenth Amendment provided relief only when a voter, as a member of a group, could show a dilution of the effectiveness of the group's voting power (*Shaw v. Reno* 509 U.S. 630; 1993).

Two years later, in *Miller v. Johnson* (1995), the Court broadened the scope of *Shaw v. Reno* (1993) by introducing a new legal standard for invalidating redistricting plans. The new standard, which considerably expanded the reach of *Shaw*, required plaintiffs to show that "race was the predominant factor" motivating the legislature's redistricting plan. District shape was now simply "circumstantial evidence" that race was the predominant factor, but shape was no longer necessary for such a determination to be made. To prove that racial considerations were predominant, a plaintiff had to show that the legislature "subordinated traditional race-neutral districting principles," such as compactness, contiguity, and respect for communities of shared interests, to racial considerations (*Miller v. Johnson* 515 U.S. 900; 1995). The Supreme Court applied the *Shaw* and *Miller* doctrines in *Bush v. Vera* (1996) and *Shaw v. Hunt* (1996) to overturn the constitutionality of the majority-minority districts at issue in those cases.

The Traditional Interpretation and Its Limitations

The Supreme Court's voting rights cases are usually analyzed from an equal protection standpoint. The traditional equal protection approach stresses the conflict between a *color-blind* Constitution which is said to prohibit the consideration of a morally arbitrary characteristic such as race in the formulation of government policy, and, a *color-conscious* Fourteenth Amendment whose very purpose in the Constitution is to ensure the inclusion of the one group – African-Americans – whose rights have been so shamefully denied over the course of the nation's history. Proponents of color-consciousness argue that the long history of slavery and discrimination has created a "tilted" playing field, one that was built by and for the benefit of whites and results in the systematic exclusion of blacks. Therefore, to treat individuals fairly, it may be necessary to enact color conscious policies to counteract the effects of racial injustice on the life chances of individuals (Fish, 1997, pp. 144–145; West, 1996, p. 32).

Proponents of color-blindness, by contrast, adopt the moral ground that "discrimination on the basis of race is illegal, immoral, unconstitutional, inherently wrong, and destructive of democratic society" (Bickel, 1975, p. 133). According to this point of view, the principle of color-blindness also applies to affirmative action (or "reverse discrimination" in the words of its detractors) because racial preferences for blacks discriminate against whites, and any kind of discrimination on the basis of color is wrong (Glazer, 1987; Sowell, 1984). As expected, those who favor a color-blind interpretation of the Constitution are usually opposed to race-based electoral districts (Thernstrom, 1987), while those who support color-consciousness claim that majority-minority districts are essential for the fair and effective representation of certain racial groups (Gutmann, 1996, pp. 109–110; Phillips, 1995).

While the traditional approach captures many of the theoretical issues at stake in minority redistricting, it has become less helpful over time. For a start, the debate has reached an impasse of sorts, with each side rehearsing what are by now familiar arguments. A further difficulty is that the Supreme Court's decisions do not adhere rigidly to a color-blind/color-conscious dichotomy, notwithstanding its rhetoric to the contrary (Kull, 1992, p. 118). Despite the Court's repeated invocation of Justice Harlan's declaration that "Our Constitution is color-blind, and neither knows nor tolerates classes among citizens" (*Plessy v. Ferguson* 163 U.S. 537; 1896), the Court has not categorically prohibited the intentional use of race, but has instead imposed strict restrictions on the *degree* to which race can be considered.[11]

The Paradox of Simultaneous Group Denial and Group Recognition

In its recent electoral redistricting decisions, the Supreme Court betrayed even more ambivalence than usual about whether and to what degree the Fourteenth Amendment permits the use of racial considerations. Rather than choosing between the principle of color-blindness and the principle of color-consciousness (or at least favoring one side over another), the Court appeared to hold several contradictory positions simultaneously.

In certain parts of the *Shaw* opinion, the Court expressed its antipathy for the use of race in redistricting. Justice O'Connor stated that racial classifications "are by their very nature odious to a free people whose institutions are founded upon the doctrine of equality" (*Shaw v. Reno* 509 U.S. 630; 1993; citing *Hirabayashi v. United States* 320 U.S. 81; 1943). Previously, the use of race in the redistricting context was considered to be compatible with the equal protection clause provided that it was used for benign or remedial purposes, such as drawing district lines to avoid the dilution of minority voting power. Justice O'Connor, however, refused to distinguish between benign and invidious uses of race on the grounds that any and all racial classifications are harmful and serve to foster illegitimate stereotypes about skin color. According to the Court, racial classifications also stigmatize members of racial groups and incite racial hostility.

The Court held that the use of race in redistricting was subject to the same strict standards that currently govern the adjudication of affirmative action in education, employment and government contracts. Relying upon its decision in *Richmond v. J. A. Croson Co.* (1989), the Court stated that equal protection analysis does not turn on the race of those benefited or harmed by a classification, and consequently all racial classifications, including those in the redistricting context, are subject to strict scrutiny.[12] This change in standard was a significant departure from the Court's previous practice of treating equal protection claims in redistricting far less stringently than equal protection claims involving other government conduct. By imposing the onus of a strict scrutiny standard, the Court signaled that almost no race-conscious redistricting plans would pass constitutional muster (*Shaw v. Reno* 509 U.S. 630; 1993).

The Court's extension of strict scrutiny review to electoral redistricting and its color-blind rhetoric suggest that racial group identity should have, at best, a marginal role in a democratic system. Given the Court's *rejection* of race as being relevant in a system of representation, it is perplexing that the Court also explicitly *recognized* the dangers facing members of racial minorities in a democratic system. In other parts of the *Shaw* opinion, Justice O'Connor endorsed the line of cases beginning with *Allen v. State Board of Elections* (1969) that addressed the problem of "minority vote dilution."

In *Allen v. State Board of Elections* (1969), the Supreme Court recognized that "the right to vote can be affected by a dilution of voting power as well as by an absolute prohibition on casting a ballot." The Court determined that certain practices, such as multimember or at-large electoral districts, can reduce or nullify the ability of minority voters, as a group, to elect the candidate of their choice, particularly when members of a racial minority vote as a cohesive unit. For this reason, the Court held that practices that dilute a minority group's voting power violate the equal protection clause of the Fourteenth Amendment. By recognizing minority vote dilution as a valid constitutional claim, the Court acknowledged in *Allen* that equal access to the polls did not assure equally meaningful political participation (*Allen v. State Board of Elections* 393 U.S. 544; 1969). In *White v. Regester* (1973), the Court struck down the constitutionality of multimember districts on the basis that they "enhanced the opportunity for racial discrimination" (*White v. Regester* 412 U.S. 755; 1973). In addition, the Court upheld the use of race-conscious districting to create districts with substantial minority populations (*United Jewish Organizations v. Carey* 430 U.S. 144; 1977).

The Court dealt a significant blow to vote dilution claims when it held in *Mobile v. Bolden* (1980) that only those electoral procedures that were adopted with a racially discriminatory *purpose* violated the Constitution, regardless of whether such procedures had the *effect* of diluting minority voting strength (*Mobile v. Bolden* 446 U.S. 55; 1980). To counteract the *Mobile* decision, Congress adopted the 1982 amendments to the Voting Rights Act to make it clear that racially discriminatory *results* violate the Act. The amended Section 2 provides that a violation exists if a class of citizens has "less opportunity than other members of the electorate to participate in the political process and to elect representatives of their choice" (42 U.S. C. § 1973(b)). Based upon the 1982 amendments, the Supreme Court developed a framework to adjudicate minority vote dilution claims in *Thornburg v. Gingles* (1986). To make a valid minority vote dilution claim under *Thornburg*, a plaintiff must show first, that the minority group is sufficiently large and geographically compact to form a majority in a single-member district; second, that the minority group votes as a cohesive political bloc; and third, that the majority group votes sufficiently as a bloc to enable it to usually defeat the minority group's preferred candidate (*Thornburg v. Gingles* 478 U.S. 30; 1986).

In *Shaw v. Reno* (1993), the Court acknowledged that certain electoral arrangements, such as at-large districts, can reduce a racial minority group's ability to elect a representative of its choice, and therefore violate the Fourteenth Amendment. The *Shaw* majority's continued recognition of the constitutional claim of minority vote dilution is simply unintelligible without the assumption that race *does* organize political preferences. Furthermore, given that state legislatures are aware that racial minorities vote cohesively (and usually for the Democratic Party), it is inevitable that districts will be drawn with some attention to race. Indeed, the *Shaw* majority acknowledged that

> . . . redistricting differs from other kinds of state decision making in that the legislature always is aware of race when it draws district lines, just as it is aware of age, economic status, religious and

> political persuasion, and a variety of other demographic factors. That sort of race consciousness does not lead inevitably to impermissible race discrimination (*Shaw v. Reno* 509 U.S. 630; 1993).

It is unclear how it is possible for a legislature to be "aware" of race in the way that it is aware of other demographic factors, yet not be so aware that it is "motivated" by an impermissible race discrimination. Even more puzzling about the Court's distinction between (permissible) awareness and (impermissible) motivation is that Section 2 of the Voting Rights Act *requires* that legislators take race into account in order to avoid minority vote dilution, and the Court's decision in *Thornburg v. Gingles* (1986) provided the standards by which states can take race into account in order to comply with the Act. To further confuse matters, the majority held that race-conscious redistricting is not unconstitutional in all circumstances (*Shaw v. Reno* 509 U.S. 630; 1993).

Within a single opinion, the Court's rhetoric swings from claiming that considerations of race have *no* place in electoral redistricting to arguing that race *must* be taken into account when drawing district lines. I refer to this vacillation as the "paradox of simultaneous group denial and group recognition," in order to take account of the Court's contradictory stance on the place of racial groups in a system of representation. To make matters even more confusing, the actual legal standard adopted by the Court does not coincide with either of these two positions. Instead, the Court floated unhappily between permitting the use of "some" race as mandated by the Voting Rights Act, and forbidding the influence of "too much" race on the basis that it presumptively violated the equal protection clause of the Fourteenth Amendment. The result is that legislatures are in the impossible position of having to avoid legal liability under the Voting Rights Act, on the one hand, and the Fourteenth Amendment, on the other. This legal dilemma occurred because the Court simultaneously denied and recognized the relevance of racial groups in a democracy.

In large part because of the Court's vacillation on the use of race in representation, these recent electoral redistricting decisions have been met by near universal criticism on the part of legal scholars. Samuel Issacharoff argued that the Court's "refusal either to condemn all reliance on race as unconstitutional or to impose a constitutional template of compactness on redistricting left the opinion without an operational core" (Issacharoff, 1995, p. 45). In a separate article, Alexander Aleinikoff and Samuel Issacharoff maintained that *Shaw*'s theory of "too much" race may be a "murky and unworkable standard" once it is applied in practice (Aleinikoff & Issacharoff, 1993, p. 624). They also stated that even the most charitable reading of *Shaw* "cannot hide the tremendous failings of intellectual coherence and practical application that attach to the ever perilous middle ground of compromise" (Aleinikoff & Issacharoff, 1993, p. 650). On a similar note, Pamela

Karlan argued that *Shaw* and its progeny "betoken a jurisprudence that is both incoherent and doctrinally unstable" (Karlan, 1995, p. 91). She further contended that the "patent insufficiency of the Court's reasoning raises the question of the Court's real agenda in issuing such a confused and confusing opinion" (Karlan, 1993, p. 271). Richard Pildes and Richard Niemi noted that "beyond casting doubt on 'highly irregular' districts, *Shaw* provides no criteria to guide reapportionment bodies or courts in judging when this line has been crossed" (Pildes & Niemi, 1993, p. 485).

Despite the validity of the critics' claims, this article suggests that much can be learned from *Shaw v. Reno* (1993) and its progeny. Instead of relying upon the traditional equal protection framework, I engage in a detailed textual analysis of the opinions in order to uncover the competing visions of democracy that lie at the heart of the Supreme Court's new jurisprudence. Although these rival understandings of democracy do not help to resolve all the doctrinal contradictions and incoherences identified by the legal scholars, they do provide important insights on how the justices conceive of (and by extension, constitute) democracy.

II: ENVISIONING DEMOCRACY

In this part, I argue that competing visions of democracy elucidate the deep divide between the majority and dissenting opinions in *Shaw v. Reno* (1993) and its progeny. The majority opinion adopted an explicit vision that I refer to as "Individualist Democracy." The dissenting opinions, by contrast, had an entirely different understanding of democracy, which I refer to as "Democracy as Power."

The Majority Opinion and Individualist Democracy

In *Shaw v. Reno* (1993), the Court held that plaintiffs can challenge a redistricting plan under the equal protection clause if it "rationally cannot be understood as anything other than an effort to separate voters into different districts on the basis of race." To understand the Court's apparent crafting of a new constitutional right to a color-blind electoral process, particular attention must be paid to the Court's portrayal of the facts. The majority decision provided a particularly lurid description of the Twelfth District. Justice O'Connor stated that the district was "approximately 160 miles long and, for much of its length, no wider than the I-85 corridor. It winds in snakelike fashion through tobacco country, financial centers, and manufacturing areas 'until it gobbles in enough enclaves of black neighborhoods.' " The Court dryly observed that "[n]orthbound and southbound drivers on I-85 sometimes find themselves in separate districts in one county, only to 'trade' districts when they enter the next county." To further underscore the peculiar appearance of the Twelfth District, Justice O'Connor quoted a state legislator who remarked that "if you drove down the interstate with both car doors open, you'd kill most of the people in the district" (*Shaw v. Reno* 509 U.S. 630; 1993). The Court employed similar rhetoric in the next case, *Miller v. Johnson* (1995). At issue in *Miller* was the bizarre shape of the Eleventh District, which spanned some 260 miles connecting black neighborhoods in Atlanta with those in Savannah. According to the Court, "the populations of the Eleventh are centered around four discrete, widely spaced urban centers that have absolutely nothing to do with each other." The majority opinion also quoted from the Almanac of American Politics, which described the Eleventh District as a "monstrosity" (*Miller v. Johnson* 515 U.S. 900; 1993).

In *Shaw v. Reno* (1993), the appearance of the Twelfth District was central to the Court's determination of its unconstitutionality. Indeed, the Court explicitly stated that "reapportionment is one area in which *appearances do matter*," even though traditional districting principles such as compactness and contiguity are not constitutionally required (*Shaw v. Reno* 509 U.S. 630; 1993; emphasis added).[13] The reason the physical appearance of the Twelfth District mattered, according to the Court, is that the district's very shape fostered and perpetuated certain harmful messages.

The *Shaw* majority identified two kinds of harms emanating from the district's appearance. The first harm was that the district reinforced "the perception that members of the same racial group – regardless of their age, education, economic status, or the community in which they live – think alike, share the same political interests, and will prefer the same candidates at the polls." The second harm caused by the Twelfth District's shape was the "equally pernicious" message sent to elected representatives. The majority argued that when "a district obviously is created solely to effectuate the perceived common interests of one racial group, elected officials are more likely to believe that their primary obligation is to represent only the members of that group, rather than their constituency as a whole" (*Shaw v. Reno* 509 U.S. 630; 1993). In an important article, Richard Pildes and Richard Niemi referred to these harms as "expressive harms" that result from "the idea or attitudes expressed through a governmental action, rather than from the more tangible or material consequences the action brings about. On this view, the meaning of a governmental action is just as important as what that action does" (Pildes & Niemi, 1993, pp. 506–507). They further argued that the Court's theory of voting rights "centers on the perceived legitimacy of structures of political representation" (Pildes & Niemi, 1993, p. 507).

A close examination of the text reveals that the Court justified the gravity of these harms by direct and explicit appeals to democratic ideals. This article suggests that the bizarrely shaped Twelfth District caused harm, in the Court's eyes, to democracy itself. As stated above, the first harm was that the district fostered the stereotype that members of the same racial group "think alike, share the same political interests, and will prefer the same candidates at the polls." Immediately following its description of the first harm, the Court stated:

> If our society is to continue *to progress as a multiracial democracy*, it must recognize that the automatic invocation of race stereotypes retards that progress and causes continued hurt and injury (*Shaw v. Reno* 509 U.S. 630; 1993; emphasis added).

The Court implied that the perception that members of the same racial group "think alike" and "share the same candidates at the polls" was not simply harmful by virtue of being a racial stereotype; it was harmful because it damaged the democratic system.

The second harm identified by the Court was that elected officials would be more likely to believe that their primary obligation would be to the majority racial group in their district rather than the entire constituency. After describing the harm, the Court proceeded to quote at length from Justice Douglas's dissent in *Wright v. Rockefeller* (1964):

> Here the individual is important, not his race, his creed, or his color. The principle of equality is at war with the notion that District A must be represented by a Negro, as it is with the notion that District B must be represented by a Caucasian, District C by a Jew, District D by a Catholic, and so on.... That system, by whatever name it is called, is a divisive force in a community, emphasizing differences between candidates and voters that are irrelevant in a constitutional sense (*Shaw v. Reno* 509 U.S. 630; 1993; citing *Wright v. Rockefeller* 376 U.S. 52; 1964).

From the *Shaw* majority's perspective, the Twelfth District damaged the integrity of the democratic system because the relationship between a representative and her constituents would be defined by membership in a particular racial group. The obvious implication left unstated by the Court was that elected officials in majority-black districts would represent the interests of black residents, but not white residents. This state of affairs, according to the *Shaw* majority, was "altogether antithetical to our system of representative democracy" (*Shaw v. Reno* 509 U.S. 630; 1993).

A close reading of *Shaw v. Reno* (1993) reveals that the Court had adopted a particular vision of democracy, which I refer to as "Individualist Democracy." In the majority's ideal vision of democracy, a system of government represents the interests of individuals, and not groups, in the political process. The term "individual" is narrowly defined as those dimensions of a person's identity that are not grounded in a racial or other affiliation; hence, in Justice Douglas's words, "the individual is important, not his race, his creed, or his color." For the *Shaw* majority, remedial race-based districting "threatens to carry us further from the goal of a *political system in which race no longer matters* – a goal that the Fourteenth and Fifteenth Amendments embody, and to which the Nation continues to aspire" (*Shaw v. Reno* 509 U.S. 630; 1993; emphasis added). Democracy aspires, in the Court's view, to become a political system in which race is no longer politically salient.

Apart from the emphasis on the individual, another important aspect of Individualist Democracy is the belief that an acknowledgment of race could lead to democratic instability. The *Shaw* Court referred repeatedly to the "particular dangers" of benign racial classifications in voting. Justice O'Connor asserted that "racial gerry-mandering, even for remedial purposes, may balkanize us into competing racial factions." The Court also quoted Justice Douglas's assertion that:

> When racial or religious lines are drawn by the State, the multiracial, multireligious communities that our Constitution seeks to weld together as one become separatist; antagonisms that relate to race or to religion rather than to political issues are generated; communities seek not the best representative but the best racial or religious partisan. Since that *system is at war with the democratic ideal, it should find no footing here* (*Shaw v. Reno* 509 U.S. 630; 1993; citing *Wright v. Rockefeller* 376 U.S. 52; 1964; emphasis added).

The *Shaw* majority adopted Justice Douglas's contention that multiracial communities would be become "separatist" and that "antagonisms that relate to race . . . rather than to political issues" would be generated. Race-based redistricting is a "divisive force" in a democratic system. The purpose of the Constitution, by contrast, is to "weld together as one" the diverse communities in the nation. The Court's concern here is that race-based redistricting affects the beliefs and behavior of *all* participants in the democratic system, and not just the beliefs and behavior of representatives and constituents in the district itself. These beliefs and behaviors are dangerous to democracy because they destabilize the sense of membership in a collective whole.

In sum, two principal themes can be deduced from the *Shaw* majority's vision of Individualist Democracy. The first is the principle that individuals, and not racial groups, are represented in a democracy. The Court put forth a vision of democracy that is based upon a strong version of the color-blindness principle: not only will government not take race into account, but racial issues will cease to emerge in political affairs. Indeed, throughout its discussion of democratic representation, the majority appeared to espouse a distinction between (illegitimate) racial interests and (legitimate) political interests, as is evident in its reliance on Justice Douglas' contention that "antagonisms that relate to race or to religion *rather than to* political issues are generated" by race-based redistricting. While the distinction between "political issues" and "racial issues" is highly implausible given the historic and contemporary salience of race, it is faithful nonetheless to the ideal of a non-racialized Individualist Democracy. The second theme is the majority's preoccupation with democratic stability. The *Shaw* Court asserted that remedial racial classifications carry particular dangers in the voting context because they run the risk of balkanizing the nation into competing racial factions. In an Individualist Democracy, by contrast, the political system has moved beyond group membership and the dangers that such identities and loyalties (allegedly) pose for its stable functioning.

The Dissenting Opinions and Democracy as Power

In *Shaw v. Reno* (1993), the dissenting justices were extremely critical of the majority's establishment of an "analytically distinct" racial gerrymandering claim. Justice White (joined by Justices Blackmun and Stevens) argued that the *Shaw* majority had "imagin[ed] an entirely new cause of action" that was at odds with the voting rights precedents. Specifically, the dissent argued that the new *Shaw* claim was invalid and unjustifiable because it was not based upon any cognizable injury such as minority vote dilution. The appellants in *Shaw*, who were white voters, had not been impaired in their ability to participate in the political process. For this reason, argued the dissent, the white voters did not suffer from an unconstitutional dilution of their voting power. As Justice White noted, white voters, who constituted 76% of the population in North Carolina, still maintained a voting majority in ten of the state's twelve congressional districts (*Shaw v. Reno* 509 U.S. 630; 1993).

At the heart of the dispute between the majority and the dissent was a fundamentally different vision of democracy. A close examination of the dissenting opinions reveals that the justices had a particular conception of democracy, which I refer to as "Democracy as Power." The dissent's alternative vision of democracy stressed the imbalance in *political power* currently existing between the dominant group and a racial minority.[14]

The dissenting justices in *Shaw v. Reno* (1993) analyzed the constitutionality of majority-minority districts by focusing on the actual power of those benefiting from the remedial redistricting. In the event that a politically powerful group manipulates electoral districts in order to further enhance its own political power at the expense of weaker groups, then, according to Justice Stevens, the "duty to govern impartially" has been abused. If, however, the politically dominant group acts to facilitate the election of a member of a politically weaker group, then the duty to govern impartially has not been violated. A group is politically weak if it is under-represented in the legislature. Justice Stevens insisted that:

> A majority's attempt to enable the minority to participate more effectively in the process of democratic government should not be viewed with the same hostility that is appropriate for oppressive and exclusionary abuses of political power (*Shaw v. Reno* 509 U.S. 630; 1993).

In other words, the act of *enabling* a minority group to participate more effectively in the "process of democratic government" should not be treated the same as the act of *disabling* a minority group from participating in a democracy. A racial gerrymander is unconstitutional not because of the racial stereotypes embodied within it, but because its purpose is to enhance the power of the majority group at the expense of the minority group, and thereby further imbalance the unequal distribution of power. The equal protection clause, in Justice Stevens's view, did not prevent a state from facilitating the election of a member of a racially identifiable group of voters, where the group lacked power in the political process. Indeed, the role of the equal protection clause is to equalize power among disparate groups and provide minority voters with an effective voice in the national assembly (*Shaw v. Reno* 509 U.S. 630; 1993).

As Justice White argued in a similar vein, race-based redistricting raises constitutional problems only when the districts have the intent and effect of unduly diminishing the influence of racial groups on the political process. Racial gerrymandering cannot be said to exist unless "the political processes ... were not equally open to participation by the group in question – that its members had less opportunity than did other residents in the district to participate in the political processes and to elect legislators of their choice" (*Shaw v. Reno* 509 U.S. 630; 1993; *White v. Regester* 412 U.S. 755; 1973).

While the dissenting justices spoke of "majority" and "minority" groups in the abstract, they also emphasized that race-conscious redistricting had to be treated in the context of the power imbalance between *blacks* and *whites* specifically. Justice Stevens argued that:

> The Court's refusal to distinguish an enactment that helps a minority group from enactments that cause it harm is especially unfortunate at the intersection of race and voting, given that African Americans and other disadvantaged groups have struggled so long and so hard for inclusion in that most central exercise of our democracy (*Miller v. Johnson* 515 U.S. 900; 1995).

For Justice Stevens, the obvious purpose of the Twelfth District, which was to enable the election of a black representative from North Carolina, did not violate the Constitution (*Shaw v. Reno* 509 U.S. 630; 1993). For this reason, he disagreed with the majority's use of the term "gerrymander" to describe the situation in which the majority shares its power with a politically weak and underrepresented group:

> [T]he Court misapplied the term 'gerrymander,' previously used to describe grotesque line-drawing by a dominant group to maintain or enhance its political power at a minority's expense,

> to condemn the efforts of a majority (whites) to share its power with a minority (African Americans) (*Miller v. Johnson* 515 U.S. 900; 1995).

For a similar reason, Justice White was deeply skeptical that the white plaintiffs in *Shaw v. Reno* (1993) were impaired in their ability to participate in the political process. Justice White noted that whites constituted 76% of the population in North Carolina and they formed a majority in 83% of the congressional districts. It was therefore ironic that the majority would recognize a new constitutional gerrymandering claim on behalf of white voters challenging a district that had sent the first black representative from North Carolina to Congress since Reconstruction (*Shaw v. Reno* 509 U.S. 630; 1993).

In sum, there are two important features of Democracy as Power. First, democracy was not conceived of as representing strictly individual interests, but rather, was presented as involving the relative *political power* of *groups* within a society. In Democracy as Power, a properly functioning democracy is one in which members of racial minority groups have the same opportunity to participate in the political process. When the ability of minority groups to elect a representative of their choice is hampered, democracy is undermined because such groups are effectively "shut out" from the process of democratic government. A legitimate democracy is not one that simply provides equal opportunity to achieve representation; instead, a legitimate democracy requires that fair representation is actually realized. Second, there was a frank recognition of the intersection of racial identity and political interests. The dissents argued that electoral redistricting issues could not be adjudicated without acknowledging the fact that African-Americans constituted a politically weak segment of society in comparison to the dominant white majority. According to the dissenting justices, denying the political salience of race undermined democracy by disempowering racial minorities.

Two Theories of Representation

It is evident that a greater contrast could not exist between the visions of democracy – Individualist Democracy and Democracy as Power – that were adopted by the majority and the dissenting opinions in *Shaw v. Reno* (1993). Where the dissent was preoccupied with the relative power of historically disadvantaged groups in the political process, the majority was committed to a deracialized and individualist vision of democracy. In this section, I briefly consider the theoretical bases of these rival understandings of democracy.

These competing visions of democracy correspond in certain ways with the two predominant conceptions of representation in political theory: the *liberal* theory of representation and the *communitarian* theory of representation. The liberal theory of representation is rooted in the principles of liberalism. A central tenet of liberalism is the fundamental equality of all individuals, which is defined as the equality of "respect which is owed to persons irrespective of their social position" (Rawls, 1999, p. 447). This principle of equality is taken to mean that "individuals have a right to equal concern and respect in the design and administration of the political institutions that govern them" (Dworkin, 1978, p. 180). In practice, "equal concern and respect" is realized through neutral procedures or what Rawls refers to as pure procedural justice. Pure procedural justice obtains when "there is a correct or fair procedure such that the outcome is likewise correct or fair, whatever it is, provided that the procedure has been properly followed" (Rawls, 1999, p. 75). What matters here is not that the outcomes are fair according to an independent standard, but rather that fair procedures are followed, leading to outcomes that are necessarily fair, whatever they happen to be. In other words, the principle of equality in liberal theory is met by ensuring the equality of opportunity.

A liberal theory of representation is based on the same principles: equality of opportunity, fair and neutral procedures, and the primacy of the individual. The state ensures the equality of opportunity by treating all individuals impartially and neutrally, without making distinctions based on morally arbitrary characteristics such as race and sex. Clearly, the majority's vision of Individualist Democracy corresponds closely with the liberal theory of representation. In an Individualist Democracy, individuals, and not groups, are to be represented in a democratic system. By creating the Twelfth District, the state violated the requirement of fair and neutral procedures because it took race into account for the purpose of ensuring representation for a particular racial group.

The communitarian conception of representation holds that liberal theory ignores the importance of *group* membership for determining political interests (Phillips, 1995; Williams, 1998; Young, 2000). Liberal theory fails to account for the social and historical context that affects the life chances and prospects of members of certain disadvantaged groups. Melissa Williams cogently argued that "[p]recisely those factors that were supposed to be "morally arbitrary" – race, class, sex, and so on – are the ones that correlate most highly with relative advantage and disadvantage" (Williams, 1998, p. 60). For this reason, the liberal doctrine of equal opportunity can produce systemically unequal results. The communitarian theory of representation has many strands, but a common theme is that socially and historically disadvantaged groups should be ensured representation in the national assembly. Some communitarians argue that descriptive representation, in which the national assembly "mirrors" the make-up of society, can provide racial minorities a voice that they would otherwise lack (Mansbridge, 1999). Clearly, the dissent's vision of Democracy as Power reflects some of the major themes of the communitarian theory of representation. Democracy as Power stresses the group-based nature of political interests, recognizes the importance of historical exclusion and discrimination, and supports the protection of minority representation.

The communitarian theory of representation reveals the serious impoverishment of the majority's ideal vision of democracy. For a start, Individualist Democracy does not grapple with the fact that it is difficult to speak of representation and voting without some reference to groups. As Justice Powell observed, "the concept of 'representation' necessarily applies to groups: groups of voters elect representatives; individual voters do not" (*Davis v. Bandemer* 478 U.S. 109; 1986). On a similar note, Lani Guinier pointed out that group-based representation is unavoidable in a representational scheme based upon geographic districts (Guinier, 1994, pp. 126–127). Indeed, every representational system is premised by definition upon groups of individuals aggregated according to shared political interests, as Melissa Williams observed:

> Individual citizens can only be represented insofar as they have identifiable interests, and the act of identifying the interests that ought to be reflected in public policy is necessarily an act of defining a group of citizens who share those representable interests. In other words, no system of representation can escape the need to aggregate citizens for the purpose of assigning a representative to them (Williams, 1998, p. 25).

It is important to note, however, that the *Shaw* majority did not question the aggregation of political interests by geography or party affiliation: it was the aggregation of political interests according to *racial identity* that the Court disdained.

The difficulty with the Court's position, however, is that political interests *are* sometimes based on racial identity.[15] By virtue of their race, African-Americans share many political interests in common. As Michael Dawson argued, "as long as African Americans continue to believe that their lives are to a large degree determined by what happens to the group as a whole, . . . African Americans' perceptions of racial group interests [would] be an important component of the way individual blacks go about evaluating policies, parties, and candidates" (Dawson, 1994, p. 57). Furthermore, as Kimberle Crenshaw pointed out, the eradication of formal barriers to equality has not eliminated the subordination of African Americans (Crenshaw, 1988, p. 1384). On a similar note, Amy Gutmann observed that "blacks – whether acting as citizens or legislators – are more likely (as a matter of contingent, historical fact) to place the interest of overcoming racial injustice near the top of their political agenda" (Gutmann, 1996, p. 154). Donald Kinder and Lynn Sanders confirmed the intuition that whites view racial discrimination as largely an artifact of a distant past, while blacks see racial discrimination as endemic and ubiquitous (Kinder & Sanders, 1996, p. 287). Furthermore, it is well known that African-Americans overwhelmingly vote for the Democratic Party; indeed, the existence of group voting patterns is the basis for the Court's jurisprudence on minority vote dilution. For these reasons, it is disingenuous for the Court to argue that because racial stereotypes are pernicious, it is therefore impermissible to acknowledge the reality that members of the same race may share similar political interests.

Although the dissent's vision of Democracy as Power has a more realistic appraisal of the intersection of race and politics, it leaves many questions and issues unresolved. It is not clear whether Democracy as Power applies to *any* minority group or only to those racial minority groups that have been historically disadvantaged.[16] The vision of Democracy as Power also has an undertheorized account of what constitutes a "group" for the purposes of representation.[17] In addition, the dissent's vision fails to adequately consider whether majority-minority districts actually enhance the power of minority racial groups. For the dissent, the purpose of majority-minority districts is to enable blacks to "participate more effectively" in the process of democratic government (*Shaw v. Reno* 509 U.S. 630; 1993). An unstated assumption in the dissent's vision is that fair and effective representation is satisfied through proportional representation. For this reason, the majority-minority districts at issue in *Shaw v. Reno* (1993) and its progeny were permissible because they provided racial minorities the ability to elect candidates in proportion to their total population in the state. It would seem, however, that "effective participation" cannot be met simply by ensuring the *presence* of minority groups in the assembly. The fact remains that African Americans are a permanent minority, and therefore would not be able to protect their policy interests even under a system of proportional representation.

According to Lani Guinier, proponents of race-conscious redistricting are implicitly endorsing the "theory of black electoral success" (Guinier, 1994, pp. 54–69). This theory, which Guinier vigorously criticized, fails to take account of whether majority-minority districts enable African Americans to actually realize their political objectives. Guinier argued that minority districts provide only a token presence in the legislature, but they do little to guarantee legislative influence over policy outcomes (Guinier, 1994, p. 55). The dissenting opinions, however, do not distinguish between legislative presence and legislative influence. Instead, there is an implicit assumption that legislative presence alone guarantees effective participation in the democratic process. Ultimately, the dissent's vision of Democracy as Power views political power as the ability to secure minority representation, rather than the more ambitious goal of realizing minority empowerment.

III: SYMBOLIC DEMOCRACY

The majority opinion in *Shaw v. Reno* (1993) embraced an ideal vision of democracy in which a system of government represents the interests of individuals rather than groups. The concept of Individualist Democracy, however, only partially captures the complexity of the majority opinion. Rather than engaging in a one-sided denunciation of race-based redistricting, the *Shaw* majority vacillated between *denying* the relevance of racial groups in a democratic political process, on the one hand, and *recognizing* the relevance of racial groups in representation and voting, on the other. Is there a coherent explanation for the *Shaw* majority's vacillation between group denial and group recognition? This article develops a theory of "Symbolic Democracy" to explain the paradox of simultaneous group denial and group recognition. Before elaborating the theory, it would be helpful to consider the meaning of "symbolism."

The concept of symbolism is perhaps best understood by contrasting it with the notion of representation. Unlike representation, which involves a precise correspondence, proxy or substitution, symbols do not resemble their referents (Cohen, 1979, p. 87; Pitkin, 1967, p. 98). Symbols aim to represent ideas or concepts rather than representing the form or shape of actual objects (Pitkin, 1967, p. 93). A symbol "may well be a recognizable object but it need not be and usually is not a representation of what it symbolizes" (Pitkin, 1967, p. 94). In other words, symbols are vehicles for the conception of what they are symbolizing. Symbols allow us to make abstractions; as such, they are "instruments of expression, of communication, of knowledge and of control" (Firth, 1973, p. 77; see also Hinckley, 1990, p. 4).

Yet the messages and ideas that are conveyed by symbols are not fixed or self-evident. It is important to note that symbols are "objects, acts, concepts, or linguistic formations that stand *ambiguously* for a multiplicity of disparate meanings" (Cohen, 1974, p. ix). The very essence of symbols lies in their multivocality, ambiguity, complexity, imprecision and dynamism (Cohen, 1979, p. 98; Turner, 1975, p. 155). Again, in contrast to representation, symbolism suggests "hidden or inner qualities rather than outward resemblance" (Pitkin, 1967, p. 95). Symbols have the power to evoke emotions and attitudes, and compel individuals to act (Cohen, 1974, p. ix; Pitkin, 1967, p. 96). Symbols are also vital for developing and maintaining a sense of public identity (Berlant, 1991, p. 24; Edelman, 1964).

The "symbolic life" of the law is fundamental to the development of a national ideology (Scheingold, 1974, p. xi). The law both constructs and reflects social meanings (Lessig, 1995). In particular, legal symbols, such as the Constitution, the Bill of Rights, and the courts, convey the legitimacy of public institutions and processes (Scheingold, 1974, p. 15). In this article, I argue that the Court in

Shaw v. Reno (1993) was deeply concerned with how legal rules and procedures symbolized certain values and ideas that, from the Court's perspective, served to either augment or undermine the legitimacy of the democratic system. I am not suggesting that these procedures and rules did *in fact* symbolize these values for large numbers of people. Instead, I am interested in the ways in which the *Shaw* majority perceived these procedures and rules as being symbolic of larger concepts and ideas.

By Symbolic Democracy, then, I am referring to an analytic lens that is focused on the *relationship* between a set of democratic institutions and procedures, on the one hand, and a collection of democratic values and aspirations, on the other. Democratic institutions and procedures stand for or symbolize certain values and aspirations. A close reading of *Shaw v. Reno* (1993) reveals that the Court was deeply concerned with the symbolic value of certain democratic procedures and institutions. In contrast to the *Shaw* majority's explicit vision of Individualist Democracy, the symbolic dimension of democracy is *implicitly* located in its decision.[18]

The Twelfth District: A Symbol of Unfairness in the Democratic Process

In *Shaw v. Reno* (1993), the Court was concerned not only with the *actual* fairness of the democratic process, but also with the *appearance* of fairness. In this section I explore how, for the *Shaw* majority, the physical appearance of the Twelfth District symbolized unfairness and illegitimacy, and thereby undermined democracy itself. A close analysis of the majority opinion reveals that the Twelfth District symbolized unfairness and illegitimacy in the democratic system in three ways. For the Court, the physical appearance of the Twelfth District symbolized first, that the *representatives* were unaccountable; second, that the *constituents* were racially stereotyped; and third that the *democratic system* as a whole excluded racial groups from democratic membership and participation.[19] Because the Court felt that the Twelfth District symbolized values that were harmful to democratic legitimacy, it forbade the use of "too much" race, and, by extension, denied the relevance of race in representation.

Representatives and Accountability

In the *Shaw* majority's ideal vision of democracy, representation is conceived of in individualist terms. Representatives should relate to each constituent on a one-to-one basis, rather than on the basis of a constituent's membership in a particular racial group. Legitimate representation must, in the Court's view, be universal in that the legislator represents, at least in theory, the needs and interests of *all* her constituents on an equal basis.[20] For the Court, representation is fair only when it is individualist, neutral and non-partisan (*Shaw v. Reno* 509 U.S. 630; 1993).

It comes as no surprise, then, that the bizarre shape of the Twelfth District symbolized, in the eyes of the Court, that representatives would not be accountable to their constituents. Specifically, the *Shaw* majority stated that the legislators' self-perceived responsibilities would be directed to "a particular racial group rather than their constituency as a whole" (*Shaw v. Reno* 509 U.S. 630; 1993). In other words, the Court implied, representative democracy would be undermined because black representatives would represent the interests of the black residents of the Twelfth District, but not the interests of the white residents. The reason this is "altogether antithetical" to the democratic system is that the white voters are, under this assumption, disenfranchised and shut out of the political process. They lack representation by virtue of their whiteness, even if they voted for the black candidate. Clearly, this state of affairs runs contrary to the majority's vision of Individualist Democracy in which a citizen's relationship to the political process is not determined by her racial identity.

The Court's argument, however, is contradictory for it is implicitly based upon the very racial stereotype that it was at pains to deny. As Justice Stevens remarked, the majority's argument assumes that black voters in a majority-minority district "share the same candidates at the polls" and so will elect a (presumably) black candidate, who will ignore white interests.[21] Not only was the Court engaging in its own stereotyping, but, to make matters worse, it has been shown that the Court's stereotype about the quality of black representation is wrong. Recent evidence suggests that black representatives in majority-minority districts *are* responsive to their white constituents (Canon, 1999, p. 4).

Constituents and Racial Stereotyping

For the *Shaw* majority, the shape of the Twelfth Districts symbolized the racial stereotyping of the constituents living in the district. The Court contended that a bizarrely shaped majority-minority district sent the message that members of the same racial group "think alike, share the same political interests, and will prefer the same candidates at the polls" (*Shaw v. Reno* 509 U.S. 630; 1993). Because the boundaries of the Twelfth District were purposely drawn to create a majority African-American district, the resulting shape of the district symbolized the idea that political interests are determined by membership in a racial group. By symbolizing a connection between race and political preferences, the appearance of the Twelfth District undermined the majority's ideal vision of an Individualist Democracy. In addition, the Court expressed concern that the values symbolized by the Twelfth District would be dangerous to a democracy because they destabilized the sense of membership in a collective whole. By representing the confluence of political interests and racial identity, the Twelfth District would, according to the Court, exacerbate race-based antagonisms, resulting in political instability and conflict (*Shaw v. Reno*, 509 U.S. 630; 1993).

While the Court was undoubtedly correct that it is stereotypical to assume that all blacks have identical opinions, its unwillingness to face the reality that *race does in fact matter* made light of the political concerns of blacks. As Justice Souter argued in dissent, a system of representation must consider the relevance of race in politics:

> It is an entirely different matter, however, to recognize that racial groups, like all other groups, play a real and legitimate role in political decision making. It involves nothing more than an acknowledgment of the reality that our concepts of common interest, geography, and personal allegiances are in many places simply *too bound up with race to deny some room for a theory of representative democracy allowing for the consideration of racially conceived interests* (*Bush v. Vera* 517 U.S. 952; 1996; emphasis added).

Representation is less democratic if the interests of minority racial groups are discounted because these interests correlate with racial identity. Furthermore, as Justice Stevens argued, most racial classifications are invidious because they are based upon irrational assumptions connecting a person's ability with her skin color. In the redistricting context, however, it is "neither irrational, nor invidious, . . . to assume that a black resident of a particular community is a Democrat if reliable statistical evidence discloses that 97% of the blacks in that community vote in Democratic primary elections" (*Bush v. Vera* 517 U.S. 952; 1996).

The Democratic System and Exclusion from Membership

The legitimacy of a democracy is based to a large degree on the extent to which all persons are included in membership and participation (Cohen, 1997; Young, 1990). For the *Shaw* majority, the Twelfth District undermined democracy because it symbolized the exclusion of racial groups from democratic membership and participation. I argue that the Court drew analogies between the Twelfth District and three forms of discriminatory exclusion that are now considered to be morally unacceptable, namely, racial gerrymandering, segregation, and apartheid.

In the majority opinion, Justice O'Connor drew analogies between the Twelfth District and historic forms of racial gerrymanders in the South. In particular, the Court compared the shape of the Twelfth District to the exclusion of black voters from the city limits in *Gomillion v. Lightfoot* (1960). In *Gomillion*, Alabama redrew the boundaries of the city of Tuskegee so as to exclude blacks voters but no white voters from the city limits. The city of Tuskegee went from being the shape of a square to an "uncouth twenty-eight-sided figure" (*Gomillion v. Lightfoot* 364 U.S. 339; 1960). The *Shaw* majority stated that it "is unsettling how closely the North

Carolina plan resembles the most egregious racial gerrymanders of the past" (*Shaw v. Reno* 509 U.S. 630; 1993).

The Court's analogy is powerful because denial of the suffrage has an important symbolic aspect. The exclusion from the right to vote is not simply the denial of an important political right – it involves the denial of personhood. Judith Shklar argued that the right to vote is symbolic in that it conveys belonging, respect, recognition and prestige (Shklar, 1991, p. 27). Those who are denied the vote "feel dishonored, not just powerless and poor" (Shklar, 1991, p. 3). In a similar vein, Charles Beitz observed that those who are excluded from the franchise "are not publicly recognized as persons at all"; indeed, they are "socially dead" (Beitz, 1989, p. 109).[22] Equal voting power is thus intimately tied with one's status as a civic equal, argued Gutmann, because "equal voting power *publicly expresses* the idea of our civic equality" (Gutmann, 1996, p. 156; emphasis added). This was particularly true for black freedmen for whom the right to vote was "*the* public sign that their years of servitude were over, and that they were citizens at last" (Shklar, 1991, p. 52). The denial of the vote is thus inextricably linked to the legacy of slavery. As Frederick Douglass memorably stated, "Slavery is not abolished until the black man has the ballot" (cited in Shklar, 1991, p. 52).

The symbolic aspect of voting involves public acknowledgment of one's status as an equal, whereas denial of the vote implies public belief in one's status as an inferior, a non-person, a slave. The *Gomillion* case is a classic example of a public statement of non-recognition, exclusion, and insult. For this reason, the *Shaw* majority's analogy of the exclusion of blacks from the city of Tuskegee with the shape of the Twelfth District strikes a powerful historic chord. A close look at the holding in *Gomillion* reveals, however, that the *Shaw* majority's analogy is deceptive. In *Gomillion*, the Supreme Court stated that the redrawing of the municipal boundary line "is solely concerned with segregating white and colored voters by fencing Negro citizens out of town so as to deprive them of their pre-existing municipal vote." The Court in *Gomillion* was not concerned with the issue of racial classification as such, but with the *result* of the redrawing of Tuskegee's boundaries:

> The essential inevitable effect of this redefinition of Tuskegee's boundaries is to remove from the city all save only four or five of its 400 Negro voters while not removing a single white voter or resident. The *result of the Act is to deprive* the Negro petitioners discriminatorily of the benefits of residence in Tuskegee, including, inter alia, *the right to vote* in municipal elections (*Gomillion v. Lightfoot* 364 U.S. 339; 1960; emphasis added).

The important issue in *Gomillion* was not that the lines were drawn racially but that blacks were excluded altogether from voting. The *Shaw* majority, however, interpreted *Gomillion* as *only* standing for the proposition that using racial classifications to draw district lines is impermissible. The majority overlooked the fact that *Gomillion* principally addressed the evil of black disenfranchisement. What is ironic about this analogy is that the black voters in *Shaw v. Reno* (1993), unlike the black voters in *Gomillion*, were *not* excluded from the democratic process. If anything, the Twelfth District *enhanced* the ability of blacks to cast a meaningful vote by preventing the dilution of minority voting power.

The *Shaw* majority also likened the Twelfth District to the historic practice of segregation. The Court struck down the district because it "cannot be understood as anything other than an effort to *segregate* citizens into separate voting districts on the basis of race" (*Shaw v. Reno* 509 U.S. 630; 1993; emphasis added). The Court was even more explicit in *Miller v. Johnson* (1995) where it compared majority-minority districts to the entire institution of segregation, as the following quotation indicates:

> Just as the State may not, absent extraordinary justification, segregate citizens on the basis of race in its public parks, *New Orleans City Park Improvement Assn. v. Detiege* (1958), buses, *Gayle v. Browder* (1956), golf courses, *Holmes v. Atlanta* (1955), beaches, *Mayor of Baltimore v. Dawson* (1955), and schools, *Brown v. Board of Education* (1954), so did we recognize in *Shaw* that it may not separate its citizens into different voting districts on the basis of race (*Miller v. Johnson* 515 U.S. 900; 1995; citations omitted).

The Court compared race-based redistricting to the segregation of parks, buses, golf courses, beaches and schools. Despite its symbolic appeal, the Court's analogy between *Brown v. Board of Education* (1954) and *Shaw v. Reno* (1993) is deeply problematic. For a start, segregation involved the radical separation of the races into different spheres. A segregated school was one that *either* black children *or* white children attended. By contrast, the Twelfth District was integrated with almost 55% African-American residents. While segregation prohibited African-Americans from entering the white sphere, the Twelfth District was open to any race to live in. The racial purpose in segregation was exclusionary, whereas the racial purpose in the majority-minority redistricting was inclusionary. In some sense, then, the Supreme Court's holdings in *Brown* and *Shaw* are opposite: where *Brown* mandated integration of the races, *Shaw* prohibited racial integration.

Segregation also placed a stigma upon blacks for it was a physical manifestation and public acknowledgment of their social inferiority to whites. I suggest that the stigmatic harms identified by the Court in the current redistricting cases are entirely different. The Court argues that majority-minority districts create the racial stereotype that members of a given race "think alike." Assuming that the Court's assessment is correct, I suggest that stereotypes of racial *sameness* are different in kind from the stigmatic harms of segregation that were rooted in notions of racial *inferiority*. Furthermore, it is unclear that majority-minority districts do stigmatize their inhabitants. As Justice Stevens argued, "I do not understand why any voter's reputation or dignity should be presumed to have been harmed simply because he resides in a highly integrated, majority-minority voting district that the legislature has deliberately created" (*Shaw v. Hunt* 517 U.S. 899; 1996).

For the Court, the Twelfth District also symbolized exclusion from democratic membership because its appearance was reminiscent of apartheid. Justice O'Connor said with reference to the Twelfth District that:

> A reapportionment plan that includes in one district individuals who belong to the same race, but who are otherwise widely separated by geographical and political boundaries, and who may have little in common with one another but the color of their skin, bears an *uncomfortable resemblance to political apartheid* (*Shaw v. Reno* 509 U.S. 630; 1993; emphasis added).

This reference to "political apartheid" was a dramatic attempt to underscore the illegitimacy of the Twelfth District by comparing it to the apartheid regime in South Africa in which blacks had no political power and were denied a host of basic civic and political rights. Far from instituting political apartheid, however, the purpose of the Twelfth District was to *ensure* political power for African-Americans. As Pamela Karlan notes, there was a deep irony on the part of the majority to use the word "apartheid" to describe what are "among the most integrated districts in the country" (Karlan, 1995, p. 94).

In the eyes of the Court, the Twelfth District symbolized unfairness and illegitimacy in the democratic process. The Twelfth District symbolized the idea that representatives are unaccountable, that the political preferences of constituents are determined by race, and that racial groups are excluded from democratic membership and participation. For this reason, the Court held that considerations of race cannot predominate when a legislature redraws district lines.

The Voting Rights Act as a Symbol of Legitimacy

In other parts of the majority opinion, however, the Court explicitly recognized the dangers facing members of racial minorities in a democratic system. I suggest that, paradoxically, the *Shaw* majority's concern with Symbolic Democracy also explains the Court's continued endorsement of race-based redistricting in the context of minority vote dilution. A democratic process that hardly ever results in the election of an African American *appears* illegitimate and therefore requires the cleansing powers of the Voting Rights Act. Given the long history of disenfranchisement of African Americans, the Voting Rights Act symbolizes legitimacy and fairness in the democratic process because of its central role in ensuring the inclusion of blacks in voting and representation. For this reason, the Court could not prohibit the use of race altogether because this would, in effect, amount to a declaration that the Voting Rights Act is unconstitutional. The Court could not undermine the Act without also undermining the legitimacy of democracy itself. For this reason, the majority had little choice but to allow the consideration of "some" race as mandated by the Voting Rights Act.

The symbolic power of the 1965 Voting Rights Act can only be understood by placing it within its historical and theoretical context. Following the Civil War, the adoption of the Fifteenth Amendment in 1870 provided blacks with a constitutionally protected right to vote. After an initial period of success in which blacks were registered to vote and elected to office, efforts to promote black enfranchisement ultimately failed (Davidson, 1992, p. 10). In the wake of the Compromise of 1877, the South engaged in a wholesale effort to disenfranchise blacks by first extra-legal and then legal means. White supremacist groups, most notably the Ku Klux Klan, terrorized and killed hundreds of blacks in a successful effort to stifle political participation (Bybee, 1998, pp. 14–15). The use of widespread political fraud, such as stuffing ballot boxes and closing poll stations, further undermined black participation in elections.

In the 1890s, southern states passed legislation and amended their constitutions to further reduce black enfranchisement without directly contradicting the Fifteenth Amendment (Grofman et al., 1992, pp. 8–10). Numerous tactics were adopted, including literacy tests, constitutional interpretation tests, good character tests, poll taxes, and property qualifications. The Supreme Court did little to protect the black franchise; indeed, it upheld the constitutionality of the white primary in 1935 (*Grovey v. Townsend* 295 U.S. 45; 1935), the poll tax in 1937 (*Breedlove v. Suttles* 302 U.S. 277; 1937), and the literacy test in 1959 (*Lassiter v. Northhampton County Board of Elections* 360 U.S. 45; 1959). It was only in 1944 that the Supreme Court decided that because the Democratic primary was integral to the election process, limiting participation in the primary to whites violated the Fifteenth Amendment (*Smith v. Allwright* 321 U.S. 649; 1944). The tide began to turn slowly once the federal government adopted the Civil Rights Acts of 1957, 1960 and 1964, which provided federal court judges and federal officials the authority to monitor voting practices in the South and intervene when neccssary (Grofman et al., 1992, pp. 12–13). These acts were ultimately unsuccessful in improving black enfranchisement, however, because the states merely evaded court decisions or switched to other disenfranchising tactics.

The exclusion of African Americans from participating in the democratic process exemplified the problem of majority tyranny. In *Federalist 51*, Madison described majority tyranny as follows:

> It is of great importance in a republic not only to guard the society against the oppression of its rulers, but to guard one part of the society against the injustice of the other part. ... If a majority be united by a common interest, the rights of the minority will be insecure (Madison, *Federalist 51*, p. 291).

Particularly dangerous to the rights of the minority, argued Madison, was the threat posed by factions.[23] Recognizing that the elimination of factions was all but impossible without endangering liberty, Madison suggested that a representative government offered a "cure" to the problem of factions. By extending the sphere of government over a broader territory, a greater number of interests would enter the field and cancel each other out in the competition for power (Madison, *Federalist 10*, p. 51). Madison argued that a plurality of factions was the best safeguard against any one faction constituting a majority and gaining dominance. As John Hart Ely pointed out, however, "the fact that effective majorities can usually be described as clusters of cooperating minorities won't be much help when the cluster in question has sufficient power and perceived community of interest to advantage itself at the expense of a minority" (Ely, 1980, p. 81).[24] Powerful majorities were able to block African Americans from participating in politics, thereby depriving them of the ability to protect their rights.

The adoption of the Voting Rights Act of 1965 was thus a watershed event in the history of voting rights. Section 2(a) of the Voting Rights Act prohibits any voting qualification, standard, practice or procedure that "results in a denial or abridgement of the right of any citizen... to vote on account of race or color." Section 5 of the Voting Rights Act requires covered jurisdictions to receive pre-clearance from the Attorney General or the U.S. District Court for the District of Columbia for any changes in "any voting qualification or prerequisite to voting, or standard, practice or procedure with respect to voting."[25] In 1966, the Supreme Court upheld the constitutionality of the Voting Rights Act in *South Carolina v. Katzenbach* (1966). The Court in *Katzenbach* heralded the Voting Rights Act for "banish[ing] the blight of racial discrimination in voting, which has infected the electoral process in parts of our country for nearly a century" (*South Carolina v. Katzenbach* 383 U.S. 301; 1966).

The symbolic importance of the Voting Rights Act for democratic legitimacy was not lost on the Supreme Court in *Shaw v. Reno* (1993) and its progeny. Indeed, the Court emphasized the "vital importance" of the Voting Rights Act to democratic legitimacy:

> The Voting Rights Act, and its grant of authority to the federal courts to uncover official efforts to abridge minorities' right to vote, has been of vital importance in eradicating invidious discrimination from the electoral process and enhancing the legitimacy of our political institutions (*Miller v. Johnson* 515 U.S. 900; 1995).

The Court recognized that the Voting Rights Act plays an important role in "enhancing the legitimacy of our political institutions." Given the long history of discrimination and violence associated with extending the franchise to blacks, the Voting Rights Act is a statute that commands a certain moral force. It represents the achievement of political equality for all citizens against the anti-democratic impulses of political domination and exclusion that governed the nation's political processes for so many years.

The Court's recognition of the symbolic power of the Voting Rights Act is also evident in the way it cautiously cast doubt on the scope of the Act without openly calling its constitutionality into question. In *Miller v. Johnson* (1995), for example, the majority held that redistricting plans for which race was the "predominant factor" violated the equal protection clause. The Court's interpretation of the equal protection clause as *prohibiting* the predominant use of race appeared to directly conflict with previous cases that interpreted the Voting Rights Act as *requiring* the consideration of race. Despite the apparent conflict, the Court refused to touch the issue of the Act's constitutionality.

The Court's cautious handling of the Voting Rights Act was even more evident in the next case *Shaw v. Hunt* (1996) (hereinafter *Shaw II*). In *Shaw II*, the Court sidestepped the District Court's finding that compliance with the Voting Rights Act constituted a compelling state interest. Rather than address the issue directly, the Court "assumed arguendo" that compliance with the Voting Rights Act *could* be a compelling state interest, and furthermore, "assumed arguendo" that a second majority-minority district was required by the Act. Nonetheless, held the Court, the redistricting plan failed to meet the requirements of strict scrutiny (*Shaw v. Hunt* 517 U.S. 899; 1996). In effect, the Court backed away from deciding whether the Voting Rights Act was constitutional. Rather than resolving the tension between the Voting Rights Act and the equal protection clause, the Court avoided the issue altogether by assuming, for the sake of argument, that compliance with the Act *could* meet the requirements of strict scrutiny.

In *Bush v. Vera* (1996), in which the Court struck down three majority-minority districts in Texas, a similar "assuming arguendo" strategy was followed. Writing for the five-member majority, Justice O'Connor held that the districts exhibited "a level of racial manipulation" that exceeded what the Voting Rights Act could justify. In an unusual move, Justice O'Connor filed a separate concurring opinion in which she asserted that compliance with the Voting Rights Act *was* a compelling state interest, and that the Act could exist in tandem with the Court's holding in *Shaw v. Reno* (1993). Justice O'Connor acknowledged the difficulty of reconciling the Voting Rights Act and the equal protection clause:

> The VRA requires the States and the courts to take action to remedy the reality of racial inequality in our political system, sometimes necessitating race-based action, while the Fourteenth Amendment requires us to look with suspicion on the excessive use of racial considerations by the government (*Bush v. Vera* 517 U.S. 952; 1996).

Justice O'Connor stated her view that the Voting Rights Act and *Shaw v. Reno* (1993) were compatible in a separate concurring opinion, which suggests that this position was not accepted by the other members of the majority. Indeed,

Justice Thomas, another member of the majority, stated unequivocally in a concurring opinion that strict scrutiny *always* applies to intentionally created majority-minority districts, and furthermore, that race *necessarily* predominates in the creation of such districts (*Bush v. Vera* 517 U.S. 952; 1996). Thomas's position suggests that districts drawn under the auspices of the Voting Rights Act would almost always be found unconstitutional, but even he did not go so far as to say that the Act was in fact unconstitutional. In his dissenting opinion, Justice Souter stated with respect to the majority's "assuming arguendo" maneuver that "it indicates that the Court does not intend to bring the *Shaw* cause of action to what would be the cruelly ironic point of finding in the Voting Rights Act of 1965 (as amended) a violation of the Fourteenth Amendment's equal protection guarantee" (*Bush v. Vera* 517 U.S. 952; 1996).

In the eyes of the *Shaw* majority, the Voting Rights Act plays an important role in the democratic system. The Court openly acknowledged that the Voting Rights Act is of "vital importance" in "enhancing the legitimacy of our political institutions." The Act symbolizes democratic inclusion and legitimacy. But because the Voting Right Act mandates race-based redistricting, the Court could not prohibit the use of race in redistricting without also raising serious doubts about the Act's constitutionality. For this reason, the Court had little choice but to permit the consideration of "some" race in electoral redistricting, despite its obvious aversion to majority-minority districts. A complete ban on the use of race in redistricting would cast doubt on the constitutionality of the Voting Rights Act, and thereby undermine the legitimacy of the democratic system itself.

CONCLUSION

I have suggested that the Supreme Court's decisions in the recent electoral redistricting cases are driven by broader concerns about our system of democracy. By determining the constitutional rules that govern electoral redistricting, the Court is essentially choosing among rival understandings of representation and democracy. To uncover these theoretical commitments, I treated the decisions as political texts in their own right. In other words, I analyzed what the justices actually say about representation and democracy, rather than relying upon the traditional equal protection approach to constitutional interpretation.

Based on this analysis, I determined, first, that the majority and the dissent adopted fundamentally different visions of democracy, and, second, that the stark contrast in these competing visions helps to explain the divergence in the cases. The majority's vision – Individualist Democracy – views democracy as system of government that represents the interests of individuals, and not racial groups, in the political process. By contrast, the dissent's vision – Democracy as Power – views democracy as mediating the relative political power of groups within a society. I also developed the concept of Symbolic Democracy to help explain a central paradox in the Court majority's decision: its simultaneous denial and recognition of the relevance of racial groups in representation.

At a broader level, I suggest in this article that the Supreme Court's visions of democracy play a fundamental role in determining the shape and contours of representative government in America. It is vitally important to consider how the Court has conceptualized and defined representative government because its actions and opinions have constructed democracy itself. For this reason, the recent electoral redistricting cases force a reappraisal of the ways in which drawing district lines has wide-ranging implications for what we mean by representation and democracy.

NOTES

1. This article focuses on the four principal cases in the Supreme Court's "new jurisprudence" in electoral redistricting: *Shaw v. Reno* (1993), *Miller v. Johnson* (1995), *Shaw v. Hunt* (1996), and *Bush v. Vera* (1996). In its most recent redistricting case, *Hunt v. Cromartie* (2001), the Court's jurisprudence took yet another turn. The Court revisited the constitutionality of North Carolina's revised redistricting plan, and held in a 5–4 decision that when blacks vote overwhelmingly for the Democratic Party, it is acceptable to place them in the same district, provided that the district is motivated by partisan politics and incumbency protection, and not by race (*Hunt v. Cromartie* 532 U.S. 234; 2001). Due to the Court's shift in approach (and space limitations), this paper does not consider the *Cromartie* decision.

2. The Court had long recognized the problem of minority vote dilution, by which "the right to vote can be affected by a dilution of voting power as well as by an absolute prohibition on casting a ballot" (*Allen v. State Board of Elections* 393 U.S. 544; 1969). Practices that diluted a minority group's voting strength were held to violate the equal protection clause of the Fourteenth Amendment (*White v. Regester* 412 U.S. 755; 1973). The Court also permitted the creation of majority-minority districts as a solution to minority vote dilution (*United Jewish Organizations v. Carey* 430 U.S. 144; 1977).

3. It is important to note that this article does not reject the equal protection approach to interpreting the Supreme Court's adjudication of electoral redistricting. Instead, I suggest that the fundamental issues in the electoral redistricting cases, including the concepts of color-blindness and color-consciousness, can be fruitfully analyzed from the perspective of democratic theory. By elaborating a new theoretical approach to the Supreme Court's recent involvement in minority redistricting and representation, this article both challenges and enriches the conventional equal protection paradigm.

4. A number of legal scholars are studying the "law of democracy," a term developed by Samuel Issacharoff, Pamela Karlan and Richard Pildes to describe the Supreme Court's cases on the political process (Issacharoff et al., 1998). These scholars are the main proponents of the "political markets" approach to the Court's decisions on political parties. Borrowing

from the corporate law field and public choice analysis, legal scholars argue that the Court should identity those institutions and rules that result in "lockups" providing permanent political advantage to either one political party or to the two-party system more generally (Pildes & Issacharoff, 1998).

5. This paper is part of a larger project that considers the visions of democracy in the Supreme Court's voting rights jurisprudence as a whole.

6. I would like to clarify that by using the word "explain," I am not attempting to provide a causative model of Supreme Court decision making. Rather than predicting the outcomes of the Supreme Court's decisions, my purpose is to reveal and analyze the visions of democracy that are embodied in the Court's reasoning.

7. Justice Frankfurter dissented from the Court's holding in *Baker v. Carr* (1962) on the ground that reapportionment was an area of political controversy that was unfit for judicial intervention. His observation that the Court was in essence choosing among competing political philosophies was meant to underscore the inappropriate nature of the Court's involvement in the political process (*Baker v. Carr* 369 U.S. 186; 1962). The intersection of voting rights law and political philosophy was also commented upon by Justice Thomas in *Holder v. Hall* (1994). According to Thomas, the "most prominent feature of the [Court's] philosophy" is its preference for single-member districts, which are favored because they help minorities win seats. Thomas argues that the Court's "theory of political participation" opts for direct political control over a fewer number of seats rather than indirect political influence over a greater number of seats. This choice, in turn, depends upon "a certain theory of the 'effective' vote, a theory that is not inherent in the concept of representative democracy itself" (*Holder v. Hall* 512 U.S. 874; 1994).

8. Ely argued that the Constitution is principally concerned with protecting processes and structures, rather than with articulating substantive values. In particular, he claimed that the Constitution is geared to ensuring a political process that is open to all citizens on an equal basis (Ely, 1980, p. 99). Ely's distinction between process and substance, however, ignores the extent to which all processes must be defended on substantive grounds. The identification of fair procedures, for example, necessarily requires a reliance on substantive values – values that tell us what fair procedures look like. Similarly, political participation is a process but it is a process we support precisely because of the values that it implies.

9. The Court is not, however, the only institution that constructs democracy – the Constitution, the executive branch, and Congress are also responsible for determining the details and contours of representative government in America. But given the Court's supposed independence from politics, its construction of democracy deserves particular scrutiny.

10. The Supreme Court did not decide whether or not the Twelfth District was constitutional. Instead, the Court remanded the decision back to the District Court to determine whether the plaintiffs' allegation of racial gerrymandering could be sustained. In the event that it was sustained, the District Court would be required to subject the redistricting plan to strict scrutiny; that is, the District Court would determine whether the plan was narrowly tailored to further a compelling governmental interest (*Shaw v. Reno* 509 U.S. 630; 1993).

11. In equal protection analysis, the Court subjects racial classifications to a "strict scrutiny" standard. Once the Court invokes strict scrutiny, the classification at issue will be deemed constitutional only if the Court agrees that the classification "is necessary to promote a compelling government interest." The strict scrutiny standard is fairly stringent, and has become increasingly demanding in the last twenty years with respect to the constitutionality of so-called benign discrimination, that is, affirmative action policies that aim to help members of racial minority groups. As Cass Sunstein observed, remedial action is

constitutional only in so far as it redresses "identifiable acts of past purposeful discrimination performed by the institution now engaging in affirmative action. Affirmative action grounded in an effort to overcome "societal discrimination" is generally unacceptable" (Sunstein, 1993, p. 331). Given the strictness of the strict scrutiny standard, and the Court majority's rhetoric on color-blindness, it is not surprising that commentators often present the issue as a choice between color-blindness and color-consciousness.

12. The Court equated the creation of majority-minority districts with classic affirmative action programs, even though there are obvious differences. Typically, affirmative action policies involve a choice that usually benefits a member of a minority racial group at the expense of a member of a majority racial group. By contrast, efforts to avoid minority vote dilution, such as creating the Twelfth District, do not injure any one racial group, unless, of course, one argues that white voters are injured by being represented by black candidates. This position, of course, is one that neither the Court nor white plaintiffs who brought suit would openly subscribe to. It can also be argued that the right to vote is different in kind to other rights because the right to vote is fundamental for the protection of all other rights. Without the right to vote, a person lacks representation and hence political power.

13. The Court previously held that traditional districting principles, such as compactness and contiguity, are not constitutionally required (*Gaffney v. Cummings* 412 U.S. 735; 1973).

14. I am not suggesting that the *Shaw* majority's vision of democracy does not involve notions of power. Instead, I use the term "democracy as power" to denote the dissent's *open* acknowledgment that questions of disparate power are at stake in electoral redistricting. Although the majority does not engage in discussions of power, it appears that in an Individualist Democracy, power resides in the individual's equal opportunity to vote for a candidate. Rather than discussing the imbalances of power between various racial groups, the majority argues that the very existence and recognition of these groups threatens democratic stability.

15. The majority's refusal to recognize the political salience of race led it to reach absurd conclusions. Because the Court made a distinction between race-neutral redistricting standards (which were acceptable) and race-conscious redistricting standards (which were subject to strict scrutiny), the states argued in response that they were following race-neutral standards, such ensuring incumbency protection and maintaining communities of interest. It just so happened, claimed the states, that race correlated with party affiliation, incumbency and communities of interest. In *Bush v. Vera* (1996), the Court held if district lines happened to correlate with race because they were drawn on the basis of party affiliation, which correlates with race, then the redistricting plan constituted a political, but not a racial, gerrymander. But, if race was used as a *proxy* to determine party affiliation, then a racial stereotype is in operation and strict scrutiny must be applied (*Bush v. Vera* 517 U.S. 952; 1996). Given that African-Americans vote overwhelmingly for the Democratic Party, and given that this political fact is widely known, the Court's distinction between acceptable political gerrymanders that happen to follow racial lines and unacceptable racial gerrymanders that happen to follow political lines is all but impossible to maintain in practice. The Court's position meant that even if the legislature was predominantly motivated by incumbency protection (and not race), the redistricting plan would be subject to strict scrutiny because the legislature used race as a proxy for party affiliation.

16. The dissenting opinions do not clarify whether the vision of Democracy as Power would apply to every politically weaker group. Do *all* minority groups, racial or otherwise, have a right to representation? Although the dissenting justices spoke of the "majority" and the "minority" in the abstract, they also emphasized that race-conscious redistricting

must be treated in the historical context of African-Americans and their exclusion from democratic participation. It seems that Democracy as Power does not apply to all racial minority groups, but rather, applies to those groups that have also suffered historical discrimination and exclusion.Complicating this picture is the fact that states have traditionally respected so-called "communities of interest" when drawing district lines. In *Miller v. Johnson* (1995), the Court held that a state is "free to recognize communities that have a particular racial makeup, provided its action is directed toward some common thread of relevant interests." In dissent, Justice Ginsburg argued powerfully that communities of interest are often based *solely* on ties of ethnicity, even when socioeconomic factors differ within the group:

> But ethnicity itself can tie people together, as volumes of social science literature have documented – even people with divergent economic interests. For this reason, ethnicity is a significant force in political life (*Miller v. Johnson* 515 U.S. 900; 1995).

Legislatures have always created voting districts on the basis of shared Chinese, Italian, Irish, Polish, or Jewish ethnic identity, but these ethnic districts have not offended or demeaned its members. Justice Ginsburg concluded that:

> If Chinese-Americans and Russian-Americans may seek and secure group recognition in the delineation of voting districts, then African-Americans should not be dissimilarly treated. Otherwise, in the name of equal protection, we would shut out "the very minority group whose history in the United States gave birth to the Equal Protection Clause" (*Miller v. Johnson* 515 U.S. 900; 1996; citing *Shaw v. Reno* 509 U.S. 630; 1993).

Justice Ginsburg's position appears to be that since it is the normal practice to recognize various ethnic groups when drawing district lines, it is therefore permissible to recognize African Americans in redistricting as well (see also Kymlicka, 1995, pp. 135–136 for a similar argument). Although Ginsburg stated that minorities "seek and secure group recognition," she did not go so far as to suggest that such groups enjoy a *constitutionally protected* right to the recognition of their group.

17. The issue of what constitutes a "group" is one of the principal theoretical problems in contemporary political theory. Given the complexity of the issue, I shall only point to the central dilemma faced by the communitarians. In general, theorists have tried to resolve a tension between recognizing the existence of group difference, on the one hand, and avoiding essentializing group identities by assuming that all individuals in a group share the same interests and opinions, on the other (Mansbridge, 1999, p. 637; Phillips, 1995, p. 167). Iris Young has suggested that a difference exists between interests, opinions, and perspectives, and she argues that members of a group share a similar perspective on the world, even though their interests and opinions may differ (Young, 1997). Other theorists argue that group membership is based on a shared history of oppression and discrimination (Williams, 1998) or shared experience (Mansbridge, 1999). The dissent's vision of Democracy as Power does not elaborate what constitutes a "group" apart from suggesting that "politically weaker groups" are those that are underrepresented in the legislature (*Shaw v. Reno* 509 U.S. 630; 1993). This definition, however, does not resolve (or for that matter, raise) the difficulty that majority-minority districts essentialize group identities.

18. It is important to clarify the difference between the "theory" of Symbolic Democracy and the majority's "vision" of an Individualist Democracy. An Individualist Democracy is

the Court's *explicit* description of an ideal vision of democracy. Symbolic Democracy, by contrast, is my externally developed framework or heuristic that captures and explains the Court's reasoning. Symbolic Democracy is thus *implicitly* located in the decision.

19. Richard Pildes and Richard Niemi referred to the first two harms as "expressive harms" that result from "the idea or attitudes expressed through a governmental action, rather than from the more tangible or material consequences the action brings about" (Pildes & Niemi, 1993, pp. 506–507). They also observed that the Court was concerned about "the perceived legitimacy of structures of political representation" (Pildes & Niemi, 1993, p. 507). I fully agree with their assessment of the Court's approach. Thinking about these issues from a "symbolic democratic" dimension, however, captures the full extent of the symbolism, allows for ambiguity in the messages sent, shows how democratic legitimacy was undermined, and explains the Court's vacillation on the place of race in representation.

20. It is impossible for any representative to literally represent the interests of all her constituents, but at least the representative should not, the *Shaw* majority seemed to be saying, be preordained to represent one racial group and not another.

21. Dissenting in a later case, Justice Stevens observed that although the representational harms identified by the Court were attributed solely to the message that was *sent out* by the legislature's districting scheme, such messages could only have a harmful impact if they were *received*, that is, that blacks did vote for the same candidates, and that these candidates ignored white voters (*Miller v. Johnson* 515 U.S. 900; 1995).

22. Beitz argued that recognition, which he defined as "public acknowledgement of one's status as an equal member of the polity," is a main component of a normative vision of democracy (Beitz, 1989, p. xiii). Procedures that convey a lack of recognition, such as gerrymandering techniques that dilute the votes of racial minorities, convey social acceptance of the inferiority of a particular group. Thus, those "singled out as less worthy are demeaned and insulted" (Beitz, 1989, pp. 109–110).

23. Madison defined a faction as "a number of citizens whether amounting to a majority or minority of the whole who are united and actuated by some common impulse of passion, or of interest, adverse to the rights of other citizens, or to the permanent and aggregate interests of the community" (Madison, *Federalist 10*, p. 46). The main cause of faction was "the various and unequal distribution of property" (Madison, *Federalist 10*, p. 47). A minority faction, claimed Madison, would cause inconvenience and disruption, but it could be defeated by the majority. By contrast, a majority faction in a popular government would be able to "sacrifice to its ruling passion or interest both the public good and the rights of other citizens" (Madison, *Federalist 10*, p. 48).

24. The "cure" to the majority tyranny problem, according to Ely, is located in footnote four of *United States v. Carolene Products Co.* (1938). In footnote four, Justice Stone suggested that the Supreme Court has a greater protective function when "prejudice against discrete and insular minorities... tends seriously to curtail the operation of those political processes ordinarily to be relied upon to protect minorities" (*United States v. Carolene Products Co.* 304 U.S. 144; 1938). Building upon this insight, Ely argued that the purpose (and justification) of judicial review is to unblock stoppages in the democratic process, such as the denial of the right to vote (Ely, 1980, p. 117).

25. Covered jurisdictions were defined in Section 4 of the Voting Rights Act so as to target those southern states with the worst records in racially discriminatory election procedures.

ACKNOWLEDGMENTS

I am very grateful for excellent suggestions on earlier versions of this paper from Patchen Markell and Lisa Wedeen. In addition, I would like to thank a number of people for their invaluable comments and conversations, including Cass Sunstein, Danielle Allen, Jacob Levy, Jeanine Bell, Austin Sarat, Jennifer Rubenstein, Sujatha Fernandes, and participants at the 2001 annual meeting of the American Political Science Association and the 2002 annual meeting of the Law and Society Association, where earlier versions of this paper were presented. I am also indebted to two anonymous reviewers for their incisive criticisms and valuable suggestions. My deep thanks as well to Azam Dawood for his unwavering support and encouragement.

REFERENCES

Aleinikoff, A. T., & Issacharoff, S. (1993). Race and redistricting: Drawing constitutional lines after Shaw v. Reno. *Michigan Law Review*, *92*, 588.

Beitz, C. R. (1989). *Political equality: An essay in democratic theory*. Princeton: Princeton University Press.

Berlant, L. (1991). *The anatomy of national fantasy: Hawthorne, utopia, and everyday life*. Chicago: University of Chicago Press.

Bickel, A. M. (1975). *The morality of consent*. New Haven: Yale University Press.

Bybee, K. J. (1998). *Mistaken identity: The Supreme Court and the politics of minority representation*. Princeton: Princeton University Press.

Canon, D. T. (1999). *Race, redistricting, and representation: The unintended consequences of black majority districts*. Chicago: University of Chicago Press.

Cohen, A. (1974). *Two-dimensional man: An essay on the anthropology of power and symbolism in complex society*. London: Routledge & Kegan Paul.

Cohen, A. (1979). Political symbolism. *Annual Review of Anthropology*, *8*, 87.

Cohen, J. (1997). Deliberation and democratic legitimacy. In: J. Bohman & W. Rehg (Eds), *Deliberative Democracy: Essays on Reason and Politics* (pp. 67–91). Cambridge: The MIT Press.

Crenshaw, K. (1988). Race, retrenchment and reform. *Harvard Law Review*, *101*, 1384.

Davidson, C. (1992). The voting rights act: A brief history. In: B. Grofman & C. Davidson (Eds), *Controversies in Minority Voting: The Voting Rights Act in Perspective* (pp. 7–51). Washington, DC: The Brookings Institute.

Dawson, M. C. (1994). *Behind the mule: Race and class in African-American politics*. Princeton: Princeton University Press.

Dworkin, R. (1978). *Taking rights seriously*. Cambridge: Harvard University Press.

Edelman, M. (1964). *The symbolic uses of politics*. Urbana: University of Illinois Press.

Ely, J. H. (1980). *Democracy and distrust: A theory of judicial review*. Cambridge: Harvard University Press.

Firth, R. (1973). *Symbols: Public and private*. Ithaca: Cornell University Press.

Fish, S. (1997). Reverse racism, or how the pot got to call the kettle black. In: F. J. Beckwith & T. E. Jones (Eds), *Affirmative Action: Social Justice or Reverse Discrimination?* (pp. 142–151). New York: Prometheus Books.

Glazer, N. (1987). *Affirmative discrimination*. Cambridge: Harvard University Press.

Grofman, B., Handley L., & Niemi, R. (1992). *Minority representation and the quest for voting equality*. Cambridge: Cambridge University Press.

Guinier, L. (1994). *The tyranny of the majority: Fundamental fairness in representative democracy*. New York: The Free Press.

Gutmann, A. (1996). Responding to racial injustice. In: A. K. Appiah & A. Gutmann (Eds), *Color Conscious: The Political Morality of Race* (pp. 106–178). Princeton: Princeton University Press.

Hinckley, B. (1990). *The symbolic presidency*. New York: Routledge.

Issacharoff, S. (1995). The constitutional contours of race and politics. *Supreme Court Review*, 45.

Issacharoff, S., Karlan, P. S., & Pildes, R. H. (1998). *The law of democracy: Legal structure of the political process*. Westbury: Foundation Press.

Karlan, P. (1993). All over the map: The Supreme Court's voting rights trilogy. *Supreme Court Review*, 245.

Karlan, P. (1995). Our separatism? Voting rights as an American nationalities policy. *University of Chicago Legal Forum*, 83.

Kinder, D. R., & Sanders, L. M. (1996). *Divided by color: Racial politics and democratic ideals*. Chicago: University of Chicago Press.

Kull, A. (1992). *The color-blind constitution*. Cambridge: Harvard University Press.

Kymlicka, W. (1995). *Multicultural citizenship: A liberal theory of minority rights*. Oxford: Oxford University Press.

Lessig, L. (1995). The regulation of social meaning. *University of Chicago Law Review*, *62*, 943.

Madison, J. (1999). Federalist No. 10. Federalist No. 51. In: A. Hamilton, J. Madison & J. Jay, *The Federalist Papers* (C. Rossiter, Ed). New York: Mentor.

Mansbridge, J. (1999). Should blacks represent blacks and women represent women? A contingent "Yes". *The Journal of Politics*, *61*, 628.

Phillips, A. (1995). *The politics of presence: The political representation of gender, ethnicity, and race*. Oxford: Oxford University Press.

Pildes, R. H., & Niemi, R. G. (1993). Expressive harms, 'Bizarre Districts,' and voting rights: Evaluating election-district appearances after *Shaw v. Reno*. *Michigan Law Review*, *92*, 483.

Pildes, R. H., & Issacharoff, S. (1998). Politics as markets: Portisan lockups of the democratic process. *Stanford Law Review*, *50*, 643.

Pitkin, H. F. (1967). *The concept of representation*. Berkeley: University of California Press.

Rawls, J. (1999). *A theory of justice* (Rev. ed.). Cambridge: Belknap Press of Harvard University Press.

Scheingold, S. A. (1974). *The politics of rights: Lawyers, public policy, and political change*. New Haven and London: Yale University Press.

Shklar, J. (1991). *American citizenship: The quest for inclusion*. Cambridge: Harvard University Press.

Smith, R. M. (1985). *Liberalism and American constitutional law*. Cambridge: Harvard University Press.

Sowell, T. (1984). *Civil rights: Rhetoric of reality*. New York: Quill.

Sunstein, C. (1993). *The partial constitution*. Cambridge: Harvard University Press.

Thernstrom, A. M. (1987). *Whose votes count? Affirmative action and minority voting rights*. Cambridge: Harvard University Press.

Turner, V. (1975). Symbolic studies. *Annual Review of Anthropology*, *4*, 145.

West, C. (1996). Affirmative action in context. In: G. E. Curry (Ed.), *The Affirmative Action Debate* (pp. 31–35). Cambridge, MA: Perseus Books.

White, J. B. (1985). *Heracles' bow: Essays on the rhetoric and poetics of the law*. Madison: University of Wisconsin Press.

Williams, M. S. (1998). *Voice, trust, and memory: Marginalized groups and the failings of liberal representation*. Princeton: Princeton University Press.

Young, I. M. (1990). *Justice and the politics of difference*. Princeton: Princeton University Press.

Young, I. M. (1997). Difference as a resource for democratic communication. In: J. Bohman & W. Rehg (Eds), *Deliberative Democracy: Essays on Reason and Politics* (pp. 383–406). Cambridge: The MIT Press.

Young, I. M. (2000). *Inclusion and democracy*. Oxford: Oxford University Press.

Cases Cited

Allen v. State Board of Elections. 1969.393 U.S.544.
Baker v. Carr. 1962.369 U.S. 186.
Breedlove v. Suttles. 1937.302 U.S.277.
Brown v. Board of Education. 1954.347 U.S.483.
Bush v. Vera. 1996.517 U.S.952.
Davis v. Bandemer. 1986.478 U.S.109.
Gaffney v. Cummings. 1973.412 U.S.735.
Gayle v. Browder. 1956.352 U.S. 903.
Gomillion v. Lightfoot. 1960.364 U.S. 339.
Grovey v. Townsend. 1935.295 U.S.45.
Hirabayashi v. United States. 1943.320 U.S.81.
Holder v. Hall. 1994.512 U.S. 874.
Holmes v. Atlanta. 1955.350 U.S. 879.
Hunt v. Cromartie. 2001.532 U.S.234.
Lassiter v. Northhampton County Board of Elections. 1959.360 U.S.45.
Mayor of Baltimore v. Dawson. 1955.350 U.S. 877.
Miller v. Johnson. 1995.515 U.S.900.
Mobile v. Bolden. 1980.446 U.S.55.
New Orleans City Park Improvement Assn. v. Detiege. 1958.358. U.S. 54.
Plessy v. Ferguson. 1896.163 U.S.537.
Richmond v. J. A. Croson Co. 1989.488 U.S.469.
Shaw v. Hunt. 1996.517 U.S. 899.
Shaw v. Reno. 1993.509 U.S.630.
Smith v. Allwright. 1944.321 U.S.649.
South Carolina v. Katzenbach. 1966.383 U.S.301.
Thornburg v. Gingles. 1986.478 U.S.30.
United Jewish Organizations v. Carey. 1977.430 U.S.144.
United States v. Carolene Products Co. 1938.304 U.S.144.
White v. Regester. 1973.412 U.S.755.
Wright v. Rockefeller. 1964.376 U.S.52.

PART II.
"MISSING PERSONS"

ACCOUNTING FOR ABSENT BODIES: THE POLITICS AND JURISPRUDENCE OF THE MISSING PERSONS ACT

Thomas M. Hawley

ABSTRACT

This paper explores the political and legal issues contained in the law and jurisprudence surrounding missing American service personnel. It argues that the Missing Service Personnel Act of 1995 is an effect of the legacy of the Vietnam War rather than a response to a particular legal problem. The essay further contends that we should be suspicious of the effort to transform the balance sheet of war into a justiciable legal question, primarily because the requirement to produce a body fails to disarm the representational economy in which the absent body constitutes a continuation of Vietnam War hostilities.

INTRODUCTION

Since the end of direct American military involvement in Vietnam in 1973, the fate of American service personnel unaccounted-for in Southeast Asia has been a source of much lingering concern in the United States. The list of those unaccounted-for, which included 2,583 names at war's end, now stands at 1,905 (DPMO website 2002).[1] Efforts to determine the fate of those on the list have generated numerous Congressional inquiries, Presidential delegations, and even civilian forays to "rescue" American prisoners of war thought still to be held

Studies in Law, Politics, and Society
Studies in Law, Politics, and Society, Volume 28, 75–95

ISSN: 1059-4337/PII: S1059433702280035

in Vietnam.[2] Currently, the accounting effort is officially conducted by the U.S. military's Joint Task Force-Full Accounting (JTF-FA), which, in conjunction with the Army's Central Identification Laboratory, Hawaii (CILHI), sends several search teams per year to Vietnam, Laos, and Cambodia to excavate graves and aircraft crash sites in an attempt to repatriate and identify the remains of soldiers who were killed in action but whose bodies were not recovered at the time of death (JTF-FA website 2002; CILHI website 2002). The issue of missing Americans has also become an enduring feature of the American political and cultural landscape, having generated numerous family organizations who agitate on behalf of missing service personnel, inspired a large number of feature films and novels, and led to the creation of the POW/MIA Flag which flies at sports stadia, government installations, and veterans' posts across the United States.[3]

To understand the effort to account for American service personnel in Southeast Asia, it is important to bear in mind that fewer Americans remain unaccounted-for from the Vietnam War than any other. Roughly 78,000 Americans remain missing from World War II, along with another 8,100 from the Korean War. Further complicating the issue is the definition of "unaccounted-for," which refers strictly to the absence of the body. The United States government does not possess verifiable evidence that any American service personnel were left behind after the cessation of hostilities in 1973 or that any Americans remain held in Southeast Asia against their will.[4] To account for a missing service member, therefore, involves not so much a determination of fate, since all unaccounted-for personnel are believed dead, but the repatriation and positive identification of human remains. This circumstance in turn means that the effort to account for Vietnam War missing must be viewed in light of the contentious legacy of the Vietnam War, particularly the fracturing of the American body politic that occurred during the war and the enduring sense of failure and defeat which has been a hallmark of American political and cultural life ever since. The return of the absent body functions metonymically in that it not only resolves questions as to the whereabouts of missing service personnel but also helps bring a sense of closure to a conflict that otherwise refuses to go away. As one searcher remarked, "The war won't really be over until they're all accounted for. We need to bring them all home" (Dillow, 1995, p. A5).

Significantly, these circumstances are not restricted to the accounting procedures used for Vietnam War-era service personnel. Indeed, the fraught cultural and political legacy of the Vietnam War and the attendant importance of the body is reflected nowhere more conspicuously than in contemporary law and jurisprudence concerning missing soldiers. The shift this represents in American legal thinking about the balance sheet of war is noteworthy, one that begins with the Missing Persons Act (MPA).[5] Since its passage in 1942, the Missing Persons Act has served as the primary instrument through which the status of missing soldiers is resolved. Its main intent is to determine the point at which the military service branches can discontinue payments and allotments to dependents of soldiers who become missing as a result of hostile action. To do so, the law permits the military Service Secretaries to issue a presumptive finding of death when "the information received, or a lapse of time without information, establishes a reasonable presumption that a member in a missing status is dead."[6]

In the aftermath of the Vietnam War, however, these presumptive findings of death generated a great deal of political turmoil, particularly among families of the missing who accused the government of administratively "killing off" their loved-ones and forsaking its duty to determine their fate and whereabouts. Such turmoil eventually led to the Missing Service Personnel Act of 1995.[7] Though not intended wholly to displace the Missing Persons Act, the 1995 law nevertheless formalized a series of personnel accounting requirements developed since the end of the Vietnam War that far exceeded those contained in the 1942 legislation. In so doing, the 1995 law expressed in legal terms the substantial anxiety over the fate and whereabouts of missing service personnel, anxiety which the law now proposes to resolve through recourse to the body. Indeed, one of the more substantial provisions of the 1995 law requires the repatriation and positive identification of human remains in order to account for a missing service member.[8] Hence, under the new law the passage of time indicates only that the service member in question has died (a circumstance which still permits the service branches to discontinue payments and benefits to dependents). This finding of death, however, does not actually account for the missing soldier in question. According to the 1995 law, accounting for the missing occurs only upon repatriation and identification of human remains.

Effectively, then, post-Vietnam War legislation pertaining to missing service personnel has instituted a distinction between death and the body to which that death pertains. This circumstance offers an important commentary on the social function of law in the post-Vietnam War era and the role to which the law aspires. In particular, the law seeks to provide a mechanism through which the extraordinary complexities of missing soldiers might be resolved and, by extension, to put to rest the cultural, political, and legal anxieties handed down from the Vietnam War. While the quest for clarity through law may not be especially remarkable in and of itself, what is noteworthy are the terms by which this clarity is to be achieved, namely, the body. These terms are especially striking in the context of Vietnam War missing. Were it the case that the United States was repatriating anything resembling the body that left for Vietnam in the 1960s and 1970s, then perhaps an accounting protocol requiring repatriation of remains would not be so conspicuous. However, due to the effects of climate and terrain, the passage of time, and the circumstances of most soldiers' disappearance, searchers in Southeast Asia must almost always content themselves with an extremely small quantity of highly fragmentary remains, a situation that in turn requires substantial conceptual and scientific effort to make the body recovered at excavation correspond with its legal counterpart. Haunting the entire process is the persistent reality of mechanized warfare – namely, permanently absent bodies – a circumstance no less true for those service members who go missing in a more contemporary context.[9]

Given these circumstances, it is difficult to escape the conclusion that the law pertaining to missing Vietnam War service personnel is designed not so much to resolve some pressing legal problem (since the Missing Persons Act still enables a determination of fate), but is instead aimed at pacifying issues that are more immediately ontological in nature. As an event with which extant interpretive structures were ill-equipped to cope, the Vietnam War remains a source of tension, one whose many divides have proven difficult to bridge despite the passage of time. Missing soldiers are an especially prominent reminder of this and it is therefore not surprising that substantial efforts are made to account for them. Yet it is precisely the importance of this issue that compels attention to the means by which is to be resolved. In particular, the law's insistence on identifiable remains to account for missing soldiers when in many cases little, if anything, remains of these bodies institutes a standard that may well be conceptually intelligible but becomes increasingly difficult to satisfy in practice as time goes by. Consequently, the law becomes implicated in the continuation of the very problem its creation was meant to solve.

To develop these issues in greater detail, the essay begins with a brief history of missing persons legislation in the United States, starting with the Missing Persons Act and continuing with some of the legal challenges that resulted from the Vietnam War. The analysis then outlines the pertinent tenets of the Missing Service Personnel Act of 1995, paying particular attention to those provisions which require identifiable remains in order to account for missing service members. Attention will also be devoted to various events that have shaped the issue of missing service personnel since the end of the Vietnam War, particularly the lists of the missing provided by the Vietnamese in 1973, discrepancy cases, and live-sighting reports. The final section elaborates on the relationship between the anxieties of the post-Vietnam War era and the law pertaining to missing service members. In particular, by requiring a body to account for the missing, the 1995 law institutionalizes a structure of accountability in which can be seen a desire to efface the political and social anxieties occasioned by the loss in Southeast Asia.

Further, since accounting for the missing is no longer tied to a determination of fate, the law in this context advances a particular kind of claim about the balance sheet of war, namely one in which the truth of "what really happened" to the missing is established via knowledge of the recovered, identified body. This truth/knowledge interface suggests most immediately that war and its aftermath are amenable to legal intervention and, ultimately, to fuller and more adequate explanation than has previously been the case. The importance of this in the post-Vietnam War era is not insubstantial given the contentious legacy of unaccounted-for soldiers. Indeed, the accounted-for body serves as a metonym in the effort to establish accountability for a lost war. However, we are wise to be wary of such claims and the attendant compulsion to transform the aftermath of war into a justiciable legal question. Such transformation ultimately furthers the wartime representational economy in which absent bodies are equivalent to the continuation of Vietnam War hostilities.

THE MISSING PERSONS ACT[10]

Since its passage in 1942, the Missing Persons Act has governed the legal status of American service personnel who become missing as a result of hostile action. As indicated, the Act was originally designed only to provide for the continuance of pay and benefits to missing soldiers and their dependents, and to determine the time at which such pay and benefits were to be terminated. Hence, it was never intended to be an accounting tool per se. A brief review of its provisions, however, shows how and why the Missing Persons Act became a *de facto* accounting tool, and how that became problematic in the aftermath of the Vietnam War.

As originally conceived, the Missing Persons Act required that pay and allowances to service members in a missing status continue at the rate in existence at the time of the service member's disappearance, and that said pay reflect any increases earned subsequently.[11] The Act also provided for payments to dependents of missing service members at the discretion of the Service Secretary (then called the "Department Head").[12] Payment of allotments was to continue for one year after the service member became missing or until the Service Secretary declared the absent member dead.[13] The law made an exception to the one-year time limit if the Service Secretary received word that the missing service member in question was still alive, or if other information was received that warranted continuation in a missing status.[14] As indicated, much of the Vietnam War-era controversy concerning missing soldiers found its source in the findings of death made by the Service Secretaries at the end of the one-year period without new information concerning the missing service member. A finding of death in the absence of remains created the impression among some families that their loved-ones were being administratively "killed-off." Some family members also feared the United States government, having declared the missing to be dead, would no longer make efforts to locate their remains.

In response to this situation, several different legal remedies were sought by families of the missing. The most significant of these was the 1973 case *McDonald v. McLucas*[15] in which the plaintiffs argued that circumstances under which the Service Secretaries could declare a missing service member dead were in violation of the Due Process Clause of the Fifth Amendment (Stahl, 1996, p. 117). In particular, the plaintiffs argued that:

> (1) no statutory criteria guided the Secretary in deciding whether to make an official report of death or presumptive finding of death, (2) Congress had not delegated rule-making authority to the Secretaries with respect to a finding of death, (3) no notice was given to the next-of-kin regarding the pendency of a status review nor any opportunity to be heard before a finding of death was made, and (4) the Missing Persons Act permitted the Service Secretary to make findings in the total absence of any evidence (Stahl, 1996, p. 117).

In response, a temporary restraining order was issued on August 6, 1973 that suspended all further status changes until a three-judge panel could rule on the Constitutional issues raised in the suit (Stahl, 1996, p. 118).

Six months later the court found in favor of the plaintiffs, noting that the sections of the Missing Persons Act which permitted the Service Secretaries to make a finding of death denied prior notice and the opportunity to be heard to those next-of-kin who were entitled to benefits under the Act.[16] While the court declined to void previous status determinations, it did require all future changes to be carried out in accordance with its decision. Consequently, the Service branches promulgated regulations in 1974 designed to bring status reviews in line with the court's ruling. Consensus held that these procedures needed to be informal rather than adversarial in nature. Hence, there would be no cross examination of witnesses, presentation of interrogatories, or recording of testimony. The Service Secretaries would send notice of pending review to primary next-of-kin and allow them to attend the hearing, while keeping all other "secondary next-of-kin" appraised by mail. The Services further agreed that primary next-of-kin would be granted access to all the information on which the status review was to be based, with the exception of classified material. In view of this, the Services agreed that the file reviewed by the military's hearing officer could not include any information not available to the next-of-kin (Stahl, 1996, p. 120).

Although these new regulations conformed with the interpretation of the law of as expressed in *McDonald*, the politically charged nature of status reviews delayed their official resumption for a further four years, during which time the United States government conducted several inquiries into the fate of missing service personnel. Among these was the House Select Committee on Missing Persons in Southeast Asia, which in 1976 concluded that "because of the nature and circumstances in which many Americans were lost in combat in Indochina, a total accounting by the Indochinese governments is not possible and should not be expected" (U.S. Congress, House, 1976, p. vii). The Committee further found that the Missing Persons Act "adequately protects the rights of the missing person and their next-of-kin" (U.S. Congress House, 1976, p. vii). A further investigation, chaired by Leonard Woodcock at the request of President Carter, concluded after a visit to Vietnam and Laos in 1977 that no Americans were being held against their will in Southeast Asia and that "normalization of relations affords the best prospect for obtaining a fuller accounting for our missing personnel and recommends that the normalization process be pursued vigorously for this as well as other reasons" (U.S. Department of State, 1977, p. 363). As a result of these inquiries, President Carter decided in August of 1977 to instruct the Department of Defense to resume official status changes in accordance with the Missing Persons Act.

THE PRE-HISTORY OF THE MISSING SERVICE PERSONNEL ACT OF 1995

Although the resumption of status changes in 1977 enabled official determinations of fate concerning soldiers missing in action from the Vietnam War (who after status changes were officially considered "killed in action/body not recovered"), questions concerning what had happened to them and the whereabouts of their remains were far from answered. Such questions were not simply the exclusive province of immediate family members but were shared by the defense and intelligence establishments, senior administration officials and members of Congress, and members of the lay public. The reasons behind this skepticism were multiple and varied, ranging from the entirely plausible to the patently false. Hence, a brief overview of various post-Vietnam War events is provided here as a means of further understanding the evolution of missing service persons legislation and jurisprudence from the end of the war up to the Missing Service Personnel Act of 1995.

One of the substantial contributing factors to the continued salience of the POW/MIA issue in the United States are the lists of missing Americans provided to the United States by the Vietnamese at the signing of the Paris Peace Accords in January 1973. Because North Vietnam viewed captured Americans as war criminals rather than as prisoners of war, it had refused throughout the Vietnam War to adhere to Geneva Conventions provisions requiring belligerents to supply each other with lists of captured personnel. Consequently, U.S. intelligence concerning the number and identity of American prisoners of war in Southeast Asia was imprecise at best, with estimates in the year prior to the ceasefire ranging from as few as 400 to as many as 1,600 POWs. Of even greater concern were Americans held prisoner in Laos. Although Laos and Cambodia had experienced heavy fighting during the Vietnam War, neither were signatories to the Paris peace agreement. The United States was thus in the essentially untenable position of seeking from North Vietnam an accounting of Americans missing in Laos and Cambodia, a request the Vietnamese consistently refused by citing the obvious sovereignty concerns this would entail. Nevertheless, the United States had strong reason to believe that both North Vietnam and the Pathet Lao were being less than forthright concerning Americans held prisoner in Laos.[17]

The controversy culminated in early 1973 when, upon the signing of the peace agreement, North Vietnam provided the United States with a list of American prisoners in its possession. Again, concern centered on the absence of any Americans on the list known to have been taken prisoner in Laos. Indeed, it was not until February 1, 1973, or five days after the signing of the peace accord, that North Vietnam finally provided a list of American detainees in Laos. Again it fell far short of expectations. At the time, 352 Americans were listed as missing in action in Laos, along with perhaps as many as forty-one prisoners of war (U.S. Congress, Senate, 1993, p. 82). Yet the February 1 list given to the United States contained a mere ten names, all of whom had been captured by North Vietnam in Laos. Thus, the list made no mention of Americans who had actually been captured by the Pathet Lao. As a result, the United States faced the prospect of negotiating the release of American prisoners with a hostile power who was not party to the peace agreement at the same time that American troops were being steadily withdrawn from the region. Although the United States momentarily considered halting its troop withdrawal, fear that the release of verified American prisoners would be jeopardized by prisoners whose existence could not be definitively proved caused the United States to renounce this threat. Operation Homecoming thus came to a close as scheduled on March 29, 1973.

Contributing to the anxiety created by the lists of the missing was a series of what came to be known as "discrepancy cases." These pertained to Americans whom the Vietnamese had acknowledged taking prisoner but whose names did not appear on any list and who did not return during Operation Homecoming. The evidence was in some instances quite compelling. On May 18, 1965, for example, Air Force Captain David Hrdlicka was shot down over Laos and captured by forces of the Pathet Lao. Over the next few years, Hrdlicka was used for propaganda purposes which included a photograph of him in captivity that appeared in the Soviet magazine *Pravda* and a Radio Peking broadcast quoting Lao sources as confirming his status as a prisoner. Nevertheless, Hrdlicka's name was not on the list of ten prisoners held in Laos given to the United States on February 1, 1973 and he did not return during Operation Homecoming (O'Daniel, 1979, p. 46). Although there can be no question that Hrdlicka survived his shoot down and was subsequently alive for a certain period of time in Lao captivity, both the Lao and the Vietnamese have consistently denied any knowledge of his fate and his remains have never been returned to the United States. A presumptive finding of death was eventually issued but because "unaccounted-for" is defined as the absence of the body rather than the absence of knowledge as to a given soldier's fate, Hrdlicka was, and still is, listed as unaccounted-for by the United States government (DPMO website 2002).

Another discrepancy case concerns Navy Lieutenant Ronald Dodge, shot down over Vietnam on May 17, 1967. Dodge managed to eject safely from his aircraft and he reached the ground alive, albeit in enemy territory. Upon completion of his descent, Dodge radioed a message to his wingman, "Here they come. I'm destroying my radio." Later that same day, a Vietnamese radio broadcast publicized the capture of a "U.S. bandit pilot" (O'Daniel, 1979, p. 46). Over the ensuing years, Dodge was also used for propaganda purposes. A photograph of him being led by his captors through an undisclosed area of North Vietnam appeared in *Paris Match* a few months after his capture and he was featured in an East German propaganda movie entitled *Pilots in Pajamas* (O'Daniel, 1979, p. 46). As with David Hrdlicka, Dodge's name was not among the prisoners to be returned upon the signing of the peace agreement and he too failed to return at Operation Homecoming. In 1981, his remains were repatriated to the United States without explanation by the Vietnamese.

While discrepancy cases do not constitute unimpeachable proof that living Americans were left behind after the Vietnam War, they nevertheless contribute much to the ambiguity that characterizes the issue of the missing. Further ambiguity comes in the form of live-sighting reports. As the name implies, live-sighting reports refer to incidents in which a living American is reported to have been seen somewhere in Southeast Asia. Such reports are sometimes first-hand, other times merely hearsay, and occasionally pure fabrications. As of August 2002, the United States had received 1,917 first-hand live-sighting reports, of which 1,897, or 98.96%, had been resolved as either Americans already accounted-for, pre-1975 sightings, or fabrications (DPMO website 2002). However, this still leaves twenty cases unresolved, which in turn means that live-sighting reports, like discrepancy cases, cannot simply be dismissed out of hand. Of the twenty unresolved live-sighting reports, nineteen pertain to Americans reportedly held in a captive environment and one to Americans in a non-captive environment (i.e. working in Vietnam or married with a Vietnamese family) (DPMO website 2002).

While the small quantity of unresolved live-sighting reports may make them appear to be a relatively minor feature of the POW/MIA issue, they have fueled considerable domestic controversy over the fate and whereabouts of unaccounted-for American service personnel. Indeed, a series of highly publicized live-sighting reports in the early 1990s put the issue back in the public view with renewed urgency. In the summer of 1991, a photograph appeared on the front page of newspapers across the United States showing three middle-aged, Caucasian men standing near some trees. The accompanying story noted that the families of each of the three men had positively identified them as American POWs John Robertson, Albro Lundy, and Larry Stevens. The ensuing media sensation was understandably intense and the photo was taken seriously by officials throughout the United States government. Not long afterward, another photograph appeared claiming to be that of Navy Lieutenant Daniel Borah, shot down over Vietnam in 1972. Borah's parents asserted their conviction that the man in the photo was their son. In the meantime, the United States Senate passed a resolution by Republican Senator Bob Smith (R-NH) calling for the creation of the Senate Select Committee on POW/MIA Affairs to look into these and other POW/MIA-related matters. Shortly thereafter, a third photo appeared purporting to show Army Captain Donald Carr, missing in action in Laos. As had been the case with the others, members of Carr's family were also convinced that the man in the photo was their relative. It seemed that all the speculation generated by live-sighting reports and discrepancy cases had turned out to be true and that perhaps the United States government really had failed to secure their return (Keating, 1994, pp. 221–237).

Subsequent analysis of the three photos revealed each of them to be frauds perpetrated by already notorious POW/MIA "activists," some of whom had long been making a living soliciting private donations in support of organizations which they claimed would soon be bringing home live American POWs. The photo of Robertson, Lundy, and Stevenson turned out to be a hoax devised in Cambodia. The three men in the picture were actually farmers and the photo had been clipped from a 1923 edition of *Soviet Life* magazine, extensively modified, and then pedaled to POW/MIA activist Eugene "Red" McDaniel who publicized the photo after failing to convince various Congressmen of its authenticity. The man in the Borah photo was later discovered to be a seventy-seven year-old, half-French, half-Lao hill tribesman. The image reached the United States through a circuitous chain of Laotian refugees, eventually coming into the hands of Senator Bob Smith – the same Senator Smith who sponsored the resolution for the creation of the Select Committee on POW/MIA Affairs. The photo of Donald Carr turned out to be an accused rare bird smuggler awaiting trial in Germany who had posed for the photo at the request of longtime POW/MIA campaigner Jack Bailey, who had then publicized the photo in an attempt to upstage rival activist Eugene McDaniel and his photo of Robertson, Lundy, and Stevenson (Keating, 1994, pp. 221–237).

Any doubt that these incidents were of significance to how Americans perceived the issue of Americans missing in Southeast Asia was dispelled by an August 1991 *Wall Street Journal*/NBC News poll in which 69% of respondents believed that Americans were still prisoners of war in Southeast Asia and 52% thought the

United States government was not doing enough to get them back (Franklin, 1993, p. xv). Further, the Borah photo served as the primary rationale behind Senator Bob Smith's resolution creating the Senate Select Committee on POW/MIA Affairs. These, then, are some of the circumstances against which subsequent legal developments relating to missing American service personnel must be viewed. In particular, the Missing Service Personnel Act of 1995 must not be seen as some sort of isolated legal phenomenon. Rather, it must be understood in relation to the controversies surrounding Americans missing in Southeast Asia and to the culture of suspicion, deceit, and misinformation those controversies have spawned. Rather than a response to a specifically legal problem, the 1995 law is an effort to explain more adequately the balance sheet of war, one which reflects an abiding faith in the ability of the body to provide this explanation.

THE MISSING SERVICE PERSONNEL ACT OF 1995[18]

With this brief history in mind, it now becomes possible to review the main provisions of the 1995 legislation on missing service members and to elaborate further the claim that the new law is as much a response to cultural and political phenomena as it is a remedy to any specific legal problem. Two provisions of the new law are especially important in this regard. The first concerns the requirement of counsel at the initial board of inquiry to determine the status of a service member believed to be missing as a result of hostile action. In addition to requiring the Service Secretary to appoint counsel for the board of inquiry, the new law also requires the Secretary to appoint counsel for the missing service member to represent only the interests of the missing individual, not the individual's family or any other interested party.[19] While this provision may at first seem relatively innocuous, it nevertheless raises two important issues. First, as Stahl argues, this provision contains the warrantless proposition that the board's counsel cannot be trusted to ensure that the interests of both the government and the missing service member are protected (1996, p. 162). Second, other than duplicating the services already provided by the board's counsel, "the missing person's counsel performs no other function. The counsel presumably will have never met the missing person and has no more knowledge of what that person would have wanted under the circumstances than the board and the Secretary. Consequently, the missing person's counsel is in the awkward position of attempting to represent a client with whom he has no attorney-client relationship and for whom he has no personal knowledge" (Stahl, 1996, p. 162).[20]

In light of the contentious politics of the POW/MIA issue, however, the significance of this new requirement is clear. In particular, what we see here is the institutionalization of the belief among family members, POW/MIA activists, and much of the lay public (as revealed by the *Wall Street Journal* poll), that the U.S. government has forsaken the Vietnam War missing. Accordingly, the missing were left behind and subsequent accounting efforts by the United States have not only been inadequate but untrustworthy. Indeed, such efforts actually furthered the problem by creating the impression that action was being taken on behalf of missing soldiers when instead it was an attempt to sweep the problem under rug. The missing service member in question must therefore be entitled to counsel at status inquiries to ensure that such injustices do not occur again. All this despite the Vietnam War's standing as America's most accounted-for war, the absence of reliable evidence to suggest that Americans were left behind in Southeast Asia following the cessation of hostilities, and the fact that no living, unaccounted-for American has returned from Vietnam in the nearly thirty years since the end of the war.

The second significant provision of the new law concerns the procedures to be followed if a status review board determines a missing soldier to be dead. To make a declaration of death, "the board must find: (1) 'credible evidence' suggesting that the person is dead; (2) 'no credible evidence' suggesting that the person is alive; and (3) that United States representatives have made a complete search of the area where the person was last seen and have examined the records of the government or entity with control of that area, unless after making a good faith effort the representatives are not granted such access."[21] Furthermore, if the board elects to declare a service member dead, it must include in its report: (1) a detailed description of the location where death occurred and the location of the body if recovered; (2) a statement of the date of death; and (3) if the body was not visually identifiable, a certification from a 'practitioner of an appropriate forensic science' that the body is that of the missing person.[22]

Again the quest for credible evidence of death is not especially remarkable in and of itself, especially when the concerns of dependents with a financial interest in such a determination are at stake. However, there are two important considerations that must be taken into account when analyzing this new accounting standard. First, "the 'credible evidence' standard of proof . . . will result in confusion because neither the new statute, case law, nor military regulations define 'credible evidence' " (Stahl, 1996, p. 166). Second, the new law disregards three standards of proof already in existence: preponderance of the evidence, clear and convincing evidence, and evidence beyond a reasonable doubt (Stahl, 1996, p. 166). Stahl argues that the middle category, clear and convincing evidence, would be most appropriate in the context of missing service personnel because it uses an historically established means to apportion the interests of the government and dependents of the missing in a manner that furthers Congressional intent to account for the missing (1996,

p. 167). Hence, the "credible evidence" standard is both legally suspect due to the absence of clear definition and ultimately unnecessary given the existence of other, legally established accounting criteria.

For present purposes, however, the more important point is not so much which legal standard ought to be employed when accounting for missing service personnel but the need for "credible evidence" to make a declaration of death in the first place. Again various elements of the Vietnam War's contentious legacy assert themselves, particularly those in which a finding of death in the absence of remains means the missing have been "forsaken." In spite of those unavoidable situations in which remains recovery will simply be impossible due to the nature of mechanized warfare, the 1995 law implements a standard of proof that effectively denies this circumstance. Positive determination of the fate and whereabouts of a given soldier can only occur through verifiable recourse to the body, meaning in turn that said soldier was not left behind or otherwise abandoned by the U.S. government. Hence the requirement for "credible" evidence in making a finding of death. Put simply, credibility in the absence of remains is no credibility at all. Credibility can no longer be established through the rigors of the accounting process but must be made manifest through positive identification of the remains of the missing service member.

In view of the above, it is possible to address more fully the relationship between the law pertaining to missing service members and the anxieties of the post-Vietnam War era. As suggested earlier, these anxieties are in some cases justifiable given the incomplete lists of missing Americans provided by the Vietnamese after the war, as well as the discrepancy cases and subsequent live-sighting reports. For some, the failure of the United States to resolve these anxieties has been interpreted as leaving soldiers behind in Southeast Asia as a political expedient. As argued earlier, this circumstance has led the law to embrace a variation on the principle of *habeas corpus*. The legal injunction to produce a body, understandable on its face, is asked, both in the context of Vietnam War missing and subsequently, to establish with more precision "what really happened" to those who failed to return home. While it may seem at first as though the law is doing little more than clarifying the terms under which resolution of missing in action cases shall proceed, it must also be recognized that the law is itself a product of the particularities of the POW/MIA issue. In other words, there is no "POW/MIA issue" on the one hand and an independently conceived "law" on the other to which litigants and other interested parties address themselves. Rather, the law helps constitute the issue as such by instituting an accounting standard in which the body becomes the basis for reflection. By legal definition, in other words, the absence of bodies becomes a problem which is then up to the law to resolve. The law functions as an active participant in, and producer of, the complexities of the POW/MIA issue.

For these reasons, one might reasonably suspect that recent legislation concerning missing service personnel has as much to do with the larger anxieties occasioned by the loss in Vietnam as it does with absent soldiers per se. This possibility becomes stronger upon consideration of the understanding of "accountability" that funds the 1995 law's requirement to produce a body in order to account for missing service personnel. On its face, of course, the requirement to produce the body is familiar enough, a standard through reference to which various kinds of accountability can be established. However, given the contentious legacy of the POW/MIA issue, the accountability in question can be seen as having less to do with a calculus of recovered versus lost bodies and more to do with a certain settling of accounts from the Vietnam War and beyond. The 1995 law's version of accountability, in other words, functions metonymically, with the body standing for the ability to explain the balance sheet of war more clearly than was the case both during and after the Vietnam War. As the material standard by way of which that explanation is secured, the recovered body becomes the unimpeachable evidence capable of adjudicating not merely all questions concerning the fate and the eventual whereabouts of missing service personnel but also the veracity of the government's version of these events. In so doing, the law neatly rehabilitates an understanding of accountability thought to have been vanquished by the Vietnam War, namely one in which the supposedly unproblematic material facts provided by the body correspond to an equally unproblematic chain of evidence concerning the service member in question. A structure of responsibility is created, with the law offering itself up as the standard through reference to which the facts of the absent body can be separated from their many and disparate fictions.[23]

As indicated earlier, however, the law cannot completely accomplish this aim, implicated as it is in the definition of the very problem it seeks to solve. Although the materiality of the body appears to offer verifiable accountability, the law is nevertheless guilty of instituting a standard susceptible to failure on its own terms. This circumstance is most obviously demonstrated by those unaccounted-for from the Vietnam War, whose remains, as indicated, are highly fragmentary and therefore escape the apparently simple identity boundaries imagined by the legal injunction to account for the missing through positive identification of remains. The risk, to put it simply, is that the standard thought to provide the ultimate resolution to the problem of missing service personnel will nevertheless fail for simple paucity of evidence. Indeed, such circumstance is already visible in the context of Vietnam War missing, whose remains are identifiable only through the most rigorous processes of forensic and genetic identification, a circumstance that casts doubt on whether the remains at issue are necessarily the same body contemplated by the accounting protocol.

Once again, however, it is important to avoid the temptation to see an accounting standard on the one hand and a body to which that standard pertains on the other. Rather, we must remain attentive to the ways in which the law *produces* the remains it seeks in order to make good on its claim to have accounted for the soldier in question. Again, the Vietnam War missing are appropriate, especially given the extreme fragmentation of recovered remains. In this context, the crux of the matter is the adjective "identifiable," since it is the act of identifying recovered remains that keeps them from being so much inconclusive artifactual data gathered at excavation. Effectively, then, by establishing the body as the standard through which the missing shall be accounted-for, the law builds a conceptual bridge between the person named on the list of the missing and the fragmentary remains recovered in Southeast Asia. Put slightly differently, the law enables a correspondence between two for-the-moment incompatible entities – the individual on the list and the fragmented body recovered in Southeast Asia. The moment of identification is therefore not a discovery in some independent, a priori sense but one that is dependent upon a particular construction of the problem and its solution.

From this vantage point, it becomes possible to speculate further on the functioning of the law in the context of missing service personnel in a manner that supplements the claim that recent pertinent legislation is less about a particular legal problem than the anxieties occasioned by the Vietnam War. Above all, the evolution from the Missing Persons Act of 1942 to the Missing Service Personnel Act of 1995 marks a decisive increase in the significance of the body. At one level, that increase might be viewed as a byproduct of the Vietnam War's peculiar metric in which body counts served as the exclusive measure of success or the lack thereof. Yet the law does much more here than simply utilize a standard drawn from an archive of past events. Rather, it advances a particular kind of knowledge claim, one in which the recovery and positive identification of a handful of bone fragments marks the point at which the hostilities of the Vietnam War are finally terminated. In so doing, the body becomes the point of application, one in which the epistemic requirements of modern forensic science dovetail with the more overtly political desire to ensure that the problem of absent service personnel is resolved.

The particulars of this knowledge claim bear elaboration. First, the law makes a statement as to what "really happened" to those service members unaccounted-for in Southeast Asia. No longer will families of the missing or the American people be forced to take the government's word for it. Instead, the law steps in to provide a mechanism in which a verifiable correspondence between circumstantial and forensic evidence is required to defeat alternative claims concerning the fate and whereabouts of the soldier in question. Again this circumstance might not be so remarkable were it not the case that the circumstances surrounding the loss of a vast majority of Vietnam War personnel strongly suggest the service member in question was simply killed in action. Nevertheless, it is precisely the ambiguity of this "suggestion" that has caused such trouble. Second, and closely related, by offering a claim as to what happened to the missing, the law states definitively that the missing soldier in question cannot be included among the discrepancy cases and live-sighting reports that have generated so much controversy since the war. Despite the extremely low odds that any of the missing survived their incident of loss for any length of time, that possibility is now definitively refuted. Third, the law imposes coherence on the ambiguous issue of missing service personnel through claims to superior evidence as to their fate and whereabouts. As seen, however, such claims are not those of a wholly external medium called "science" but are a product of the law's installation of the body at the center of the accounting protocol. These claims thus derive their efficacy not from being "more right" than competing claims but from a particular definition of the problem.

In advancing a particular kind of knowledge claim, the law also suggests how truth is to be constituted in this context. In other words, by staking a claim to knowledge of missing soldiers' fate and whereabouts, the law states that the truth of that knowledge is secured only through material, verifiable evidence of their return to the United States. In the absence of said evidence, the possibility of life and the possibility of death remain legal equivalents. The effect of this truth claim is the activation of a mode of discernment in which questions concerning the fate and whereabouts of the missing can ultimately be adjudicated only through reference to a verifiable chain of evidence, and this despite the often overwhelming circumstantial evidence which suggests in no uncertain terms that the soldier in question perished during the incident of loss. Here again, however, the contentious legacy of the Vietnam War reappears, this time in the guise of a legal standard imagined to provide the ultimate closure to one of the Vietnam War's most vexing problems. In the absence of identifiable remains, we can't really know what happened to those missing, and what we do know can't be considered true.

The salience of these circumstances was revealed in *Hart v. United States*[24] in which the wife, mother, and daughter of Air Force Lt. Col. Thomas Hart filed suit against the government over the accuracy of the identification of his remains. Hart was shot down over Pakse, Laos in December 1972 along with fifteen other crew members, two of whom parachuted to safety, five to six of whom were buried by friendly Lao forces in a nearby collective grave, and one of whom was positively identified at the crash site. Originally listed as missing-in-action, Hart's status was changed to killed-in-action/body not recovered following the resumption of status changes in 1978. In February 1985 a CILHI team excavated the crash site, recovering some 50,000 bone and tooth fragments, ID tags, and personal affects. Though none of these fragments was specifically correlated to Lt. Col. Hart, CILHI informed Mrs. Hart that it had made a positive identification of her husband, along with thirteen other crew members, through process of elimination and by virtue of the circumstantial knowledge that Hart was aboard the aircraft in question. Wondering how thirteen individuals could have been identified if five of the crew were buried in the collective grave, Mrs. Hart sued for permission to have CILHI's findings reviewed by an outside expert, who concluded that it was impossible to tell whether the fragments in question came from Lt. Col. Hart or any other individual. CILHI subsequently rescinded its identification of Hart and the others.

On this basis, Mrs. Hart refused to accept the remains and filed suit in October 1986 under the Federal Tort Claims Act (FTCA) for the intentional infliction of emotional distress as defined by Florida law. In particular, the family members alleged that CILHI had knowingly made a false positive identification of Lt. Col. Hart's remains, that it persisted in this identification despite evidence to the contrary, and that they refused to return Lt. Col. Hart to unaccounted-for status after rescinding his identification. Though the family initially prevailed in district court, the government successfully appealed on the basis of the discretionary function exemption of the FTCA, which shields the actions of government employees from judicial interference if no specific policy has been violated. The important point here is that despite overwhelming circumstantial evidence, the absence of the positively identified body means that questions as to the fate and whereabouts of Lt. Col. Hart remain unanswered, and this despite the formal change of status that occurred in 1978. The Missing Service Personnel Act of 1995 enshrines this peculiar logic in the law.

CONCLUSION

The legal wrangling over how best to account for missing American service members is not confined to questions concerning arcane elements of the law. Instead, what must be noticed are the ways in which the increased significance of the body within the accounting process transforms the balance sheet of war into a justiciable legal question. No longer are absent soldiers an unavoidable, if unpleasant, reality of mechanized warfare. No longer do the statements of those who might otherwise be trusted to know suffice to explain this unpleasant reality. There are at least three reasons to be dubious about this shift. First, large-scale military engagements inevitably entail the loss of bodies. All American wars fit this profile. Hence, the Vietnam War and its aftermath are unique not because of the missing but because the missing from this war became a problem, one which it is imagined the law might resolve. This is problematic because – moving on to the second reason – the law seeks accountability and responsibility where in some cases there simply is none. The aftermath of war and the question of who comes back and who does not simply does not admit of the kinds of intervention contemplated by the law's insistence on a subject who can be held responsible and a calculus through which such responsibility can be determined. A particular brand of post-Vietnam War social and political anxiety has been foisted upon a legal mechanism ill-equipped to provide the answers sought.

Most significantly, however, is the way in which the entire issue of warfare and its aftermath is redefined when it is treated as a legally justiciable question. The question of absent service members is reduced to a mathematical calculus in which the absence of material proof of fate and whereabouts is equivalent to a lie, and the absence of material proof of death constitutes credible evidence of life apart from even the strongest circumstantial evidence to the contrary. Evidence for this comes from the aftermath of the Persian Gulf War. In January 2001, the Department of Defense elected to reclassify Commander Michael Speicher from killed in action/body not recovered to missing in action. Speicher, a Navy pilot shot down by enemy fire on January 17, 1991 during the first day of the air campaign over Iraq, was initially classified as killed in action through a presumptive finding of death after a Navy status review board found "no credible evidence" to suggest Speicher survived his shoot down. The finding was reaffirmed in September of 1996 following a thorough excavation of the crash site by investigators from the Central Identification Laboratory, Hawaii. However, additional analysis and the receipt of new information persuaded the Navy to change Speicher's status to missing in action.[25] The Defense Department was not precise about the "new information" it claimed to have received concerning Speicher's case but it was believed to include several live-sighting reports over a period of years. Following familiar precedent, government officials acknowledged that the evidence was circumstantial but that at the same time, they could not rule out the possibility that Speicher could still be alive since Iraq had failed to account for him through repatriation of his remains.

Unfortunately, the rationale behind Speicher's status change – a rationale the law has firmly embraced – is entirely circular and self-generating. Because there is no identifiable body, one can't be sure that the soldier in question is deceased, and since one can't be certain the soldier is deceased one cannot rule out the possibility that he is still alive, and since one cannot rule out the possibility that he is still alive we must maintain that soldier in a "missing" status until the materiality of the body can verify his fate – verification that will then be taken not as proof of the soldier's death but of the possibility of his continued life. In short, because there is no proof of death to give, its absence will be taken as proof of life. The quest to vanquish the ambiguity occasioned by the absent body now exceeds itself on its own terms. Materiality, which formerly provided the ultimate resolution to the uncertainty occasioned by the absence of the body, is confounded by interpretive commitments in which continued *uncertainty* becomes the higher value. That the law should be complicit in this turn of events must rank as one of the most unfortunate elements of the Vietnam War's contentious legacy.

NOTES

1. This is the official website of the Department of Defense Prisoner of War/Missing Personnel Office (DPMO), the organization within the United States government charged with achieving the fullest possible accounting of Americans missing from all wars. http://www.dtic.mil/dpmo

2. Congressional investigations include the House of Representatives' 1975 Select Committee on Missing Persons in Southeast Asia (U.S. Congress, House, 1976), and the Senate's 1993 Select Committee on POW/MIA Affairs (U.S. Congress, Senate, 1993). Presidential delegations include the Woodcock Commission, sent by President Carter in 1977 (U.S. Department of State, 1977), and those by Gen. John W. Vessey (Ret.), who in 1988 at the behest of President Reagan commenced a long series of negotiations with the Vietnamese on matters related to unaccounted-for Americans. Among the more infamous private "rescue missions" are those conducted by retired Marine colonel James "Bo" Gritz, whose failed exploits in Southeast Asia required only minor tweaking to become the basis for several feature-length POW rescue films, *Rambo: First Blood, Part II* (dir. George Cosmatos, Artisan, 1985) being among the more well-known.

3. The largest and most well-known family organization is the National League of POW/MIA Families. The POW/MIA Flag was designed under their auspices in 1971. Their web site can be viewed at http://www.pow-miafamilies.org.

4. The return from Vietnam of Marine Pfc. Robert Garwood in 1979 is cited by some as proof the United States left prisoners behind in Southeast Asia. According to the U.S. government, however, Garwood was never technically unaccounted-for, having been suspected of collaborating with the enemy since his capture near Da Nang on September 28, 1965. He was court-martialed and convicted for this offense in 1980. For a discussion of the Garwood case, see Mather (1994, p. 43) and Franklin (1993, p. 115).

5. 37 U.S.C. §§ 551–59 (1988 & Supp. V 1993) and 5 U.S.C. 5561–69 (1988 & Supp. V 1993).

6. *Id.*, § 556(b).

7. The National Defense Authorization Act for Fiscal Year 1996, Pub. L. No. 104–106, § 569, 110 Stat. 186 (1996), codified at 10 U.S.C. §§ 1501–1513 (West Supp. May 1996).

8. 10 U.S.C. § 1507(b)(1)–(4).

9. Indeed, the United States government officially acknowledges that the remains of 661 soldiers from the Vietnam War will never be recovered, either due to loss over water or inaccessible terrain (DPMO website 2002).

10. The following discussion of the Missing Persons Act is indebted to Major Pamela M. Stahl (1996, pp. 75–177).

11. Missing Persons Act, ch. 166, 56 Stat. 143 (1942) (current version at 37 U.S.C. § 552(a) (1988) and 5 U.S.C. § 5562(a) (1988)).

12. *Id.* § 4 (current version at 37 U.S.C. § 553 (Supp. V 1993) and 5 U.S.C. § 5563 (1988)).

13. *Id.* § 3.

14. *Id.* §§ 3–4.

15. 371 F. Supp. 837 (S.D. N.Y. 1973); 371 F. Supp. 831 (S.D. N.Y. 1974) (three-judge court), *aff'd mem.*, 419 U.S. 297 (1974).

16. McDonald v. McLucas, 371 F. Supp. 831, 836 (S.D. N.Y. 1974) (three-judge court), *aff'd mem.*, 419 U.S. 297 (1974).

17. The Vietnamese consistently claimed not to have had a military presence in Laos or Cambodia during the Vietnam War and further declaimed any influence over the ruling government in Laos, the Pathet Lao, concerning their ability to account for missing Americans. While these assertions were clearly disingenuous, the United States had been party to similar deceptions throughout the "secret" wars in Laos and Cambodia and had even gone so far as to falsify the location of loss for all American personnel lost in those two countries, listing them instead as lost over South Vietnam. In addition to the problems this was later to cause with the families concerned, such falsification often meant that even the United States could not always be sure that a particular soldier had been lost where claimed.

18. The following discussion of the Missing Service Personnel Act of 1995 is indebted to Major Pamela M. Stahl (1996, pp. 75–177).

19. 10 U.S.C.A. § 1503(f)(1).

20. Stahl continues with the observation that, "The only individuals who may know what the missing person may want are the person's family members. Therefore, either the counsel is left to decide alone what is best for the missing person or the counsel may attempt to discover the client's wishes by consulting family members. If the missing person's counsel decides on this latter approach, the counsel risks becoming embroiled in arguments between spouses, children, parents, and designated persons over what these individuals believe the missing person would have wanted. The entire situation is magnified considerably when the missing person's counsel must represent several 'clients' subject to the same board review" (1996, pp. 162–163).

21. 10 U.S.C.A. § 1507(a)(1)–(3).

22. 10 U.S.C.A. § 1507(b)(1)–(4).

23. Of interest here is the law's requirement that the United States government be responsible for accounting for missing soldiers even though that government has frequently been accused by family members and others of not doing enough to account for the missing. That these same individuals would actively support legislation that ultimately places further responsibility for the accounting effort in the hands of an organization they have long believed to be central to the problem is a further example of the contorted politics of the POW/MIA issue.

24. 894 F.2d 1539, 1542 (11th Cir. 1990), *cert. denied*, 498 U.S. 980 (1990).

25. "Navy Changes Status of Cmdr. Michael Scott Speicher." Jan. 11, 2001. http://www.dtic.mil/dpmo/newsre/2001/010111_osd_pr016

REFERENCES

CILHI website, http://www.cilhi.army.mil.

Dillow, G. (1995). Vietnam Search Goes on for POWs. *Honolulu Advertiser*, (March 5), A5.

DPMO website, http://www.dtic.mil/dpmo.

Franklin, H. B. (1993). *M. I. A. or mythmaking in America: How and why belief in live POWs has possessed a nation.* New Brunswick, NJ: Rutgers University Press.

JTF-FA website, http://www. pacom.mil/jtffa.htm.

Keating, S. K. (1994). *Prisoners of hope: Exploiting the POW/MIA myth in America.* New York: Random House.

Mather, P. (1994). *M. I. A.: Accounting for the missing in Southeast Asia.* Washington, DC: National Defense University Press.

O'Daniel, L. J. (1979). *Missing in action: Trail of deceit.* New Rochelle, NY: Arlington House Publishers.

Stahl, P. (1996). The new law on department of defense personnel missing as a result of hostile action. *Military Law Review, 152,* 75–177.

U.S. Congress. House. Select Committee on Missing Persons in Southeast Asia (1976) *Americans missing in Southeast Asia: Final report of the House Select Committee on missing persons in Southeast Asia.* Washington, DC: GPO.

U.S. Congress. Senate. Select Committee on POW/MIA Affairs (1993). *Report of the Select Committee on POW/MIA Affairs, United States Senate.* Washington, DC: GPO.

U.S. Department of State (1977). Presidential Commission Visits Vietnam and Laos to Seek Information on Missing Americans (Woodcock Commission Final Report). *Department of State Bulletin.* Washington, DC (April 18), 363–374.

SURVIVING LAW: DEATH COMMUNITY CULTURE

Patrick Hanafin

ABSTRACT

Law attempts to govern life and death through the appropriation of images which give a fantasy of control over death. The functioning of the thanatopolitical state is underpinned by a perceived control over death and its representation. This means of controlling death is challenged when someone wishes to die in an untimely fashion. Death may be timely when the State engages in the officially sanctioned killing of the death penalty but not when the individual assumes such a power to decide. When an individual goes before the law to obtain a right to die, instead of confronting death, legal institutions evade the issue and instead talk about life, and its sacred and inviolable nature. Yet, in the same move, many exceptions to this sacred quality of life are carved out. One can see an example of this phenomenon in the area of Supreme Court decision making on physician-assisted suicide. In Washington v. Glucksberg the applicants had died by the time of the Supreme Court's decision. Where did they go? Were they ever really there for the law? The Supreme Court decision attempts to recompose the notion of identic wholeness in the face of bodies associated with death and decay. It is, in other words, an attempt to arrest the process of death by composing a narrative which valorises life. The case becomes a narrative about the threat to life or, more precisely, a threat to a particular way of life. In other words, the state's interest in preserving life becomes the interest in preserving the life

Studies in Law, Politics, and Society
Studies in Law, Politics, and Society, Volume 28, 97–115

ISSN: 1059-4337/PII: S1059433702280047

of the state. The state must live on. The question then moves from being one of whether the individual applicant in a case concerning physician-assisted suicide should live or die, to one which asks should we the court live or die?

Differer la mort, c'est aussi l'exhiber, la souligner (Jean-Luc Nancy, *L'Intrus*, 2000).

"Thou shalt not kill" obviously means: "do not kill he who will die in any case" and means: "because of that, do not infringe on dying, do not decide the indecisive, do not say: this is done, claiming for yourself a right over this 'not yet' (Maurice Blanchot, *The Step Not Beyond*, 1992).

How could one know the law and truly experience it, how could one force it to come into view, to exercise its powers clearly, to speak, without provoking it into its recesses, without resolutely going ever farther into the outside into which it is always receding? (Michel Foucault, *Maurice Blanchot: The Thought From Outside*, 1987).

We have entered the age of vital politics (Nikolas Rose, *The Politics of Life Itself*, 2001).

INTRODUCTION

Survival, as Zygmunt Bauman reminds us, is "the meaning of life" (Bauman, 1992, p. 199). This aspect of modernity has several manifestations, from attempts to prolong the lives of the dying to seeking the perfect body through dieting and exercise. Indeed Jean Baudrillard would hold that such bodily commodity fetishism incorporates the search for the perfect death.[1] Similarly at the level of political symbolism, the state attempts to give the impression of living on eternally. This vitalist political ontology has its roots in classical liberal notions of the state as body politic.[2] In order to give the illusion of achieving this impossible goal of eternal life the body politic attempts to immunise itself against anything which would disrupt its equilibrium. As Nikolas Rose puts it:

> Life itself, the vital reality of a people, must become the overriding responsibility and criterion that should guide the exercise of political authority (Rose, 2001, p. 2).

For the body politic one such disruptive presence is that of death, that which spells nothingness.[3] The law in its turn attempts to manage death, to engage in what Jean Baudrillard has termed "death control," in order to give the illusion that nothing escapes its regulatory grasp (see Baudrillard, 1993, pp. 125–194).

However, as with all such attempts to foreground life and sequester death, what occurs is the foregrounding of death. This is played out when the law encounters death, or those who symbolise it, in cases concerning end of life decision making, as it is euphemistically called in bioethical circles. It is as if one can make a decision with respect to death, as if death can be controlled. For example, in *Cruzan v Director, Missouri Department of Health* (497 U.S. 261 (1990)), a case involving the issue of treatment withdrawal for individuals in a persistent vegetative state, the employment of vitalist rhetoric by Justice Scalia exhibits this stance towards death. Scalia employs the metaphor of the Court destroying itself if it were to decide affirmatively in cases concerning the right to die. The Court, according to Scalia, must save itself by employing the language of the law against the introduction of such a right:

> Our salvation is the Equal Protection Clause, which requires the democratic majority to accept for themselves and their loved ones what they impose on you and me. This Court need not, and has not, and has no authority to, inject itself into every field of human activity where irrationality and oppression may theoretically occur, and if it tries to do so, it will destroy itself (497 U.S. 261, pp. 300–301).

Scalia believes in the differentiation between legislative policy making which he associates with rationality, and judicial decision making which, in such cases, he associates with "irrationality and oppression." While the Court "has no authority to inject itself into every field of human activity" the legislature on the other hand has. In allowing individuals to determine when their life should end the Court according to Scalia "will destroy itself."[4] Baudrillard could have scripted this metaphor. For indeed, in the eyes of the system and its agents, death is the ultimate threat and its presumed deferral keeps the system in balance. In cases like *Cruzan* modernity's paradigmatic bare life (see further Agamben, 1998, p. 186) is resuscitated rhetorically only to be allowed to die. In cases concerning sentient terminally ill persons who seek to die with physician-assistance, the law seeks to assert its control against yet another attempt to wrest its monopoly over death control. Thus, cases involving an individual's search to obtain a right to die raise profound questions about the political community in which we are situated.

LAW AND VITAL POLITICS

Today, according to Nikolas Rose, vital politics is no longer about the direct management of life through public health and other government interventions, but has moved towards a form of individual governance of the self. Rose captures this new vitalist politics in the term "ethopolitics":

> By ethopolitics I mean to characterize ways in which the ethos of human existence – the sentiments, moral nature or guiding beliefs of persons, groups, or institutions – have come to provide the 'medium' within which self-government of the autonomous individual can be connected up with the imperatives of good government. In ethopolitics, life itself, as it is lived in its everyday manifestations, is the object of adjudication. If discipline individualizes and normalizes, and biopower collectivizes and socializes, ethopolitics concerns itself with the self-techniques by which human beings should judge themselves and act upon themselves to

> make themselves better than they are. While ethopolitical concerns range from those of lifestyle to those of community, they coalesce around a kind of vitalism: disputes over the value to be accorded to life itself, "quality of life," "the right to life" or "the right to choose," euthanasia, gene therapy, human cloning and the like (Rose, 2001, p. 18).

The imperative to survive comes from within the individual, but can be linked ultimately to a cultural construction of the healthy self which is predicated on a fear of death. Thus, there has been a move from state intervention to a more insidious self-government, influenced by dominant cultural modes of thinking, in which the agonised self must act to change her situation. Within the framework of ethopolitics as Rose reminds us, there is an apparent self-actualisation:

> In advanced liberal democracies, biological identity becomes bound up with more general norms of enterprising, self-actualizing, responsible personhood (Rose, 2001, p. 18).

However, this apparent self-actualisation disguises a lack of freedom, as groups based on biological identity have to go before the law in order to obtain recognition. Every decision in relation to biological identity becomes a legal decision. This vitalism which appears enabling is yet another form of biopolitical management.

Groups united by their desire to obtain the right to die by assistance fall into this biological identity paradigm outlined by Rose. Thus, according to Rose, such individuals:

> use their individual and collective lives, the evidence of their own existence . . . they demand civil and human rights . . . They call for recognition, respect, resources . . . control over medical and technical expertise (Rose, 2001, p. 19).

Rose addresses the case of individuals who struggle against biodiscrimination in the context of screening for genetic illness. However the struggle for legal recognition of a right to control the time of one's death is equally part of this ethopolitical framework. The issue of physician-assisted suicide has also spawned groups who virulently oppose the practice. This conflict within the field of vital politics becomes a legal conflict as it is inevitably dressed up in the language of rights.

One such moment in constitutional jurisprudence was the Supreme Court's adjudication in *Washingon v. Glucksberg* (521 U.S. 702 (1997)). The case came about as the result of conflicting decisions on the issue of physician-assisted suicide by the Second and Ninth Circuit Courts of Appeal. The Second Circuit Court of Appeal in *Quill v Vacco* (80 F.3d 716 (2d Cir. 1996) held that the Equal Protection Clause of the Fourteenth Amendment rendered statutes which prohibit assisted suicide unlawful. Noting that New York legislation permitted a competent person to refuse medical treatment even if this resulted in the individual's death, the Court held that assisted suicide should also be permissible on the ground that like persons be treated alike. An *en banc* panel of the Ninth Circuit Court of Appeal in

Compassion in Dying v. Washington (79 F.3d 790 (9th Cir. 1996) (*en banc*)) held that the Washington state statute prohibiting a physician from assisting a patient to die was unconstitutional, as it was contrary to the substantive component of the Fourteenth Amendment's Due Process Clause. Both cases were consolidated for hearing by the Supreme Court in January 1997. The Chief Justice delivered two opinions for the Court in June 1997 overruling both the Second and Ninth Circuits' decisions. In these opinions he was joined by Justices O'Connor, Scalia, Kennedy and Thomas. However Justice O'Connor filed a separate concurrence joined by Justices Ginsberg and Breyer. In addition Justices Stevens and Souter filed separate concurrences. Taken together these concurrences cast a doubt on the majority pronouncements and display a far greater uncertainty on the issue than the opinions of the Chief Justice would care to admit. It would appear that the decision is itself being subverted from within, thus deciding yet not deciding simultaneously. In this particular set of challenges, the Supreme Court deemed that the Due Process and Equal Protection challenges must fail, but noted that this may not always be the case, depending on the particular facts of the challenge.

When reading the case, one is struck by the manner in which the multiple voices in the decision reflect the simultaneously existing yet divergent stances towards physician-assisted death on the part of the wider community. It is as if within the text of the judgment is displayed fleetingly another way of seeing the community's relation to death. Within the space of the judgment a transgressive alternative to the dominant construction of death emerges briefly, only to disappear just as quickly into the recesses of the law. Thus, law reveals that which would transgress it at the same time as prohibiting such a practice. The case, moreover, reveals the failure of rights discourse to enable one to decide the time and manner of one's death. In fact it affirms that death control is the norm. The law purports to make the "dead in motion"[5] die again and freeze the almost dead but too alive on the threshold between life and death. It attempts to give the impression that death is being man aged yet in the same move denies that life is being managed. Courts often note that their remit ends at the point where they are called upon to decide on controversial ethical issues. Thus, for example, Justice Blackmun notes in *Roe v. Wade* that:

> We need not resolve the difficult question of when life begins. When those trained in the respective disciplines of medicine, philosophy, and theology are unable to arrive at any consensus, the judiciary, at this point in the development of man's knowledge, is not in a position to speculate as to the answer (Cited in Johnson, 1987, p. 193).

Yet in deciding not to decide on when life begins or indeed when it ends, the Court does engage in a form of decision making. By imposing thresholds on when pregnancy termination may occur and when a right to die is permissible the Court makes normative decisions. This etiquette of vitalism would appear to contradict

Blackmun's disingenuous remark. The law when faced with ethical dilemmas, constantly notes that it is not capable of making such decisions, yet then proceeds to lay down a threshold which the law will not allow the citizen to transgress.

Indeed such attempts at downplaying the extent of death control are futile, as the greater the effort the Court makes to deny such a phenomenon, the more its existence is revealed. As Baudrillard observes, the selection of one life over another is already a daily fact:

> The same objective that is inscribed in the monopoly of institutional violence is accomplished as easily by forced survival as it is by death: a forced 'life for life's sake' (kidney machines, malformed children on life-support machines, agony prolonged at all costs, organ transplants, etc.). All these procedures are equivalent to disposing of death and imposing life, but according to what ends? Those of science and medicine? Surely this is just scientific paranoia, unrelated to any human objective. Is profit the aim? No: society swallows huge amounts of profit. This 'therapeutic heroism' is characterised by soaring costs and 'decreasing benefits': they manufacture unproductive survivors . . . the system is facing the same contradiction here as with the death penalty: it overspends on the prolongation of life because this system of values is essential to the strategic equilibrium of the whole; economically, however, this overspending unbalances the whole. What is to be done? An economic choice becomes necessary, where we can see the outline of euthanasia as a semi-official doctrine or practice . . . Euthanasia is already everywhere, and the ambiguity of making a humanist demand for it (as with the 'freedom' to abortion) is striking: it is inscribed in the middle to long term logic of the system . . . there is a clear objective behind all these apparent contradictions: to ensure control over the entire range of life and death. From birth control to death control, whether we execute people or compel their survival . . . the essential thing is that the decision is withdrawn from them . . . Just as morality commanded: 'You shall not kill,' today it commands: 'You shall not die,' not in any old way, anyhow, and only if the law and medicine permit. And if your death is conceded to you it will still be by order . . . death proper has been abolished to make room for death control and euthanasia . . . (Baudrillard, 1993, p. 174).

The Court in adjudicating on an issue like physician-assisted suicide is merely performing its part in the biopolitical management of the population. By ruling that an individual cannot die by assisted suicide or that someone shall be executed, the Court is engaged in the banal management of life. Such instances of killing are deemed either acceptable or not depending on the State's stance towards a particular act of killing. Thus, state executions and killing in time of war are approved of because they appear in the rhetoric of the elite to uphold the safety or integrity of the community. They give the appearance of societal solidarity, binding it together against the intruder. On the other hand there is less willingness to support physician-assisted suicide as it does not bind the community together but is an example of worklessness.

In its role as killer, the state is also maintaining a fantasmatic control over death. Austin Sarat's study of the death penalty raises the question of the killing state and law's contradictory stance towards violence (Sarat, 2001). Sarat notes that the state attempts to justify the death penalty by employing arguments based on sovereignty and legitimacy. This legitimation process implies "making [the] act of the executioner violence that can be approved and rationally dispensed" (Sarat, 2001, p. 128). Physician-assisted suicide is violence in the eyes of the state. The state fears killing when it isn't in the state's interests, when violence is out of its control. The state's interest in preserving life becomes the interest in preserving the life of the state. The state must live on. It is thus the case, as Baudrillard reminds us, that the state must have a monopoly on violence. Violence which escapes the state's monopoly is deemed subversive (Baudrillard, 1993, p. 175). Even though, as Baudrillard puts it:

> Murder, death and violation are legalised everywhere, if not legal, provided that they can be reconverted into value in accordance with the same process that mediatises labour. Only certain deaths, certain practices, escape this convertibility; they alone are subversive (Baudrillard, 1993, p. 175).

One such subversive act is suicide.[6]

WASHINGTON v. GLUCKSBERG: A "STRANGE KIND OF PROSOPOPOEIA"[7]

The decision in *Glucksberg* was made against the cultural background of a society which participates in the management of mortality on a grand scale (see further Agamben, 1998). In a sense, it fits perfectly into the contemporary biopolitical order. It is yet another example of the management of life by judicial *fiat*. The law decides if you live or die in the service of maintaining some semblance of control over mortality. In *Washington v. Glucksberg* the plaintiffs had died before the law could tell them that they could not die by assisted suicide. The Court then wrote a judgment addressed in part to the dead, a dead letter, which as Miller reminds us is "like an inefficacious speech act" (Miller, 1990, p. 158). The plaintiffs' inadvertent deathly performance allowed one to witness this *reductio ad absurdum* of modernity's vitalist imperative.

The law in facing death would rather reanimate the dead than recognise the fact of death, that which undoes law's vitalist politics. Within the judgment the law attempts to summon a living figure, a Lazarus bound tightly in his death shroud, or a Eurydice in the eyes of Orpheus. What the law refuses to see is the Lazarus inside these ligatures, the rotten corrupted one, the excess, the negative, or as Blanchot would have it, the:

> Lazarus in the tomb and not Lazarus brought back into the daylight, the one who already smells bad, who is Evil, Lazarus lost and not Lazarus saved and brought back to life (Blanchot, 1981, p. 46).

Law's Orphic gaze cannot bring the dead back to life. On the contrary, to borrow a phrase from J. Hillis Miller:

> this prosopopoeia does not constitute a mastery over death or the thing. It initiates instead an interminable series of repetitions that arrests death, holds it off (Miller, 1990, p. 158).

The law refuses to see the absence that is death, it summons forth an image of life or a right to life which cannot be trumped by a right to die. Thus, when the law looks at death, it sees not the corpse but that whose absence it marks, the living Lazarus or Eurydice.

However, the language of legal judgments reveals at the same time as it conceals this deferral of death. The law is always confounded by language's ability to "indiscriminately change both meaning and sign" (Blanchot, 1981, p. 60). Maurice Blanchot writes of the tension in literary texts between fragmentation and unity, and how this tension holds the text together. There is no overarching unity, only the competing tensions which make up the whole. In any work, according to Blanchot, there are two versions of rhetoric, which are engaged in a circular play with one another. On the one hand there is rhetoric as "a means of defence, effectively conceived to avert the danger" (Blanchot, 1959, p. 323), and on the other hand a rhetoric which operates as a means of attracting the excessive, calling it forth:

> to attract, while turning it away, the speaking boundlessness; to be a jetty thrust out in the middle of the agitated sand, and not a charming, little rampart visited by people on their Sunday strolls" (Blanchot, 1959, p. 323).

These competing versions of rhetoric are equally present in legal works, one upholding the integrity of language, the other an invitation to fragmentation. Legal judgments which address issues concerning control over death thus "visualise even as they conceal what is too dangerous to articulate openly but too fascinating to repress successfully" (Bronfen, 1992, p. xi). What is enacted in the legal judgment is the very tension which is found in the play of power and transgression.

Chief Justice Rehnquist commences his observations in *Washington v. Glucksberg* in defensive rhetorical mode and, in so doing, evinces the law's failure to recognise those who would wish to die otherwise than in the legally sanctioned way:

> our laws have consistently condemned, and continue to prohibit, assisting suicide. Despite changes in medical technology and notwithstanding an increased emphasis on the importance of end of life decision making, we have not retreated from this prohibition. Against this backdrop of history, tradition, and practice, we now turn to respondents' constitutional claim (521 U.S. 702 (1997) 719).

The backdrop or default is set. The individual is bound by the "rights" which the state accords her. The Supreme Court's obsessive hailing of legal traditions, history, and practices in *Glucksberg* mirrors the obsessional neurotic's attitude toward death, one of procrastination and hesitation. Rehnquist speaks in the rhetoric of warfare: "we have not retreated." He goes on to construct a particular legal relation to assisted death and in so doing reveals a certain conception of community:

> We now enquire whether this asserted right has any place in our Nation's traditions. Here ... we are confronted with a consistent and almost universal tradition that has long rejected the asserted right, and continues to reject it today, even for terminally ill, mentally competent adults. To hold for respondents, we would have to reverse centuries of legal doctrine and practice, and strike down the considered policy choice of almost every state (521 U.S. 702 (1997) 721–723).

In this passage, the Chief Justice creates the illusion that there is a uniform view on this contested ethical issue. This however does not give due consideration to the several contradictory views and practises. He is interpreting the Constitution in a manner which would give the appearance of unity. Rehnquist appeals to a particular interpretative method and, in so doing, is hailing a particular conception of the nation. In this regard, as Douzinas points out:

> Law's strategy is clear: the more threatening the exclusion and the fear, the stronger does the court deny them by proclaiming the wholeness and the integrity of the political community, and by offering a paean to the supremacy of the law ... The trauma is denied through the erection of an imaginary scenario of a complete law and a unified polity (Douzinas, 2000, pp. 364–365).

The Chief Justice's attempt to repress societal disagreement on the issue is not successful. Physician-assisted suicide in Rehnquist's schema would appear to act as a threat to a certain construction of communal identity; one built on a unified body of national history, legal traditions and practices. However not every state is in agreement on the prohibition of physician-assisted suicide. In Oregon voters have assented to a limited legislative scheme of physician aid in dying, for example. This, coupled with more informal practices of hastening the death of the terminally ill, gives lie to the Chief Justice's attempt to create a consensual societal attitude towards the issue.[8] Rehnquist's "prefragmentary writing of the totality which is based on continuity" (Gregg, 1994, p. 99) is interrupted both within the Supreme Court decisions and in certain of the lower court judgments on the issue. Rehnquist's interpretation is one of several possible interpretations. Indeed these possible competing interpretations are also supplied by the lower courts whose decisions are under review. The 9th Circuit Court of Appeals reminded us in its decision in *Glucksberg v. Washington* that rights are not frozen in the text and that history is not a definitive guide to interpretation:

> Although in determining the existence of important rights ... the Court examines our history and experience, it has stated on a number of occasions that the limits of the substantive reach of the Due Process Clause are not frozen at any point in time ...

> . . . the fact that we have previously failed to acknowledge the existence of a particular liberty interest or even that we have previously prohibited its exercise is no barrier to recognizing its existence . . .
>
> . . . historical evidence alone is not a sufficient basis for rejecting a claimed liberty interest (http://www.rights.org/deathnet/us9.html, pp. 11–12).

In *Glucksberg* the Supreme Court is engaged in a simultaneous imposition and questioning of what constitutes legal tradition. This confirms from within the judgment that there is no single history or tradition. In other words, physician-assisted suicide is not inconsistent with a unified tradition or history but with a *particular* conception or ideology of community. The majority's attempt to disguise the widespread juridico-medical management of death is contradicted from within the judgment itself. That which is repressed emerges at points within the Supreme Court's judgment. Justice Stevens in his opinion points to the law's project of death control in referring to the death penalty:

> But just as our conclusion that capital punishment is not always unconstitutional did not preclude later decisions holding that it is sometimes impermissibly cruel, so it is equally clear that a decision upholding a general statutory prohibition of assisted suicide does not mean that every possible application of the statute would be valid. A State, like Washington, that has authorized the death penalty and thereby has concluded that the sanctity of human life does not require that it always be preserved, must acknowledge that there are situations in which an interest in hastening death is legitimate. Indeed, not only is that interest sometimes legitimate, I am also convinced that there are times when it is entitled to constitutional protection (521 U.S. 702 (1997) 741–742).

Stevens went on to further illustrate the indeterminacies extant in cases which refer to death control:

> The *Cruzan* case demonstrated that some state intrusions on the right to decide how death will be encountered are also intolerable. The now deceased plaintiffs in this action may in fact have had a liberty interest even stronger than Nancy Cruzan's because, not only were they terminally ill, they were suffering constant and severe pain . . .
>
> . . . Although there is no absolute right to physician assisted suicide, *Cruzan* makes it clear that some individuals who no longer have the option of deciding whether to live or to die because they are already on the threshold of death have a constitutionally protected interest that may outweigh the State's interest in preserving life at all costs . . . It is an interest in deciding how, rather than whether, a critical threshold shall be crossed (521 U.S. 702 (1997) 745).

In Stevens's opinion we witness a move from a *threshold* to a *critical threshold*. In this move we can see a shift from the normative prohibition on assisted suicide – *the whether* – to the regulatory practise of death control – *the how*. This judicial recognition of the how opens a space in which a different attitude towards the issue may emerge but this space almost immediately recedes back into a more prohibitive approach. Justice Stevens went on to point out that the Court's decision here was far from definitive:

> I do not, however, foreclose the possibility that an individual plaintiff seeking to hasten her death, or a doctor whose assistance was sought, could prevail in a more particularized challenge. Future cases will determine whether such a challenge may succeed (521 U.S. 702 (1997) 750).

Stevens points tantalisingly to other interpretations but does not cross the normative threshold. He speaks of regulating the how but then in the same move defers the decision. He continues to speak in boundary talk. The raising of the possibility of a critical threshold at least acknowledges that the law participates in death control, rather than the disingenuous speech of some of the majority who seek an uncomplicated right or wrong answer to the dilemma.

Justice Souter speaks in a similar manner to Stevens, but ultimately decides to defer, when he observes:

> There can be no stronger claim to a physician's assistance than at the time when death is imminent . . .
>
> . . . the importance of the individual interest here . . . cannot be gainsaid. Whether that interest might in some circumstances, or at some time, be seen as "fundamental" to the degree entitled to prevail is not, however, a conclusion that I need to draw here, for I am satisfied that the State's interests . . . are sufficiently serious to defeat the present claim (521 U.S. 702 (1997) 781–782).

Both Souter and Stevens admit that a right to physician-assisted suicide may be possible and desirable and supported by constitutional tradition, but not in this case. The circumstances of the current case are never quite right; they do not match the court's vague principle of a right to die. This magical case is always in the future, always to come yet never to arrive, echoing the Doorkeeper in Kafka's "Before The Law": "It is possible . . . but not at the moment" (Kafka, 1978).

This constant repetition/invocation of the ideal case is another example of deferral in the service of denial. Thus, what is manifested in juridical discourse is the modernist desire to live on indefinitely. Indeed the person who goes before the law to obtain the right to die could be seen as being: "neither under the law nor in the law" (Derrida, 1991, p. 204). In other words, the individual who seeks such legal permission is both before the law in the sense that she cannot enter the realm of rights discourse, and is, as such, outside the law. Thus, the Court's discursive power here is, to paraphrase Derrida:

> . . . *difference*, an interminable *difference*, since it lasts for days and "years," indeed up to the end of (the) man. *Difference* till death, and for death, without end because ended. As the doorkeeper represents it, the discourse of the law does not say "no" but "not yet," indefinitely (Derrida, 1991, p. 204).

The Supreme Court's perfect future here is like its perfect past, never really there, always vague, always just gone or about to come. It is never here, never in the present, but always present. The law creates its own past and tradition out of the ritual recitation of precedent. It tells a story to itself which although filled with contradiction makes sense to itself about itself. This prosopopoeiac act of composition is uttered in judgments which narrate an uninterrupted present leading to a perfect future, built on an idealised past. Through the ritual incantation of precedent the judges dawdle on their self-constructed boundary between life and death. This attempt to screen the Real of death as traumatic cannot, of course, succeed. As Hal Foster observes: "this very need *points* to the real, and it is at this point that the real *ruptures* the screen of repetition (Foster, 1996, p. 42). It is in this sense that law's prosopopoeiac writing reveals death as the absolute master.

Heather Schuster has made a link between the non-visibility of citizens in the obsessive compulsive ritual of citation, repetition and reinterpretation and the law's need to maintain its own futurity. She argues:

> When a judge decides a case it is never in the present, with, by and for fully realized citizens. Court decisions, through the citation of the past, are always already in the future. There cannot be a legal present anymore than there can be a full citizen in the present. This is why the L/law must control the deployment of performativity: to defer the present in which full citizenship would be realized, and to deflect the abject. [The] excessive bodily performance ruptures the L/law's performative authority, ushering the present and abjecting the L/law (Schuster, 1999, p. 202).

Thus, in *Washington v. Glucksberg*, that these plaintiffs have died is of no import to a law that never recognises or decides for fully realized citizens. The overdetermination of the body in legal discourse leads to its disappearance, an object revealed as absent by its very presence, like the corpse. Law seeks to contain the violent and unruly precisely to maintain its dominance over violence. As Schuster puts it:

> in seeking to arrest infectious violence, the L/law must constantly reproduce itself mimetically through the performative use of precedent to create new case law, which is seen as the promise of a limit. In its mimesis, the L/law is also always violent and without end (Schuster, 1999, p. 192).

Death is only timely when the State kills and gives the appearance of controlling the time and place of death. Hence law's dead letter to the posthumous plaintiffs in this case. Thus, the more law constructs this ideal living body, the more it engages in a stance of wilful blindness to death.

BEYOND THE LAW?

The individual who goes before the law to seek assistance in dying falls into the bind of seeking the approval of the law for her transgressive desire. The person in other words remains within law's imaginary domain where she is:

> already marked in [her] difference through [her] symbolic devaluation. The problem [is] not that difference [is] recognised, but that it [is] recognised as not being of equivalent value (Cornell, 1995, p. 54).

The attempt to overcome the law by using the law must fail. By coming before the law in order to secure a right to die by assistance, the individual's lack of freedom is underlined. The appeal to the Constitution to uphold this argument marks the individual as being before and outside the law. This workless subject, attempting to die within the space of legal permission, is absorbed into the law's space.[9] In this case, to paraphrase Derrida, the discourse of the law: "operates at the limit, not to prohibit directly, but to interrupt and defer the passage" (Derrida, 1991, p. 203).

This legal discourse posits a particular societal relation to death which in Blanchot's terms is embodied in homogeneity, immanence and the enforcement of law (Blanchot, 1983, p. 70). In this case one could argue that what is valued most of all is a transcendent being in common of community. The death which builds this form of community is the death of the patriot, a community bound together through death and worship of the war dead. Death in time of war for one's country is valorised as adding to the life of the community. Similarly such a relation to death would valorise the death penalty, self-defence and killing in time of war, as necessary for the security of the body politic. This relation is built into the law's normative framework in the natural law model of the sanctity of life, which allows of exceptions in the aforementioned cases. This may help to explain how an inalienable right to life is undone when the body politic needs to defend itself or one of its citizens against transgression. The law authorises its own transgression in eliminating the transgressor. This relation to death can be seen as looking to the enforcement of law and exclusion. In managing death and repelling the enemy, the body politic aims to survive. Indeed as Tom Dumm has observed:

> In this framework, security comes to supersede freedom . . . the discourse of freedom as security allows for there to be a strategic use of the rhetoric of freedom to intensify control over populations at large . . . The securing of self is more and more closely tied to participation in or acknowledgement of one's designated place on the (largely) demographically and economically determined scales of meaning (Dumm, 1996, p. 132).

Death as the ultimate intruder must also be repelled in such an understanding of community. The exclusion of physician-assisted suicide from the list of exceptions to the sanctity of life doctrine might be explained by looking on this death as an instance of worklessness. It adds nothing to the survival of the community. It has no utility, it does not defend the state or individual against attack. It is pure excess, a death which does not sublate into building community. This is the ultimate threat to the body politic.

In transgressing the law one always remains within the space of law, as is the case with the carnivalesque which occupies a ludic space set up by the law. This is the bind in which we find ourselves when talking of asserting freedom in the space of the law. In order to challenge the law one must set up an alternative symbolic universe (Mitchell, 1984, p. 291). Juliet Mitchell explains this very well when she observes:

> You cannot choose the imaginary, the semiotic, the carnival as an alternative to the symbolic, as an alternative to the law. It is set up by the law precisely as its own ludic space, its own area of imaginary alternative, but not as a symbolic alternative. So that politically speaking, it is only the symbolic, a new symbolism, a new law, that can challenge the dominant law (Mitchell, 1984, p. 291).

This thinking of a new symbolic may lead us to look more closely in those spaces of transgression which exist at the limits of the law. An act such as suicide or assisted suicide, which so upsets the equilibrium of the law, may be one such insubordinate act, which points to an alternative relation to death. This insubordinate act of dying outside the law may fall within Blanchot's alternative positing of a societal relation to death. In *The Inavowable Community*[10] Blanchot posits this other relation to death as one of heterogeneity, alterity and the suspension of law (Blanchot, 1983, p. 59). Thus, to paraphrase Blanchot, death is the outsider which "perturbs the untroubled continuity of the social and does not recognize prohibitions" (Blanchot, 1983, p. 59). Instead of rigidly delineating a boundary between life and death, death is always already on the inside. It is the foreign body within the body politic without which life cannot go on. This affirmation of finitude may be an opening to an alternative discourse.

Thinking death otherwise requires a discourse other than the limited and limiting discourse of the law. It involves a questioning of why it is that the law presumes to be in control of language. It involves a certain refusal to submit to the law, to be insubordinate. In *L'Amitie* Blanchot speaks of a community founded on "the friendship of this No, certain, unshakeable, and exacting which holds men united in solidarity" (Blanchot, 1971, p. 130). What this "no" affirmed according to Leslie Hill was:

> the necessity of rupture: of a break in continuity in politics, so to speak, and one that put at the centre of political discourse an interval and a disjunction – beyond being and non-being, so to speak (Hill, 1997, p. 212).

Such a politics consists in a refusal of politics based on power, and is one in which the individual bears the responsibility to decide for oneself.

One can gain an insight into what this alternative politics might be by looking at the *Declaration On The Right to Insubordination In The Algerian War*, which Blanchot helped to draft. This document according to Marguerite Duras, one of the co-signatories, attempted to:

> place those to whom it was addressed before an essential and solitary responsibility, which was the responsibility to decide both for themselves and in relation to themselves (cited in Hill, 1997, p. 213).

This politics of refusal is also a refusal of a certain kind of juridico-political language. As Leslie Hill points out, Blanchot refuses all language, which is authoritarian, self-assured, peremptory, repetitive, and oppressive (Hill, 1997, p. 215). The language of law fits securely into this description of the language of power. Blanchot, in his own encounter with the law after the state instituted criminal legal proceedings against the co-authors of this insubordinate document, experienced how legal language robbed the individual of his own speech. Blanchot appeared before an examining magistrate during the course of the proceedings in order to give a statement. The magistrate then dictated Blanchot's words to the court clerk. However this was not a direct transcription of Blanchot's words but the magistrate's summing up of what Blanchot had said. In referring to this incident Blanchot notes:

> There is a seriously deficient point in this affair, which is the debate between a man with a wealth of legal expertise at his fingertips and another who has perhaps few words and does not even know the sovereign value of speech, of *his* speech. Why is it that the judge has the right to be sole master of language, dictating (in what is already a *diktat*) the words of another, as seems appropriate to him, reproducing them not as they were said, stuttering, meagre and unsure, but made worse, because finer, more consistent with the classical ideal, and, most of all, more definitive (Blanchot, 1993, p. 11).

Blanchot in describing the rationale behind the Declaration elaborated on the importance of the use of the term "right" to insubordination in this context:

> I believe that the whole force of the Declaration, its whole power of disturbance, comes from the authority with which it utters the single word insubordination, a solemn word, signifying utmost refusal: the Right to insubordination. I say Right and not Duty . . . an obligation refers to a prior moral code that shields, guarantees, and justifies it; wherever there is duty, all that is necessary is to close one's eyes and carry it out blindly; everything is then quite straight forward. The right to do something, on the other hand, refers only to itself, to the exercise of that freedom of which it is the expression; a right is a free power for which each individual, for himself and with regard to himself, is responsible and which binds him completely and freely: nothing is stronger, nothing is more serious. That is why it is essential to say: the right to insubordination: each person takes their own sovereign decision (cited in Hill, 1997, pp. 213–214).

In the context of the current study, assisted suicide could be seen as that absolute right without concomitant duty, which somehow escapes state power. Blanchot in writing elsewhere of the absolute right to suicide notes:

> Suicide is an absolute right, the only one that is not the corollary of a duty, and yet a right which no real power doubles or reinforces. It would seem to arch like a delicate and endless footbridge

> which at the decisive moment is cut and becomes as unreal as a dream, over which nevertheless it is necessary really to pass. Suicide is a right, then, detached from power and duty, a madness required by reasonable integrity and which, moreover, seems to succeed quite often (Blanchot, 1982, p. 105).

It is a dying which widens law's limit point.[11] Thus, to paraphrase Blanchot, even though the law uses death in order to impose itself (Blanchot, 1987, p. 99), what in effect occurs is that law's power is undone in this move.

I have outlined above how in *Glucksberg* one can see how this undoing of the law occurs within its own discourse.[12] The absent body gives presence to the nation in the case of the patriot, but in the case of physician-assisted suicide the absent body disturbs the biopolis. If the law cannot control the dead how can it control the living? It is vital then from the point of view of legal and political elites that death is *seen* to be managed. In lying beyond law's grasp the plaintiffs' deathly performance may point to that space of resistance wherein is traced "the flashing line that causes the limit to arise" (Foucault, 1977a, p. 35).

NOTES

1. Baudrillard observes:

> people . . . demand their death as their own good . . . it leads to investment in the 'immovable' property of death, not only as a preoccupation with the 'third home,' such as the tomb or the burial ground have become . . . but as the demand for a 'quality of death' . . . this is the inalienable right constituting the perfected form of bourgeois individual law . . . death must once again become the final object in this collection and, instead of going through this inertia as the only possible event, it must itself re-enter the game of accumulating and administering things (Baudrillard, 1993, p. 176).

2. Nancy sums up this thinking of living on eloquently when he writes:

> Depuis l'epoque de Descartes, au moins, l'humanite moderne a fait du voeu de survie et d'immoralite un element dans un programme general de "maitrise et possession de la nature." Elle a programme ainsi une etrangete croissante de la "nature." Elle a ravive l'etrangete absolue de la double enigme de la mortalite et de l'immortalite. Ce que les religions representaient, elle l'a porte a la puissance d'une technique qui repousse la fin en tous les sens de l'expression: en prolongeant le terme, elle etale une absence de fin: quelle vie prolonger, dans quel but? (Nancy, 2000, p. 24).

3. As J. Hillis Miller puts it: " 'Death' is a catachresis for what can never be named properly" (Miller, 1990, p. 172).

4. Scalia's assertion here points to the actual question which the court asks in cases concerning end of life decision making (or more correctly, death control) – not one which demands "*should the plaintiff live or die?*" but "*should we the court live or die?*" Scalia's violent metaphors point to an anxiety about upsetting borders, between life and death,

between the judiciary and the legislators. It is a logic within which the twin fantasies of textual integrity and societal wholeness must be upheld.

5. A phrase coined by Giorgio Agamben (1998, p. 186) when he writes of the case of Karen Ann Quinlan:

> Her life is maintained only by means of life-support technology and by virtue of a legal decision. It is no longer life but only death in motion.

Here again the decision whether such death in motion should be prolonged is a legal one.

6. As Baudrillard notes:

> suicide . . . has taken on a different extension and definition, to the point of becoming, in the context of the offensive reversibility of death, the form of subversion itself (Baudrillard, 1993, p. 175).

7. The phrase is taken from J. Hillis Miller (1990, p. 158). The complete sentence reads:

> If prosopopoeia in one of its meanings is the ascription of a face, a voice, or a name to the dead, a letter sent to a dead person is a strange kind of prosopopoiea.

8. As the 9th Circuit Court of Appeals decision in *Washington v. Glucksberg* acknowledged:

> Running beneath the official history of legal condemnation of physician-assisted suicide is a strong undercurrent of a time-honored but hidden practice of physicians helping terminally ill patients to hasten their deaths. (http://www.rights.org/deathnet/us9.html, p. 16).

The Supreme Court's assertion of a universal tradition which eschews euthanasia and physician-assisted suicide is countered here by an alternative tradition of physician assistance in dying which occurs outside formal legal structures. Indeed the irony of all attempts to secure a right to die within the law is that, if secured, it would extend death control even further. As Tierney (1997, p. 74) points out in Baudrillardian mode:

> the irony of our late-modern situation lies not just in the idea that the right to assisted suicide is becoming an important element of personal freedom, but also in the realization that one of the greatest threats to this freedom may be the medical and legal recognition of suicide as a right.

9. As Blanchot reminds us:

> There is not, to begin with, law, prohibition, and then transgression, but rather there is transgression in the absence of any prohibition, which eventually freezes into Law, the Principle of Meaning (Blanchot, 1980, p. 75).

10. Jean-Luc Nancy, in speaking of the link between the two texts which Blanchot examines in *The Inavowable Community* (Nancy's own *The Inoperative Community* and Marguerite Duras' *The Malaldy of Death*), observes:

> Il les distingue . . . comme deux textes dont l'un resterait a une consideration negative ou en creux du "desoeuvrement," tandis que l'autre donnerait acces a une communaute non pas "oeuvree" mais operee en secret (l'inavouable) par le partage d'une experience de l'amour et de la mort, de la vie meme exposee a ses limites.
>
> Peut-etre dit-il . . . que ces deux acces a l'essence sans essence de la "communaute" se recoupent quelque part, entre les deux parties du livre comme entre l'ordre social-politique et l'ordre passionel-intime (Nancy, 2001, p. 46).

11. Indeed it would be interesting to explore at length the link between this politics of refusal and Foucault's discussion of "non-positive affirmation." Foucault notes the potential link when, in writing of Blanchot's notion of "contestation," he observes:

> This philosophy of non-positive affirmation is, I believe, what Blanchot was defining through his principle of "contestation." Contestation does not imply a generalized negation, but an affirmation that affirms nothing, a radical break of transitivity. Rather than being a process of thought for denying existences or values, contestation is the act which carries them all to their limits and, from there, to the Limit where an ontological decision achieves its end; to contest is to proceed until one reaches the empty core where being achieves its limit and where the limit defines being (Foucault, 1977a, p. 34).

12. As Hill notes:

> the language of power [is] ultimately always vulnerable: vulnerable not to the challenge that might come from a rival code of values ... but vulnerable instead to the infinite scepticism affirmed by the language of writing itself (Hill, 1997, p. 215).

REFERENCES

Agamben, G. (1998). *Homo sacer: Sovereign power and bare life*. Stanford, CA: Stanford University Press.

Baudrillard, J. (1993). *Symbolic exchange and death*. I. Hamilton Grant (Trans). London: Sage.

Bauman, Z. (1992). *Mortality, immortality and other life strategies*. Oxford: Blackwell.

Blanchot, M. (1959). *Le livre a venir*. Paris: Gallimard-Idees.

Blanchot, M. (1971). *L'Amitie*. Paris: Gallimard.

Blanchot, M. (1980). *The writing of the disaster*. A. Smock (Trans.). Lincoln, NA: University of Nebraska Press.

Blanchot, M. (1981). *The gaze of Orpheus and other literary essays*. L. Davis (Trans.). Barrytown, NY: Station Hill Press.

Blanchot, M. (1982). *The space of literature*. A. Smock (Trans.). Lincoln, NA: The University of Nebraska Press.

Blanchot, M. (1983). *La communaute inavouable*. Paris: Minuit.

Blanchot, M. (1987). Michel Foucault as I imagine him. In: *Foucault/Blanchot*. J. Mehlman (Trans.). New York: Zone Books.

Blanchot, M. (1992). *The step not beyond*. L. Nelson (Trans.). Albany, NY: State University of New York Press.

Blanchot, M. (1993). Pour l'amitie. In: D. Mascolo (Ed.), *A la Recherche d'un Communisme de Pensee, Entetements* (pp. 5–16). Paris: Editions fourbis.

Bronfen, E. (1992). *Over her dead body: Death, femininity and the aesthetic*. Manchester: Manchester University Press.

Cornell, D. (1995). Bodily integrity and the right to abortion. In: A. Sarat & T. Kearns (Eds), *Identities, Politics and Rights* (pp. 21–84). Ann Arbor, MI: The University of Michigan Press.

Derrida, J. (1991). Before the law. In: D. Attridge (Ed.), *Jacques Derrida: Acts of Literature* (pp. 181–220). New York: Routledge.

Douzinas, C. (2000). The end of human rights: Critical legal thought at the turn of the century. Oxford: Hart publishing.

Dumm, T. (1996). *Michel Foucault and the politics of freedom.* London: Sage.
Foster, H. (1996). *The return of the real.* Cambridge, MA: MIT Press.
Foucault, M. (1977a). A preface to transgression. In: D. F. Bouchard (Ed.), *Language, Counter-Memory, Practice: Selected Essays and Interviews* (pp. 29–52). D. F. Bouchard and S. Simon (Trans.). Ithaca, NY: Cornell University Press.
Foucault, M. (1987). Maurice Blanchot: The thought from outside. In: *Foucault/Blanchot.* B. Massumi (Trans.). New York: Zone Books.
Gregg, J. (1994). *Maurice Blanchot and the literature of transgression.* Princeton, NJ: Princeton University Press.
Hill, L. (1997). *Maurice Blanchot: Extreme contemporary.* London: Routledge.
Johnson, B. (1987). *A world of difference.* Baltimore, MD: The Johns Hopkins University Press.
Kafka, F. (1978). Before the law. In: *Wedding Preparations in the Country and Other Stories.* W. Muir & E. Muir (Trans.). Harmondsworth: Penguin.
Miller, J. H. (1990). *Versions of pygmalion.* Cambridge, MA: Harvard University Press.
Mitchell, J. (1984). *Women: The longest revolution – essays on feminism, literature and psychoanalysis.* London: Virago.
Nancy, J.-L. (2000). *L'Intrus.* Paris: Galilee.
Nancy, J.-L. (2001). *La Communaute Affronte.* Paris: Galilee.
Rose, N. (2001). The politics of life itself. *Theory, Culture & Society, 18*(6), 1–30.
Sarat, A. (2001). *When the state kills: Capital punishment and the American condition.* Princeton, NJ: Princeton University Press.
Schuster, H. (1999). Reproduction and the state: Between bodily performance and legal performativity. *Angelaki: A Journal of the Theoretical Humanities, 4*(1), 189–206.
Tierney, T. (1997). Death, medicine and the right to die: An engagement with Heidegger, Bauman and Baudrillard. *Body & Society, 3*(4), 51–77.

Cases Cited

Cruzan v. Director, Missouri Department of Health. 497 U.S. 261 (1990).
Quill v. Vacco (80 F.3d 716 (2d Cir. 1996).
Washington v. Glucksberg. 9th Circuit Court of Appeals, en banc, (1996), March 6, http://www.rights.org/deathnet/us9.html.
Washingon v. Glucksberg. 521 U.S. 702 (1997).

EXTRATERRITORIAL CRIMINAL JURISDICTION: REPLACING "OBJECTIVE TERRITORIALITY" WITH "DEFENSIVE TERRITORIALITY"

Ellen S. Podgor

ABSTRACT

This article begins by exploring the development of extraterritoriality in the United States. It notes the expansion of extraterritorial provisions within federal criminal legislation and how these provisions permit prosecutors to proceed with criminal actions for conduct occurring outside this country. It also reflects on the use of an "objective territorial principle" by the judiciary, that permits criminal prosecutions whenever the conduct of the actor has a substantial effect in the United States. As an alternative to using "objective territoriality," this article advocates for using a "defensive territoriality" approach. This article stresses the benefits of using a "defensive territoriality" approach to decide whether to prosecute an extraterritorial crime.

INTRODUCTION

A foreign corporation may be prosecuted in the United States under the Sherman Act even though the price-fixing activities occur outside this country (*Nippon v. United States*, 1997). Likewise, individuals selling drugs may never step foot on

Studies in Law, Politics, and Society
Studies in Law, Politics, and Society, Volume 28, 117–135

ISSN: 1059-4337/PII: S1059433702280059

United States soil, yet find their conduct subject to a United States prosecution (*Chua Han Mow v. United States*, 1984). So too, individuals operating in Pakistan who are alleged to be part of a conspiracy that resulted in the death of a journalist from the United States, may find themselves indicted by a United States grand jury (*United States v. Sheikh*, 2002). Extraterritorial criminal jurisdiction permits United States prosecutors to proceed with each of these criminal cases.

Individuals who reside outside the United States may find themselves extradited (*Chua Han Mow v. United States*, 1984), kidnapped (*United States v. Alvarez-Machain*, 1992), or lured (U.S. Department of Justice, Attorney's Manual § 9–15.630, 1997), to the United States to face criminal charges in this country (*United States v. Best*, 2002). Corporations may find themselves subject to United States criminal penalties even though they are foreign corporations acting outside this country.

The limits of criminal law are not determined strictly by examining the national law where an act occurs. Extraterritoriality adds another dimension to the boundaries of criminal law. With increased globalization, this new dimension plays a prominent role in shaping the contours of criminal law. Recognizing that the term "globalization" is a term of enormous breadth with substantial legal jurisprudence reflecting on its many dimensions (Twining, 2002), it is noted here that the term as used in this paper is one of a simplistic nature. The term "globalization" as used throughout this paper is to recognize increased internationalization on economic, political, social, and cultural levels.

In past articles, I have discussed the concept of extraterritoriality in specific contexts. I argued for using a "defensive territoriality" approach, as opposed to the existing "objective territoriality approach," in the specific context of extraterritorial business crimes (Podgor, in press). In addition, I have previously contended that Congress should speak clearer in drafting white collar criminal statutes to address whether an extraterritorial application should be authorized (Podgor, 1997). I have also advocated for limiting national jurisdiction in the context of international computer fraud crimes (Podgor, 2002b). Although there are strong arguments for limiting extraterritorial applications in specific contexts (Podgor, 2002b), there are equally strong arguments for extending extraterritorial applications in appropriate cases.

In this article I will extend the principles that I discussed in my prior pieces to look comprehensively at all crimes. Here, I will focus generally on criminal law and explore the deficiencies of one of the key principles of extraterritoriality used by the United States, namely, "objective territoriality." It is contended here that applying "defensive territoriality" as a replacement for "objective territoriality" provides a methodology that is better attuned to globalization. "Defensive territoriality" offers a more restrained approach in the context of crimes not directed against the United States, as with business offenses that do not involve the government. It encourages, however, an extraterritorial application when acts are perpetrated against the government of this country.

This article begins by exploring the development of extraterritoriality in the United States. It notes the expansion of extraterritorial provisions within federal criminal legislation and how these provisions permit prosecutors to proceed with criminal actions for conduct occurring outside this country. It also reflects on the use of an "objective territorial principle" by the judiciary, that permits criminal prosecutions whenever the conduct of the actor has a substantial effect in the United States. With globalization, it is common for conduct outside the United States to affect this country. As such, using an "objective territorial principle" allows prosecutors enormous discretion in their decisions of whether to proceed with criminal actions that involve extraterritorial conduct.

As an alternative to using "objective territoriality," this article advocates for using a "defensive territoriality" approach. It defines and provides specific applications to understand the boundaries of this term. This article stresses the benefits of using a "defensive territoriality" approach to decide whether to prosecute an extraterritorial crime.

CRIMINAL JURISDICTION

Historically, criminal jurisdiction was predominantly a function of "territorial" jurisdiction (Podgor & Wise, 2000, pp. 28–71). The country where the act occurred, prosecuted the crime (Extraterritorial Application of Criminal Law, 1991). The law of that nation was usually the controlling law. When a conflict of jurisdiction arose, such as when two jurisdictions wished to proceed, the issue was often resolved by an international tribunal (*France v. Turkey*, 1927). This strict "territorial" approach differed from that used in civil cases, where rules of minimum or substantial contacts developed (*Int'l Shoe Co. v. Washington*, 1945).

In 1922, the Supreme Court's decision in *United States v. Bowman* (1922) routed criminal jurisdiction in a new direction. The *Bowman* case involved an alleged conspiracy to defraud the Fleet Corporation, of which the United States was a stockholder. The lower court rejected criminal jurisdiction on one of the counts that referred to acts committed on the high seas. Finding no explicit legislative authority for criminal jurisdiction, the lower court refused to permit the extraterritorial application (*Bowman*, 1922, p. 97).

The Supreme Court reversed this position. The Court stated that "[t]he necessary locus, when not specifically defined, depends upon the purpose of Congress as evinced by the description and nature of the crime and upon the territorial limitations upon the power and jurisdiction of a government to punish crime under the law of nations" (*Bowman*, 1922, pp. 97–98). The Court then expounded on two different classes of crimes: (1) crimes "against individuals or their property" such as "assault, murder, burglary, larceny, robbery, arson, embezzlement, and fraud" (*Bowman*, 1922, p. 98) and (2) "criminal statutes which are, as a class, not logically dependent on their locality for the government's jurisdiction, but were enacted because of the right of the government to defend itself against obstruction, or fraud whenever perpetrated, especially if committed by its own citizens, officers, or agents" (*Bowman*, 1922, p. 98). Cases in this second category were considered appropriate for an extraterritorial application.

Bowman set the stage for numerous decisions that permitted extraterritoriality. Courts "routinely infer[ ] congressional intent to provide for extraterritorial jurisdiction over foreign offenses that cause domestic harm" (*United States v. Plummer*, 2000, pp. 1304–1305). Thus, while it is difficult to say whether the increase in investigation of overseas crimes resulted in an increased number of criminal prosecutions, or whether the increase in desire to prosecute abroad caused an increase in criminal investigations in foreign countries, it is nonetheless evident that over time *Bowman* has been extended well beyond its contextual setting (Johnston, 1995; Lippman & Smith, 1996).

EXTRATERRITORIALITY

Extraterritoriality from a United States perspective can be a function of statutory language that specifically authorizes an extraterritorial application or judicial interpretation that reads into the statute an extraterritorial intent. In some cases courts will also consider international law and principles of jurisdiction that are internationally recognized. Despite the historical presumption against extraterritoriality in criminal cases (Estey, 1997), it is rare that courts restrain a prosecutor from proceeding with an extraterritorial prosecution (*United States v. Boots*, 1996).

Explicit Statutory Authority for Extraterritoriality

Statutory language that explicitly authorizes a prosecution of conduct outside the United States leaves little room for contesting the authority of the prosecutor to proceed with the extraterritorial application. The language can appear as legislation that is directly focused on extraterritorial conduct, as in the Foreign Corrupt Practices Act (15 U.S. C. §§ 78dd-1, 78dd-2, 78ff, 1977; See also The Export Administration Act, 1994) that directly addresses bribery occurring outside the

United States. Alternatively, Congress can speak clearly with regard to extraterritoriality, by providing a provision within a statute that authorizes an extraterritorial application (Podgor, 1997). For example, the key perjury statute permits prosecution irrespective of whether the statement is "made within or without the United States" (18 U.S. C. § 1621). Whether the statute is directly focused on extraterritorial conduct, or provides explicit reference to extraterritorially in a statutory provision, there is no issue in these cases as to whether prosecutors have authority to proceed with the criminal action. It is clear here that Congress has authorized an extraterritorial application.

Congress has explicitly authorized extraterritorial applications in a growing number of federal statutes. This clear expression of extraterritoriality by Congress furthers increased consistency and predictability in the law. When Congress authorizes extraterritoriality directly within the statute's language, there is little room for a conflicting interpretation of whether an extraterritorial application is permitted. Examples of recent legislative pronouncements of extraterritoriality include provisions within crimes of money laundering (18 U.S. C. § 1956), computer crimes (18 U.S. C. § 1030; see also U.S. A. Patriot Act, 2001), and terrorism (18 U.S. C. § 2332(b)). In some cases the extraterritoriality provision may apply to all conduct under the statute, as with the false declarations statute, which states that "this section is applicable whether the conduct occurred within or without the United States" (18 U.S. C. § 1623(b); see also 18 U.S. C. § 1512). In other cases, however, as with one of the money laundering statutes, the statute may specifically limit when an extraterritorial application will be permitted (18 U.S. C. § 1956(f)).

Judicial Interpretation Permitting an Extraterritorial Application

Questions usually arise when the statute omits reference to whether an extraterritorial prosecution is permitted. In these instances, courts are left to interpret whether Congress intended extraterritoriality and whether this application is permitted under international norms. Consistency and predictability can be flawed when lower courts disagree on whether Congress intended for a statute to have an extraterritorial application (*United States v. Boots*, 1996; but see *United States v. Trapilo*, 1997).

Historically, the omission of specific language of extraterritoriality was an indication that this extension of jurisdiction should not be allowed. This position, however, has clearly changed over time. Although courts are left with little guidance in trying to decide whether Congress intended for a statute to have an extraterritorial application, it is rare that they find otherwise (*United States v. Boots*, 1996). In addition to referencing the distinction enunciated in *Bowman* between crimes "against individuals or their property" and "criminal statutes which are, as a class, not logically dependent on their locality for the government's jurisdiction" (*Bowman v. United States*, 1922, p. 98) courts will also reference international law in trying to discern whether an extraterritorial application is permitted. It is here that one finds enormous breadth in permitting an extraterritorial application.

The international norms that the United States uses for determining whether extraterritoriality should be allowed originate from a Harvard study in international law (Harvard Research, 1935). That study provided for criminal jurisdiction premised upon "territoriality," "nationality," "passive personality," the "protective principle," and "universality." Courts that use these bases of jurisdiction do not always rest the determination of extraterritoriality on one base as an exclusive authority for an extraterritorial application (*United States v. Evans*, 1987). One can find decisions with more than one international base used as the rationale for allowing the prosecutor to proceed with a criminal case that involves extraterritorial conduct (*Chau Han Mow v. United States*, 1984).

The "territorial principle" accepts jurisdiction when the act occurs within the territory ("Restatement III," 1989, § 402(1)). The "nationality principle" permits jurisdiction premised upon the nationality of the perpetrator (Watson, 1992), while "passive personality" jurisdiction exists when jurisdiction is premised upon the nationality of the victim (Watson, 1993). The "protective principle" of jurisdiction is typically premised upon national security (Cameron, 1994). The "universality principle" of jurisdiction is often premised upon a violation of human rights (Randall, 1988).

Not all countries approach extraterritoriality in a like fashion (Council of Europe, 1992, pp. 446–447). Although many find "territorial jurisdiction" an accepted norm, countries have different ways of interpreting what is included within a territory. For example, some countries approach territoriality to include the "doctrine of ubiquity" (Council of Europe, 1992, p. 446). This "means that an offence as a whole may be considered to have been committed in the place where a part of it has been committed" (Council of Europe, 1992, p. 446). Moreover, "not all [countries] require that the offender must have intended the effects of his act to occur in the territory of the state claiming jurisdiction" (Council of Europe, 1992). In recent years the "territorial principle" in the United States has been extended to include conduct that does not occur within the strict territorial limits of a country (*United States v. Wright-Baker*, 1989). This adaptation, known as the "objective territorial principle," is often the basis for a court's finding of extraterritorial jurisdiction. This common base of criminal jurisdiction will be the focus of the next section of this article.

Courts also use principles from the Restatement (Third) of Foreign Relations Law regarding jurisdiction to prescribe (1989, § 402) limits on this jurisdiction

(1989, § 403). Although the Restatement could serve to limit extraterritorial prosecutions because it contains language of when jurisdiction should be held unreasonable, courts do not use this section to reject a prosecutor's desire to proceed with a prosecution of extraterritorial conduct (Podgor, 2002b).

Prosecutorial Discretion to Proceed Extraterritorially

Irrespective of whether the statute specifically authorizes an extraterritorial application, or whether courts allow for this approach, prosecutors have enormous discretion in deciding when to proceed against criminal conduct occurring outside the United States. The Department of Justice guidelines, which require authorization when the prosecution involves international conduct, provide some assistance in making these decisions (U.S. Department of Justice Manual, 1997, § 9–47.00; see also U.S. Department of Justice Manual, 2000, § 9–2.400). Because the U.S. Attorney's Manual specifically provides that it "may not be relied on to create any rights, substantive or procedural, enforceable at law," the propriety of an extraterritorial prosecution is only a concern in the internal administrative review process (U.S. Department of Justice Manual, 1997, § 1–1.000; see also *United States v. Caceres*, 1973).

The increased number of federal criminal statutes with extraterritorial provisions, and growing number of judicial decisions that permit prosecutors to proceed when the conduct has an effect on the United States, leaves prosecutors with few limits on their decisions to prosecute criminal conduct committed outside the United States (Waller, 2000). Absent an explicit treaty precluding an extradition or authorizing a specified procedure, the executive branch of government has enormous power to decide the method for proceeding against an individual in a foreign country. Even when the method used to obtain a defendant to the United States is a "shocking" abduction, and when the procedure "may be in violation of general international law principles," the prosecution in the United States will not be precluded (*United States v. Alvarez-Machain*, 1992).

"OBJECTIVE TERRITORIALITY"

Courts have added a dimension to the "territorial principle" by using a principle known as "objective territoriality." Use of this principle provides prosecutors with enormous breadth to find extraterritoriality to prosecute criminal acts that occur outside the United States. After discussing the breadth of the "objective territorial" principle, I will discuss the ramifications of this application.

The Breadth of "Objective Territoriality"

The breadth provided to prosecutors in proceeding with extraterritorial actions is heightened by the use of the "objective territorial" principle. When Congress has not directly addressed extraterritoriality within the statute and the prosecutor is proceeding on the basis of the conduct having a substantial effect on this country, the principle of "objective territoriality" is a key basis for this jurisdiction.

"Objective territoriality" originated from a decision by Justice Oliver Wendall Holmes in a case involving conduct between two states (*Strassheim v. Daily*, 1911). It permits extraterritoriality for "[a]cts done outside a jurisdiction, but intended to produce and producing detrimental effects within it" (*Strassheim v. Daily*, 1911, p. 285). This doctrine is a prime source used by prosecutors to uphold prosecutions of conduct beyond the borders of the United States (Coffin, 2000).

With globalization, there are few restraints on jurisdiction when a principle such as "objective territoriality" is used as the basis for proceeding against a defendant (Born, 1992). It is easy to claim that the conduct has a substantial effect on this country. If the victims of the crime reside in the United States, or if there is an economic result felt in this country, using an "objective territorial" principle may be justified. Prosecutors have used "objective territoriality" to proceed on extraterritorial drug prosecutions (*United States v. MacAllister*, 1998; see also *United States v. Postal*, 1979), unlawful entry of aliens (*United States v. Castillo Felix*, 1976) and business crimes (*United States v. Nippon Paper Industries Co., Ltd.*, 1997). They have even gone as far as using the "objective territoriality" principle to proceed on an assault and battery case occurring on a foreign vessel, when there was "a nexus between the foreign vessel and the United States" (*United States v. Pizdrint*, 1997, pp. 1112–1113). However, courts have not always required a nexus to the United States when individuals aboard a vessel are engaged in drug activity (*United States v. Caicedo*, 1995). Requiring merely a substantial effect on the United States provides prosecutors with nearly limitless discretion (Coffin, 2000).

The Ramifications of Using "Objective Territoriality"

The ramifications of permitting an increased number of extraterritorial prosecutions and leaving the discretion to proceed with these cases in the hands of prosecutors warrants reconsideration. Because of globalization, an "objective territoriality" principle allows prosecutions that are well beyond the historical position that leaned against the extraterritorial application of criminal laws. This means that national law might be usurped by another country's national law

(Raimo, 1999). Cultural differences may be lost when a country that is unfamiliar with these differences is bringing the criminal charges (Laufer & Taka, 1995). Individuals in countries that might not criminalize certain conduct, or countries that decide that civil remedies are more appropriate, may find themselves subject to a United States prosecution merely because the conduct substantially affects this country.

If other countries were to take an approach of "objective territoriality," then conduct that might be perfectly legitimate in the United States might be subject to a criminal prosecution in another forum. For example, in the United States we have a first amendment right to free speech. Other countries may limit these rights more extensively than the United States. But are we willing to accept that an individual in the United States should be subject to a criminal violation of another countries laws because they placed on the world wide web something that is legal under our standards, but illegal when received in the other country (Germany and U.S. Clash, 2001; see also *Yahoo, Inc. v. LaLigue Contre Le Racisme Et L' Antisemitisme*, 2001)? These concerns are particularly noteworthy in the context of computer criminality that exceeds the borders of the United States (Podgor, 2002b).

"Objective territoriality" also raises comity concerns as the use of this principle provides the United States with the authority to proceed on every world crime that has a substantial effect on this country (Grippando, 1983). Although discretion may be tempered in one administration, another may be more aggressive in its approach (*United States v. Nippon Paper Industries Co., Ltd.*, 1997). A consistent approach in the law can suffer as a result of the breadth of the "objective territoriality" principle.

Because of globalization, the "objective territoriality" principle provides enormous discretion that could be abused by some prosecutors. The legal structure of the United States is undermined by individual decision makers that have few restraints on their conduct (Podgor, 2000; see also Griffin, 2001). As such, it is argued here that "objective territoriality" is an outdated concept that needs to be reconfigured. Although it worked well pre-globalization, the change in world communication and travel warrants reconsideration.

"DEFENSIVE TERRITORIALITY"

In contrast to an "objective territoriality" principle, approaching extraterritoriality defensively places some restraints on the allowable conduct upon which prosecutors can proceed. Under "defensive territoriality," criminal conduct that is individual to specific persons and does not have an effect on a governmental function, is suspect as a basis for an extraterritorial application. "Defensive territoriality," however, does include conduct that is aimed at harming the United States, including a deliberate avoidance of jurisdiction, as when one goes outside the country to perpetrate a crime on the United States (Podgor, 2002b). Thus, the relationship to a government function is the essence of "defensive territoriality." The difficult line drawing arises in deciding when is conduct aimed at the government, as opposed to being merely aimed at individuals within the country.

"Defensive territoriality" does not preclude the use of other bases of extraterritorial jurisdiction. For example, the individuals who perpetrated the acts against the World Trade Center and the individuals therein, on September 11th, 2001 could easily be prosecuted under a strict "territorial principle." The acts occurred within the United States and therefore this country has jurisdiction. There is no need to use an extraterritorial application when the conduct occurs on United States soil. Although extradition may be necessary to secure individuals outside this country who perpetrated these acts, there is no question that the United States has "territorial" jurisdiction to prosecute the acts occurring in New York City on September 11th. Likewise, instances when the "nationality principle," the "protective principle," "universality," and the "passive personality principle" might be a legitimate basis for jurisdiction, are not impeded by replacing an "objective territorial" approach with that of "defensive territoriality."

"Defensive territoriality" is not synonymous with the "protective principle," although there are clearly some overlapping themes. The "protective principle" usually arises in situations when there is a threat to national security (*United States v. James-Robinson*, 1981, pp. 1344–1345). It can also arise when someone is interfering with the "operations of [ ] government functions" (*United States v. Gonzales*, 1985, p. 938). "Defensive territoriality" covers a wider range of conduct than what is included within the "protective principle." For example, "[t]here seems to be a tendency in some countries to stretch the concept of 'essential' interests to include such interests as the capital market, national shipping and aviation, the environment and certain industrial and commercial interests, for instance, industrial secrets, though this is not a general trend." (Council of Europe, 1992, pp. 451–452).

Although "defensive territoriality" is not contingent on whether the conduct has an effect on the United States, as with the "objective territorial" principle, it does extend beyond issues of national security and government functions. For example, committing a fraud against the United States might not rise to the level of the "protective principle." It would, however, be included within "defensive territoriality." When individuals perpetrate crimes against the United States government, irrespective of the crime involved, the government needs to be able to defend itself through appropriate judicial means (Smith, 1991).

"Defensive territoriality" is in keeping with the historical approach to when criminal conduct should be prosecuted extraterritorially. In *Bowman* not only was the government the victim of the act, but the government was also affected by the conduct. The judicial philosophy enunciated in *Bowman*, and the specific language used in that Supreme Court decision, is clearly in keeping with a "defensive territorial" approach to extraterritoriality (*United States v. Bowman*, 1922).

The Boundaries of "Defensive Territoriality"

Two factors are considered in understanding "defensive territoriality." First, who will be making the determination of the boundaries of this principle (Council of Europe, 1992, p. 456). Second, when does conduct fall within the range of that subject to the "defensive territoriality" principle. As with all issues that consider the line between national and international law, comity concerns need to be at the forefront of the decision-making process (Pearce, 1994).

The answer to the question of who should be deciding whether extraterritorial conduct should be subject to prosecution considers a wider number of parties than presently exists under the "objective territorial" approach. "Defensive territoriality" needs to be a concept considered by both legislators and courts. In contrast to "objective territoriality," that finds its place only when the judiciary is reviewing an extraterritorial application and only when a statute omits specific reference authorizing a prosecution outside the United States, "defensive territoriality" should be both a statutory rule of construction and a consideration by the judiciary.

Legislators drafting laws need to consider whether an extraterritorial application is warranted. In so doing, they need to approach the extension of a statute beyond the borders of the United States with considerable restraint. Merely because individuals in this country might be affected by criminal conduct, should not mean that the conduct should be subject to our laws. International agreements, international tribunals, and the courts of other countries may be better suited to punish conduct that is unsatisfactory to individuals in our country.

Placing broad language in a statute that allows it to be applied extraterritorially, fails to consider the broad range of conduct that might be subject to a United States prosecution. For example, the extensive language added to the computer fraud statute, as part of the "Uniting and Strengthening America by Providing Appropriate Tools Required to Intercept and Obstruct Terrorism Act of 2001" ("U.S. A. Patriot Act, 2001"), is not limited to terrorist activity, which was the original purpose for that act. This statutory modification to the computer fraud statute, 18 U.S. C. § 1030, includes fraudulent acts that might have no relation to government functions (Podgor, 2002a). What might be strictly a civil dispute in another country, could rise to the level of a criminal action here because of the extraterritorial application added within this statute.

In deciding the appropriate extraterritorial lines, the legislature needs to consider not only comity concerns, but also the effect of an extraterritorial provision on international affairs. Legislation needs to be specific to when conduct outside this country will be defeating a government function.

Courts will also have authority to consider the boundaries of whether extraterritoriality should be allowed. In this regard, the courts will be interpreting clear legislative language and also be considering statutes that omit language of extraterritoriality. In discerning the intent of Congress and considering international principles, a principle that is not as far reaching as "objective territoriality" is a more appropriate norm for all of society.

"Objective territoriality" covers nearly every imaginable criminal act. After all, in a globalized society, what does not have an effect on this country? In contrast, "defensive territoriality" protects government functions, while also allowing national laws of each country to maintain the primary position in controlling criminal conduct that occurs within the boundaries of that country.

Two exceptions to "defensive territoriality" need to be recognized. When a United States citizen specifically goes outside this country to participate in criminal activity that might not be covered by the laws of that nation, immunity for these activities should not be provided. Deliberate avoidance of the laws in the United States should be an exception that will allow extraterritorial jurisdiction despite the fact that it does not meet the "defensive territorial" restraints.

A second exception to "defensive territoriality" is when another country welcomes the United States to proceed with a prosecution to which the country has jurisdiction. In those instances when another country recognizes a superior law enforcement ability in the United States, and prefers the United States to proceed, "defensive territoriality" should not bar the extraterritorial application.

Both of these exceptions should be allowed under "defensive territoriality." Both deliberate avoidance of jurisdiction and welcomed prosecution, do not raise the comity concerns that normally accompany an "objective territorial" approach.

Contextual Application of "Defensive Territoriality"

"Defensive territoriality" is decided based upon the connection of the act to a government function. The graver the harm and the greater the effect on the government, the stronger the case for the need of the government to defend itself from this criminal conduct. When the harm is insignificant, or when the conduct is merely between private parties, the United States government should not be playing a role in punishing the extraterritorial conduct.

Looking at the three examples in the opening section of this paper, it is apparent that using "defensive territoriality" would preclude prosecutions that are presently allowed in the United States. "Defensive territoriality," however, could serve to expand extraterritorial jurisdiction when conduct occurring outside this country is deliberately aimed at harming a government function.

Under "defensive territoriality," foreign corporations that engage in price-fixing outside the United States would not be subject to indictment in this country, unless the corporation had a direct tie to a government function or the price-fixing activity was related to a United States government contract. Although the conduct might have an effect on the United States, under "defensive territoriality" the activity would not be the subject of a criminal indictment in this country. Price fixing, a legitimate activity in some countries, would be outside the boundaries of extraterritoriality if a "defensive territorial" model were used.

Likewise, individuals selling drugs outside the United States would not be subject to United States prosecution unless they entered the United States or conducted activities here in this country. The continual employment of mules to transport the drugs into the United States would not subject those who are outside this country to a United States prosecution. The fact that drug trafficking has an effect on the United States would not be a basis for a United States prosecution.

The immunity to drug dealers who act outside the United States, should not be considered a defeat to the legal system. Alternatives methods of enforcing the drug laws in this country need to be considered. For example, the continual indictment of those who do bring drugs into this country, followed by strong publicity of these indictments in the originating country, should serve to deter those doing the transporting from continuing to participate in these activities. Further, international agreements can be used to motivate other countries to engage in stronger prohibitions to drug trafficking. Thus, although certain drug trafficking might be outside the scope of a United States prosecution, the conduct should not be considered acceptable.

A more problematic example arises in cases where pollution started in one country enters the United States through the air or water. The extent to which the United States should be able to prosecute the polluters is questionable because, although an act is occurring here in the United States, the initial conduct is occurring in a foreign country. Thus, under "defensive territoriality," international treaties and mutual agreements, as opposed to the criminal system of the United States, should rightfully resolve these situations (but see Fettig, 2002).

"Defensive territoriality" would also preclude the indictment of those individuals in Pakistan who are alleged to have conspired in the murder of United States journalist Daniel Pearl. As is presently occurring, the trial of these individuals belongs to the territory in which the act occurred, namely, Pakistan (Pakistan Resists U.S. Extradition, 2002). It can be argued that this act was a direct affront to the United States government, and therefore within the scope of "defensive territoriality." If in fact the perpetrator's intent behind this killing was directed at the United States government, as opposed to a general opposition to the United States people, then the prosecution might fall within the scope of "defensive territoriality."

Further, if Pakistan had refused to proceed with this prosecution, then alternatives would need to be considered for punishing those responsible for death of a United States citizen. Use of the "passive personality principle," a principle premised upon the victim being a United States citizen, could be used to proceed with this prosecution. International tribunals could also step in when a country was fearful to proceed with a prosecution within its territorial limits.

Although each of these initial examples might not find their way into a United States tribunal if "objective territoriality" is discarded, there would be other conduct that could be subject to prosecution through adoption of a "defensive territorial" approach. For instance, when the United States is defending itself, prosecution needs to be allowed and encouraged. Thus, when a United States embassy outside this country is subjected to terrorist activity, the United States should have the ability to proceed against the perpetrators of these acts. Although the United States may opt for prosecution in the jurisdiction where the actual act occurs, the option to proceed should likewise be with the United States. Clearly if the evidence, witnesses, and preliminary investigation occur in another country, the United States could be motivated to let the territory with immediate jurisdiction prosecute the criminal acts. But prosecuting individuals who attack an institution of the United States needs to be included within this country's jurisdiction in order to deter future criminal conduct.

In addition, the principle of "defensive territoriality" needs to be universally accepted. Other countries need to acquiesce to allowing the United States to prosecute conduct that may be within the territorial limits of those other countries. Likewise, where crimes occur in this country that are directed at the government of another country, the United States needs to allow that country the right to prosecute. However, when the act against another country occurs in the United States, and is by a United States citizen, allowances may need to be made to protect that individual's constitutional rights. Nonetheless, the United States needs to be equally respectful to the rights afforded to citizens of another country.

Conduct directed at a United State embassy is but one example of extraterritorial criminal conduct that might be directed at our government. A cyberterrorist that aims his or her conduct against a defense department computer system is another example of when individuals outside the United States might be subject to prosecution here. Each of these individuals is targeting a government body or function, and as such, should be subject to penalties by the country that is the victim of the criminal act.

Benefits of Using "Defensive Territoriality"

In a globalized world, increased extraterritorial applications can have a negative effect on how other countries perceive the United States. Foreign governments have reacted negatively to existing extraterritorial practices (Griffin, 1998). Cooperation in prosecutions that merit action in the United States could be fostered if this country were to approach extraterritoriality from a global perspective. Using "objective territoriality," without recognizing the ramifications to other countries, fails to consider the global dimension in approaching the fight against crime.

If the United States continues to operate as the regulator of crime that has an effect on this country, there is the possibility that other countries will employ a similar approach in their own territories. Thus, United States citizens could be subject to the criminal laws of these countries even though they have not stepped foot in the other country, and despite the fact that they are a United States business. In a world environment it is important to recognize the boundaries of national law and to also recognize the long term effects of not respecting the national laws of each country.

It is important to note that the United States needs the assistance of other countries in its prosecutions. In a global environment, evidence is not exclusive to one jurisdiction (Podgor & Wise, 2000, pp. 318–347). It can be important to secure the assistance of other countries to pursue criminal activity here. Usurping international jurisdiction norms could easily become problematic for the United States in its efforts to proceed in prosecutions that have an international dimension.

Additional benefits of using "defensive territoriality" as opposed to "objective territoriality" can be seen. For example, cultural differences are more apt to be considered if national law boundaries are respected. In cases where the line between civil and criminal law may be "blurred" (Coffee, 1992, pp. 1876–1877; see also Mann, 1992) as in many business offenses, imposing the law of the United States on individuals or corporations of another country could have the effect of making something civil into a criminal matter. Furthermore, if a country does not criminalize the conduct, then it can be argued that people have not been properly notified of the possible criminal ramifications. It is questionable that due process, an essential ingredient in the United States system, will be fostered when deterrence is emanating solely from the punishment, as opposed to a knowing violation of a criminal law. (Podgor, 2002b, pp. 305–306). Also, using "defensive territoriality" places limits on prosecutorial discretion, as prosecutors will no longer have unrestrained decision-making authority to proceed on actions outside the United States.

"Defensive territoriality" also increases the extraterritorial range when the United States is the victim of a crime. Although the conduct might not rise to the level of being covered by the "protective principle" or might not be an issue of national security, the fact that the United States government is the victim should allow this country to proceed criminally (Congress May Validly Enact Legislation, 1961). Because the conduct is targeted against the United States, it is appropriate to respond legally through a judicial process to deter others from committing like offenses. In order to preclude its continuation and reoccurrence, the United States deserves to defend itself and to punish conduct that is aimed at the government.

CONCLUSION

Globalization requires that we rethink the boundaries of criminal law. The extraterritorial application of a nation's law needs to be considerate of the laws of other nations. Although mutual treaties and international agreements will often resolve the boundary lines, it is important to realize the ramifications of those instances that may not be covered under these agreements.

The existing "objective territorial" principle permits a wide range of conduct to be subject to extraterritorial prosecution. Although this concept, when originally conceived, was appropriate to stop criminal acts that affected individuals in the United States, it also now needs to be reconsidered in light of globalization. With the boundaries of countries lost to telephones, faxes, computers, airplanes, and world travel, we must recognize that much can be affected by what happens outside this country. Although we need to protect the processes of our government, we also need to respect the processes used by other countries. Absent an international tribunal to resolve these differences, we need to redefine the boundary lines of national law.

ACKNOWLEDGMENT

The author wishes to thank research assistant David Walker for his assistance in preparing the final paper.

REFERENCES

Born, G. B. (1992). Reappraisal of the extraterritorial reach of U.S. law. *Law & Policy in International Business, 24*, 1.

Cameron, I. (1994). *The protective principle of international criminal jurisdiction*. Aldershot England: Dartmouth Publishing Co.

Congress may validly enact legislation embodying protective theory of criminal jurisdiction. (1961). *University of Pennsylvania Law Review*, 110, 5.

Coffee, J. C., Jr. (1992). Paradigms lost: The blurring of the criminal and civil law models – and what can be done about it. *Yale Law Journal, 101*, 1875.

Coffin, J. T. (2000). The extraterritorial application of the economic espionage act of 1996. *Hastings International & Comparative Law Review*, 527.

Council of Europe Committee on Crime Problems. (1992). Extraterritorial criminal jurisdiction. *Criminal Law Forum, 3*, 441.

Chua Han Mow v. United States, 730 F.2d 1308 (9th Cir. 1984).

18 U.S. C. § 1512 (2000).

18 U.S. C. § 1956 (1994).

18 U.S. C. § 1621 (1994).

18 U.S. C. § 1623(b) (2000).

18 U.S. C. § 1030 (2000).

18 U.S. C. § 2332(b) (1994).

Eighty-Fifth Annual Meeting of the American Society of International Law. (1991). Extraterritorial application of criminal law. *American Society of International Law & Procedure, 85*, 283.

Estey, W. (1997). The five bases of extraterritorial jurisdiction and the failure of the presumption against extraterritoriality. *Hastings International & Comparative Law Review, 21*, 177.

Export Administration Act, 50 U.S. C. §§ 2401–2420 (1994).

Foreign Corrupt Practices Act, 15 U.S. C. §§ 78dd-1, 78dd-2, 78ff. (1994).

Fettig, K. (2002). Criminal and civil remedies for transboundary water pollution. *Transnational Law, 15*, 117.

France v. Turkey, P. C. I. J., Ser. A, No. 10 (1927).

Germany and U.S. clash over efforts to crack down on neo-nazi web sites in the U.S. (2001, February). *International Enforcement Law Report No. 2, 17*, VI.A64.

Griffin, J. P. (1998). Foreign governmental reactions to U.S. assertions of extraterritorial jurisdiction. *George Mason Law Review, 6*, 505.

Griffin, L. C. (2001). The prudent prosecutor. *Georgetown Journal of Legal Ethics, 14*, 259.

Grippando, J. M. (1983). Declining to exercise extraterritorial antitrust jurisdiction on grounds of international comity: An illegitimate extension of the judicial abstention doctrine. *Virginia Journal of International Law, 23*, 395.

Harvard Research in International Law. (1935). Jurisdiction with respect to crime. *American Journal of International Law, 29* (Supplement), 437.

International Shoe Co. v. Washington, 326 U.S. 310 (1945).

Johnston, D. (1995, April 17). Strength is seen in a U.S. export: Law enforcement. *The New York Times*, pp. A1, A8.

Mann, K. (1992). Punitive civil sanctions: The middleground between criminal and civil law. *Yale Law Journal, 101*, 1795.

Nippon v. United States, 109 F.3d 1 (1st Cir. 1997).

Laufer, W. S., & Taka, I. (1995). Japan regulatory compliance, and the wisdom of extraterritorial social controls. *Hastings International & Comparative Law Review, 18*, 487.
Lippman, T. W., & Smith, J. R. (1996, August 20). FBI plan to expand overseas, *The Washington Post*, p. A1.
Pakistan resists U.S. extradition. (2002, May 6). *The Wall Street Journal*, p. A18.
Pearce, B. (1994). The comity doctrine as a barrier to judicial jurisdiction: A U.S. – E.U. comparison. *Stanford Journal of International Law, 30*, 525.
Podgor, E. S. (1997). Globalization and the federal prosecution of white collar crime. *American Criminal Law Review, 34*, 325.
Podgor, E. S. (2000). The ethics and professionalism of prosecutors in discretionary decisions. *Fordham Law Review, 68*, 1511.
Podgor, E. S., & Wise, E. M. (2000). *International criminal law: Cases and materials*. New York: Matthew Bender & Co.
Podgor, E. S. (2002a). Computer crimes and the USA patriot act. *Criminal Journal Magazine, 17*, 61.
Podgor, E. S. (2002b). International computer fraud: A paradigm for limiting national jurisdiction. *University of California at Davis Law Review, 35*, 267.
Podgor, E. S. (in press). "Defensive territoriality": A new paradigm for the prosecution of extraterritorial business crimes. *Georgia Journal of International & Comparative Law*.
Raimo, T. (1999). Winning at the expense of law: The ramifications of expanding counter-terrorism law enforcement jurisdiction overseas. *American University International Review, 14*, 1473.
Randall, K. C. (1988). Universal jurisdiction under international law. *Texas Law Review, 66*, 785.
Restatement of the Foreign Relations Law of the United States (3rd ed.) (1989). St. Paul, MN: American Law Institute.
Smith, B. T. (1991). Assertion of adjudicatory jurisdiction by United States courts over international terrorism cases. *Army Law* (October), 13.
Strassheim v. Daily, 221 U.S. 280 (1911).
Twining, W. (2002). *Globalisation and legal theory*. Evanston, IL: Northwestern University Press.
United States Department of Justice. (1997). *United States Attorney's Manual* §§ 9–1.100, 9–15.630, 9–47.00.
United States Department of Justice. (2000). *United States Attorney's Manual* § 9–2.400.
United States v. Alvarez-Machain, 504 U.S. 655 (1992).
United States v. Best, 2002 WL 31080306 (3rd Cir. 2002).
United States v. Boots, 80 F. 3d 580 (1st Cir. 1996).
United States v. Bowman, 260 U.S. 94 (1922).
United States v. Caceres, 440 U.S. 741 (1973).
United States v. Caicedo, 47 F.3d 370 (9th Cir. 1995).
United States v. Castillo Felix, 539 F.2d 9 (9th Cir. 1976).
United States v. Evans, 667 F. Supp. 974 (S. D. N. Y. 1987).
United States v. Gonzales, 776 F. 2d 931 (11th Cir. 1985).
United States v. James-Robinson, 515 F. Supp. 1340 (S. D FL 1981).
United States v. MacAllister, 160 F.3d 1304 (11th Cir. 1998).
United States v. Nippon Paper Industries Co., Ltd., 109 F.3d 1 (1st 1997).
United States v. Pizdrint, 983 F. Supp. 1110 (M. D. Fla. 1997).
United States v. Plummer, 221 F.3d 1298 (11th Cir. 2000).
United States v. Postal, 589 f.2d 862 (5th Cir. 1979).
United States v. Sheikh, Indictment, U.S. D.C. D. N. J., March 12, 2002.
United States v. Trapilo, 130 F.3d 547 (2d Cir. 1997).

United States v. Wright-Baker, 784 F.2d 161 (3rd Cir. 1989).
USA Patriot Act, H. R. 3162, 107th Cong. § 814 (2001).
Waller, S. W. (2000). The twilight of comity. *Columbia Journal of Transnational Law*, *38*, 563.
Watson, G. R. (1992). Offenders abroad: The case for nationality-based criminal jurisdiction. *The Yale Journal of International Law*, *17*, 41.
Watson, G. R. (1993). The passive personality principal. *Texas International Law Journal*, *28*, 1.
Yahoo, Inc. v. LaLigue Contre Le Racisme Et L'Antisemitisme, C-00-21275 JF, (D. Cal. 2001).

PART III.
THE CHALLENGES OF (AND TO) RIGHTS

"SUBJECTIVITY IS A CITIZEN": REPRESENTATION, RECOGNITION, AND THE DECONSTRUCTION OF CIVIL RIGHTS

Jonathan Goldberg-Hiller

INTRODUCTION

The progressive limits to rights mobilization have become starkly apparent in the past two decades. No new suspect classes have been forthcoming from the Supreme Court since 1977 despite continued demands for legal recognition by lesbians and gays, indigenous peoples and others interested in expanding civil rights doctrine. Public tolerance for civil rights measures has likewise dried up. Since the 1960s, referenda on civil rights have halted affirmative action programs, limited school busing and housing discrimination protections, promoted English-only laws, limited AIDS policies, and ended the judicial recognition of same-sex marriage, among other issues. Nearly 80% of these referenda have had outcomes realizing the Madisonian fear of "majority tyranny"[1] and signaling the Nietzschean dread of a politics of resentment (Brown, 1995, p. 214; Connolly, 1991, p. 64).

While frequently inchoate, recent debates over the extension of civil rights protection to new groups have been framed around a persistent asymmetry. Proponents of civil rights recognition have asked for rights as a hallmark of citizenship while claiming present laws to be inadequate for their recognition and protection; their opponents have argued that citizenship is not at stake, that new rights are

Studies in Law, Politics, and Society
Studies in Law, Politics, and Society, Volume 28, 139–188

ISSN: 1059-4337/PII: S1059433702280060

redundant if not excessive, and consequently, the identities sought to be protected are artificial or misrepresented (Burlein, 2002; Cooper, 1998; Goldberg-Hiller, 2002; Patton, 1995; Schacter, 1997, p. 684). "Post-civil-rights era"[2] discourse has thus been marked both by challenges to the tactics and rhetoric of recognition as well as the boundaries of political bodies in which citizenship ought now inhere, propelled as much by language and the social movements which help generate it, as it is by broader changes in social and economic organization that have fueled anxieties. This paper explores two recent debates over civil rights in Hawai'i – one over same-sex marriage and the other over constitutional recognition of indigenous rights claims – in an effort to deconstruct these newer civil rights discourses and the way that civil rights law now comes to constitute political subjectivity.

My approach to these debates is inspired by studies of legal mobilization which have urged us to decenter our attention from the formal character of rights to the ways in which actors and discourses bring law into social action.[3] The cases I study here ask us to also consider the ways in which law is pushed away, rights argued to be morally and politically inappropriate for social organization. I show that pushing rights away paradoxically may tend to recenter law through new ideas about political sovereignty, fashioning post-liberal ideas of citizenship and assumptions of the self.[4] These ideas are politically ambivalent. In some forms and contexts, this discourse of sovereignty – the rhetoric that invokes it, the ontological ideas that it depends upon (and which depend upon it) – has inhibited progressive civil rights movements. In other contexts, post-civil-rights sovereignty discourse works to sustain progressive forms of collective action. My goal in this article is to open this discourses to criticism, to show the social constructions that underlie claims to be naturally emergent, in order to advance our understanding of law and enhance progressive efforts of legal mobilization.

I do this by presenting two case studies. In the case of same-sex marriage, I show how sovereignty discourse can work to build democratic majorities opposed to civil rights advances by creating stable political identities unavailing of self-criticism in the very manner in which they resist civil rights appeals. In the case of indigenous rights struggles, I demonstrate the ability of some proponents to deconstruct these barriers and question the ontological certainty that surrounds this discourse. My deconstruction is shadowed by critical international relations scholarship which has urged that we creatively move beyond sovereignty[5] and the works of Emmanual Lévinas who rejected its ontological premises in his ethical critique.

I first sketch a theoretical approach to the discourse of sovereignty that modulates these civil rights conflicts.[6] Sovereignty invites deconstruction, I argue, for the pervasive assumptions about subjectivity and community that it depends upon, and the silences that it enforces as a political and legal idiom. After presenting my two case studies, I explore implications of this deconstruction for alternative political practice. Throughout this analysis I endeavor to show the scholarly and practical importance of taking seriously discourses aligned against civil rights.

RECOGNITION AND ORDER

The presumption of liberal civil rights models to protect the "discrete and insular minority"[7] – as individual and as faction – from the tyranny of the majority has its genealogy in a Hobbesian imagery of sovereignty and its construction of social ordering. Against the frightening image of a state of nature in which life devoid of political agreement is famously solitary, poor, nasty, brutish and short, Hobbes arrays an artificial image of the self in which sovereignty is to be alienated.

> For by Art is created that great LEVIATHAN called a COMMON-WEALTH, or STATE ... which is but an Artificiall Man; though of greater stature and strength than the Naturall, for whose protection and defence it was intended; and in which, the *Soveraignty* is an Artificiall Soul, as giving life and motion to the whole body ... by which the parts of this Body Politique were at first made, set together and united, resemble that *Fiat*, or the *Let us make man*, pronounced by God in the Creation (Hobbes, 1968 [1651], pp. 81–82).

How well this artificial man can salve "the multiplicity of allergic egoisms which are at war with one another and are thus together" (Lévinas, 1991, p. 4) depends in part on what the artificial soul of the sovereign body politic recognizes as its limits. For one, it matters how this artificial soul problematizes[8] the Other, for as Shane Phelan notes, "The trope of the body politic works powerfully to transform contests within society into attacks on society" (1999, p. 58). For another, the success of the sovereign construct turns on how well the artificial languages – such as civil rights – convey this recognition.

As many criticisms of the Hobbesian project recognize, biases abound in the very assumptions of political sovereignty, particularly in the privileging of reason, but also in the philosophical and political alchemy of the body politic into ideas of identity/difference, self/other, inside/outside, History/contingency and imminence/transcendence.[9] In Bryan Turner's words,

> The Hobbesian problem of order was historically based on a unitary concept of the body .... However, the regime of political society also requires a regimen of bodies and in particular a government of bodies which are defined by their multiplicity and diversity. The Hobbesian problem is overtly an analysis of the proper relationship between desire and reason, or more precisely between sexuality and instrumental rationality. This problem in turn can be restated as the proper relationship between men as bearers of public reason and women as embodiments of private emotion (Turner, 1984, pp. 113–114).

In the democratic – as opposed to Hobbesian absolutist – state, this tension between reason and desire continues, but not strictly in the form of a gendered alterity identified by Turner. As markers of citizenship and standing, civil rights can shift these boundaries, but by a similar logic, rights for new groups will only be protected where reason can dictate an expansion.

Left lingering in the sovereign rush, however, is what remains unmarked and unremarked (as some critical race scholarship on intersectionality has made plain).[10] Civil rights operate as a sign of inclusion in the body politic only to the extent that they continue to mark particular bodies as capable of generality, of remaining in Marx's words "an imaginary participant in an imaginary sovereignty . . . filled with an unreal universality" (Marx, 1977 [1844], p. 46). Sovereignty thus serves as an epistemological ground prior to the political subject in that it limits the basis for self-presentation as it simultaneously limits the state. As Ashley notes,

> The sign of 'sovereignty' betokens a rational identity: a homogeneous and continuous presence that is hierarchically ordered, that has a unique centre of decision presiding over a coherent 'self,' and that is demarcated from, and in opposition to, an external domain of difference and change that resists assimilation to its identical being . . . . The sign of 'anarchy' betokens this residual external domain: an aleatory domain characterised by difference and discontinuity, contingency and ambiguity, that can be known only for its lack of the coherent truth and meaning expressed by a sovereign presence. [Sovereignty is invoked] as an originary voice, a foundational source of truth and meaning . . . that makes it possible to discipline the understanding of ambiguous events and impose a distinction . . . between what can be represented as rational and meaningful (because it can be assimilated to a sovereign principle of interpretation) and what must count as external, dangerous, and anarchic (1988, p. 230).

The powerful compulsion of this construct can be seen in recent public debates over civil rights in which access to anti-discrimination law is refigured as illegitimate, dangerous, and anarchic excess. These claims reinvest in the homogeneity and hierarchy that have long been utopian conditions for discourse in the public sphere. For this reason, sectarian religious sentiments that have exercised some recent anti-rights activism are nonetheless publicly suppressed in favor of more universalist positions. Of course, this does not mean that all differences are restrained. Women, gays, people of color – all those who are figured as passionate more than rational – are marked with a "surplus corporeality" (Berlant, 1997) that softens sovereign boundaries through excess or weakness, making them vulnerable to penetration (Bordo, 1993; Butler, 1990; Phelan, 1999; Stychin, 1999). As Warner argues,

> The ability to abstract oneself in public discussion has always been an unequally available resource. Individuals have to have specific rhetorics of disincorporation; they are not simply rendered bodiless by exercising reason . . . . The subject who could master this rhetoric in the bourgeois public sphere was implicitly, even explicitly, white, male, literate, and propertied. These traits could go unmarked, even grammatically, while other features of bodies could only

be acknowledged in discourse as the humiliating positivity of the particular (Warner, 1992, p. 382; see also Wildman, 1995).

The implicit association of unmarked bodies and universal, rational subjects is endangered by courts that can compel speech and demand a defense of privilege. (Witness, for example, the politics attempting to derail the 1996 trial in Hawai'i[11] where the state was forced to defend – unsuccessfully – its preference for heterosexual marriage.) It is for this reason that sovereignty serves as an idiom, an explicit rhetoric invoked for its ability to discipline silence through control of state access. As I have argued elsewhere (Goldberg-Hiller, 2002), sovereignty today becomes effectively distinguishable from the state when invoked in these civil rights debates. Its contemporary return in political discourse, therefore, competes with alternative forms of recognition that bypass a sovereign logic. Thus, some "particular" bodies – including lesbians and gays, and indigenous peoples – are symbolically *re*marked as valuable through commodification, or integrable due to sanctioned political memory, acceptable lifestyle, or protected legal status, and conceptually united through common consumption of public symbols (Clarke, 2000, 30ff; Evans, 1993).

These are all concerns that Foucault, in his narrative of modernity, has called a resurgence of the *social*: discourses comprising what he has termed a governmentality inclusive of, but extending beyond, the boundaries of political sovereignty. Foucault has urged us to "see things not in terms of the replacement of a society of sovereignty by a disciplinary society by a society of government; in reality one has a triangle, sovereignty-discipline-government" (Foucault, 1991, p. 102).[12] This triangular relationship suggests that autonomy, rationality, and the like are frequently evaluated not as ends in themselves, but as specific values promoting identifiable social interests. It is for this reason that the ability of civil rights law to mark the appropriate generality associated with citizenship and inclusion in the sovereign community is never far removed from the specific social rationales for inclusion.

In turn, these social rationales modify sovereign discourse which becomes increasingly a form of counter-memory, "a transformation of history into a totally different form of time," "a parody" that takes identity as real and power as a fiction (Foucault, 1977, 160ff). Sovereignty, then, is not critical for it fails to reveal power as much as circulate it as forms of remembrance and forgetting to reinforce hierarchy and repel rights language. Burlein has playfully called this ignorance-power.

> Foucault coined the phrase knowledge-power to denote the ability of words and facts, disciplines and institutions to produce subjects who perform certain relations of power simply as a condition of becoming a subject who speaks and knows. Playing off Foucault, I use the term ignorance-power to denote the ability of the Right's counter-memories to produce subjects who perform supremacist relations of power not just through what people say and know, but also and primarily through what people need not say and can afford not to know: the fears and aggressions, silences

> and desires that circulate through what is best in people, their highest ideals and deepest hopes. The power of such ignore-ance stems less from individual prejudices and more from its structural placement. Ignorance haunts culture because it inhabits the structures of everyday life so deeply that it need not speak its name in order to take effect (Burlein, 2002, ms).

As conservative social movements are driven by and through ignorance-power to oppose civil rights or other policies advancing claims of social equality, the silences that Burlein notes above skew public debates. One manifestation of this structural bias is that public discourse fails to force a real recognition of social need, hiding socially dominant subjects from self-knowledge and a meaningful, ethical engagement with the body politic in which the Other is conceived. It is this violent refusal to take the Other as real, to question self-consciousness, and to discover "new ways of knowing and understanding, of engaging and being, of perceiving and communicating with Self, Other, and World" (Ruiz, 1999, p. 643) that limit the power of rights appeals and animate the need for deconstruction. Because Lévinas' ethical deconstruction targets the ontological framework of ignorance-power, I turn to a brief discussion of his philosophy below.

Lévinas and the Ethics of Encounter

The ethics of encounter that Lévinas proposes to escape the violence of Western ontology[13] and its historical "truths" involves a vulnerability to and recognition of the Other. The Other is experienced phenomenologically at the level of sensibility, prior to thought and rationality – "Alterity's plot is born before knowledge" (Lévinas, 1999, p. 101) – which Lévinas argues to be integral to subjectivity itself. In order to realize that subjectivity and remain open to the other, it is necessary to lessen the hold of social and political languages that freeze historical relations – what Lévinas has called the *same*. In his mature work, this distinction is drawn between the *Saying* and the *Said*.[14] "Saying is not a game. Antecedent to the verbal signs it conjugates . . . it is the proximity of one to the other, the commitment of an approach, the one for the other, the very signifyingness of signification" (Lévinas, 1991, p. 5).

> The 'said' for Lévinas is constituted by the reigning philosophical discourse within which interpersonal encounters are conceptually contained. It is the domain of obtuse consciousness, a consciousness that elides the past and present, closing off history. Consciousness thematizes the past, depluralizing it and inhibiting the effects of encounters. In contrast, the proximity of the Other in conversation is a saying that disrupts the incorporation of the other's past into a thematized said (Shapiro, 1999, p. 67).

The disruptive proximity of the Other is in some sense literal for Lévinas. The encounter of the Other is face-to-face and is corrosive to the pretense of a sovereign self-consciousness and the language forms and enforced silences in which this subjectivity is embedded. "The activity of speaking robs the subject of its central position; it is the depositing . . . of a subject without refuge. *The speaking subject is no longer by and for itself; it is for the other*: obligated to response and responsible for the other, without ever having chosen this responsibility" (Peperzak & Lévinas, 1993, p. 221 emphasis added).

Without discounting the dangers inherent in a radical alterity, this ethical stance, as Derrida notes, takes seriously the asymmetry of same and Other (paralleling the asymmetry of civil rights debates), but seeks a transcendence through an encounter not limited by the totalizing language of the said.

> What, then, is this encounter with the absolutely-other? Neither representation, nor limitation, nor conceptual relation to the same. The ego and the other do not permit themselves to be dominated or made into totalities by a concept of relationship. And first of all because the concept (material of language), which is always *given to the other*, cannot encompass the other, cannot include the other. The dative or vocative dimension which opens the original direction of language, cannot lend itself to inclusion in and modification by the accusative or attributive dimension of the object without violence. Language, therefore, cannot make its own possibility a totality and *include* within itself its own origin or its own end (Derrida, 1978, p. 95).

Reducing the totalization of language permits a breach between Lévinasian ethics and a politics which interests me here.[15] For it is not the case that the state can never be justified in the face of the Other.[16] Nonetheless, an approach to the state – such as that of Hobbes and Locke – that takes self-preservation and self-interest as a sovereign given, subordinates ethics to politics (Simmons, 1999, p. 91), as could any approach to the dyad of self and Other where selfishness or infatuation might overtake ethics, or where politics is localized by privileging only face-to-face relationships.

In order to account for justice beyond sovereignty and the dyad, Lévinas introduces the idea of the Third.

> The third party is other than the neighbor, but also another neighbor, and also a neighbor of the other, and not simply his fellow . . .. The other stands in a relationship with the third party, for whom I cannot entirely answer, even if I alone answer, before any question, for my neighbor . . .. The third party introduces a contradiction in the saying whose signification before the other until then went in one direction. It is of itself the limit of responsibility and the birth of the question: What do I have to do with justice? (Lévinas, 1991, p. 157).

Justice opens the ambivalent possibility that ethics can be universalized, but also that it can be totalizing, erasing the ethical duty to the other, and thus becoming violent.[17] In order to bring ethics back in, to dissolve the "sovereign conceit" (Butler, 1996) of the said and shatter the illusion of sovereignty (Cornell, 1992, p. 72), it is also necessary to move consciousness and debate beyond the simple equation of subjectivity and citizenship.

> The original locus of justice, a terrain common to me and the others where I am counted among them, that is, where subjectivity is a citizen with all the duties and rights . . . can be established only if I, always evaded from the concept of the ego, always desituated and divested of being, always in non-reciprocatable relationship with the other, always for the other, can become an other like the others (Lévinas, 1991, pp. 160–161).

It is necessary for justice, therefore, to establish the primacy of alterity.

Herzog makes clear that for Lévinas, putting alterity first as an ethical paradigm raises the problem of representation. At one level, we can never fully escape ontology for as Lévinas acknowledges, "even when we deconstruct [it] we are obliged to use its language" (Levinas quoted in Herzog, 2002, p. 206). Nor is politics capable of elimination, for "it is in a political context that I discover the misery in the face of the Other and my responsibility for him/her that comes before all politics" (Ibid., p. 211). Nonetheless, liberal political schemas often eschew this conceptual and institutional ambivalence, relying instead upon an ontology of interest and a politics of representation (e.g. enfranchisement) that tend to "reduce the alterity of the other to sameness" (Ibid., p. 217). The third is a reminder of that limit.

> The notion of third articulates the two dimensions of politics . . . that of representation and that of disturbing absence. The disturbance, which *is* the trace of the Other and of the others, is the disturbance of hunger, of actual hungry people who never are, who cannot be taken into account. Politics and its surplus, its peace, appear together with the 'entry' of the third (Herzog, 2002, p. 221).

Politics with justice demands, then, the utopian: an active inclusion into the sovereign of those left out, as well as a realization of and commitment to their experience of their own dignity.

Certainly, it would be surprising were such a radical alterity be made a common part of political encounter and legal debate. Indeed, as Shapiro (1999), Campbell (1998), and others have noted, Lévinas' own justifications of Zionism and refusals to take women's agency seriously reaffirm Derrida's criticism that Lévinas had not successfully transcended Western ontology, suggesting that conscious attempts to reduce ethics to politics recapitulate the dangers of the said. The reminder to remain open to the other, as incommensurate as that may become, is nonetheless an important ethical caution in any debate over citizenship with its inevitable reduction to the "we" of community.

My purpose in sketching this brief introduction to Levinasian ethics is not to inject a level of idealism nor, I hope, of unnecessary theoreticism into the attention to the fate of civil rights. Nor is it to intimate that civil rights mobilization is always an exercise in futility because of the alienated forms in which "the said" of law is embedded. But I will suggest, following these studies, that the ethical deconstruction of sovereignty discourse might provide more room in which to maneuver by pointing to new possibilities in civil rights discourse.

THE CIVIL *RITES* OF SAME-SEX MARRIAGE

Nothing is a game. Thus being is transcended (Lévinas).[18]

In 1993, the Hawai'i Supreme Court ruled in *Baehr v. Lewin* that same-sex couples could not be denied a marriage license under state constitutional prohibitions against gender discrimination without showing a compelling state interest. The first of its kind in the world, the ruling surprised the plaintiffs and their supporters as much as it shocked the state and the nation. A series of political maneuvers designed to derail the case, including statutory legislation in Hawai'i, an unsuccessful defense of state discrimination at trial, and a state commission on the issue of same-sex marriage, finally succeeded when a constitutional amendment preserving legislative control of marriage law was passed in 1998. During the intervening years, even though not one same-sex marriage was performed, the issue captivated public attention and dominated public debate in Hawai'i.

Opponents of same-sex marriage struggled to find appropriate languages to deny what the Court had declared were essentially constitutional rights to be free of discrimination. To some extent, the anti-discrimination logic could be seen as an extension of amendments passed in 1984 that had removed procreation as the stated purpose of marriage since it unfairly discriminated against the handicapped, elderly and others. With those amendments, marriage had become a nearly-universal entitlement, access to which the state governed merely by unspoken assumptions about the appropriate sex of its participants. Nonetheless, the Court refused to explicitly add lesbians and gays to the same protected status it was willing to provide others who might be disadvantaged by the rejection of the procreation rationale. Generally, fluidity of legal and social identities can offer some tactical advantage to social movements and has long been exploited by some lesbian and gay activists. Yet such fluidity can also work against some forms of political action where strategic essentialism can congeal identities and enhance commitments of principals and allies (Bravmann, 1997; Gamson, 1996; Seidman, 1997). The refusal to recognize a fixed legal identity in the *Baehr* opinion permitted right wing maneuvers to disrupt strategic identity formation around rights mobilization. But obstruction of rights mobilization holds its own risks as it goes against long-standing liberal traditions and calls upon new political and moral languages for its legitimation.

Opposition to gay and lesbian rights and identities has frequently been couched in terms of disease and immorality in the United States, but by the 1980s this tactic stalled as it was increasingly alienating likely allies (Herman, 1997). While personal vilification of gays and lesbians was voiced by some of Hawai'i's opponents, the local pride in social tolerance, the highest court's declaration of a right, and the gaze of national attention combined to encourage a different rhetoric, one directly concerned with the social place of civil rights. One idiom, borrowed from the fight over Colorado Amendment 2 in 1992 that would have denied antidiscrimination protection for gays and lesbians (Gerstmann, 1999, 99ff; Goldberg, 1994; Keen & Goldberg, 1998), was the language of special rights illustrated below.

> I oppose [same-sex marriage] because it legitimizes the idea that we have to give special rights to people because they engage in homosexual behavior. By passing [enabling legislation], you would be sending the message that people who engage in behavior that is harmful to themselves and society will be given special protection.[19]
>
> I am grieved by the trend in our society both in Hawai'i and the mainland toward recognizing homosexual relationships, lifestyle and behavior as a normal and legitimate alternative lifestyle. I particularly reject the idea of homosexuals being recognized as a minority group with special rights because of that status.[20]

The accusation of special rights has its genealogy in negative reactions to and anxieties about civil rights movements; in the twentieth century, special rights claims were used to defuse demands for women's suffrage, and were explicitly manifest as a tactic to delay and destroy the Civil Rights Act of 1964. Since then, special rights discourse has been applied to other types of conflicts. In each of its sites of enunciation, however, special rights arguments are used to delegitimate some rights claims and the institutions, resources, identities, and other meanings that undergird them, while calling upon another set of institutions, resources, identities and meanings that are upheld as contrasting supports for "equal rights" or its equivalent. In short, the binary between special rights and equal rights – what Schacter (1994) has called a "discourse of equivalents" – invokes a set of power dynamics with broad political and social consequences (Goldberg-Hiller & Milner, 2001). To those who use the special rights idiom falls a double task: demonstrating that some subjects are unfit for citizenship while showing that an "equal rights" space – citizenship generally – is not in question. In the case of same-sex marriage, upholding the equal rights space of citizenship was complicated by the fact that the courts had already ruled for the plaintiffs; opponents of same-sex marriage had to argue that courts are not the legitimate guardians of civil rights.

In the discussion below, I illustrate several means by which the discourse of sovereignty was mobilized to maintain the special rights/equal rights boundary in the successful efforts to pass an amendment to derail the court case. I am interested in how the excess ascribed to the problem of special rights limits the moral appeals of civil rights. Why lesbians and gays were not more successful in gaining support, I argue, has much to do with the way that sovereignty rhetoric obstructed an ethical self-criticism that rights talk demanded.

Marriage Rites and Special Rights

The binary opposition between equal rights and special rights is especially complex and is often maintained through efforts that appear to violate its integrity. One of the problems of the same-sex marriage controversy is that it is not apparent why extending marriage status to those previously denied the right infringes the interests of those married under different rules. Special rights claims were used to solve this problem by renaming culturally valued institutions as the minority interests to be protected from civil rights advances (Patton, 1993). This rhetorical position is glaringly evident in the title of the federal Defense of Marriage Act (1996) which permits states more latitude in denying recognition of same-sex marriages conducted in other states as though such unions were a direct imposition upon heterosexual marriage. This rhetoric is also evident in the voiced concern that gay and lesbian demands victimize the majority through a straitjacket of hate speech. Anti-same-sex marriage activists sometimes imagined this as a form of public rape by gay activists:

> I believe that a small minority of homosexual marriage advocates are trying to force their values down the throats of the people of Hawai'i. I do not think that they're evil. I think they have an agenda. . . . And anyone who disagrees with them is labeled a homophobe, or is labeled a gay basher.[21]
>
> I do not wish to condemn or judge a homo-sexual life style, only *God* may do so. Our society prohibits same sex marriage because it is unnatural, immoral and unhealthy. Homo-sexual's have rights but what is happening to our rights. We, the people of Hawai'i, are having our family values violated and eroded.[22]

This inversion can also be seen in the following newspaper advertisement (Fig. 1) that names homophobia as a form of hate speech. In this ad, the majority is rhetorically reversed into a victimized minority, thereby obscuring the identities and demands of lesbians and gays. The failure of courts to protect "real" victims of gay rights abuse permitted the sovereign community to be reimagined without the intercession of court backed civil rights. This ad's response is that "one word can set you straight – YES," a punning reference to the voting position the defensive reader should take on the amendment plebiscite. The insistence on "one word" refuses the intrusion of further debate – a position akin to the military policy of "don't ask, don't tell," in which the "saying" of certain sexual identities are held to disrupt social and political order. Voice is analogized in this inversion to an affront rather than a plea for engagement and recognition.

Implicit in these examples is the argument that civil and individual rights must yield to "the people," as the argument below makes explicit.

> The tremendous cost to society at large and the individual families in which the victims live, should lead us to rethink what we have done in liberalizing our regulation of homosexual conduct. It is time to let the people of Hawai'i have a voice in the full range of issues regarding

Fig. 1. *Source*: Honolulu *Star Bulletin* (28 October 1998), p. A14.

public concerns with homosexuality. Just focusing on marriage licenses is insufficiently narrow. Please undertake to give the people of Hawai'i the right to exercise their political will and vote on a constitutional amendment to prohibit special rights of any kind to homosexuals.[23]

Reinforcing the political imagery of the sovereign people were common accusations that "outsiders" were making the demands for special rights. For opponents of same-sex marriage, the local faces of the plaintiffs were collectively a façade for the conspiratorial "homosexual agenda" bankrolled by East Coast gay rights organizations. (Although the resources for plaintiffs' case were entirely local in the early years, this accusation became a self-fulfilling prophecy when the vehement reaction by opponents made these "outsiders" feel compelled to join in later.) Supporters of the plaintiffs likewise pointed to the millions of dollars given by the Mormon Church in Utah to indicate that the rejection of courts was not indigenous. The special rights/equal rights frame, however, is not an equal opportunity division; it is an instantiation of power relations, an argument that an opponent is making an excessive claim, and that excess is an improper intrusion of politics corrupting the universalism of law. Rather than attacking the premises, such tit-for-tat arguments by proponents unwittingly buttressed the legitimacy of the sovereign idiom.

Fig. 2. *Source*: Honolulu *Advertiser* (30 September 1998), p. A11.

The hostility to meddling outsiders reflects the long struggles against colonial control in Hawai'i. In Fig. 2, an advertisement in support of the amendment against the *Baehr* decision, the juxtaposed images of one dark-skinned heterosexual couple wearing lei and one white skinned gay couple in mainland formal attire align sovereign boundaries with ethnic relations as a reminder that same-sex marriage is likely the next assault on local dignity and values. The text also raises the suspicion of the gay legal agenda beyond ethnicity, suggesting that gays may not be what they seem. "In most political campaigns, it's considered a bad thing to mention the opposition. But in this case the opposition is the bad thing. They're trying to deceive you." One form of implied deception in this ad is that gays are relatively wealthy (as are many haole [Caucasians, foreigners] in Hawai'i) and therefore are too powerful, rich, and successful to need civil rights protection. Rights would only give gays an unfair advantage.

> While comprising less than 2% of the population, homosexuals do not constitute a discriminated minority but in reality are better educated with a higher level of income and are more politically sophisticated than the average population. In fact, they are a radical liberal special interest group using their political and economic clout to force their radical agenda on the majority of the population. Their agenda is not about civil rights, but an agenda for special prividges [sic] based upon sexual preference.[24]

The fear of deception among gays invokes Ashley's specter of the irrational, external, dangerous, and anarchic[25] for several reasons. One is related to the specific strategies and epistemologies of social identity. The political articulation of lesbian and gay self-knowledge and self-projection privileges "coming out" (Blasius, 1992; Stychin, 1995, 143ff) – not coming across boundaries, but emerging already from within suburban and urban life, family and workplace, church and organization. This boundary subversion involves challenging or "queering" the dominant sovereign social codes of nation, history, space, culture and property (Berlant, 1997; Bravmann, 1997; Davies, 1999; Patton, 1997). As Patton (1997) has made clear, the queer strategy of boundary subversion has been mimicked by right-wing opponents, a contest that aids the rhetorical delamination of nation, state, and sovereignty in the reimagination of the boundaries of community.

The conservative alarm over violation of once-certain boundaries is magnified by a second factor: lesbians' and gays' uncertain legal subjectivity. *Romer v. Evans* (1996) implicitly overruled the denial of rights to privacy by which gays and lesbians were subjected in *Bowers v. Hardwick* (1986). That earlier case cited the authority of a sovereign majority's historical, ethical, Biblical and natural "entitlement to hostility"[26] to homosexuality. Nonetheless, by finding that Colorado's discrimination against lesbians and gays merely fell short of a legal standard of rationality, gays and lesbians have at most acquired from the *Romer* standard what one commentator has called "thin gay rights" (Massaro, 1996). Shed of criminal suspicion yet lacking suspect class standing, gays are left without clear legal identities, suspected of "deceptive" analogy to "authentic" civil rights subjects and burdened by the uncertain mapping of legal to social and political space (Gerstmann, 1999).

In response to claims that gays were deceptive, a counter-argument was made in the local newspapers. Against a background of lawbooks, four ethnically "local" leaders supporting same-sex marriage announced, "*Don't be fooled! A 'Yes' Vote on the Constitutional Amendment has nothing to do with traditional marriage.*" The ad copy tried to link the concern about sovereignty to the usual disgruntlement with the legislature:

> A yes vote on the constitutional amendment sends the same-sex marriage issue right back to the legislature, where they will have to take up the issue all over again. But more frightening to our basic democracy is that a yes vote gives the legislature the power to overrule the supreme court and change our Bill of Rights. Is that what you really want?

The suggestion that the legislature could also subvert sovereign aims questioned institutional legitimacy but did nothing to challenge the arguments about deception and the importance of reasserting a popular sovereignty based in transparency as a norm of citizenship.

This became clear as advertising and debate rhetoric increasingly emphasized common sense as a means to question the fitness of gay identities for civil rights and to reject the role of the courts.

> It is incredible that all this time, energy, and money is being wasted. That most of the people in this room are being robbed of precious family time with their children by having to come down here and speak out against something that is so obviously wrong. Why? Because three Supreme Court Justices do not understand the definition of marriage. Because three judges simply lack basic *common sense*.[27]

One advertisement featured a local man in an aloha shirt leaning against a tree and looking sincerely at the camera. The copy read, "The marriage Question on the November ballot isn't about civil rights; its about common sense. Radical gays are hiding behind civil rights because they know Hawai'i will vote against same-sex marriages." Another showed a heterosexual family and asked "Why are the same-sex marriage people playing 'Hide and Seek' with the issue? They hide behind civil rights while the people of Hawai'i seek only the truth – the real, common-sense issue that asks if we should preserve marriage between one man and one woman." In these advertisements, civil rights is the stand-in for duplicity while common sense signifies democratic reason.

The boundary between reason and deception constitutes an asymmetrical relation of power. By naming these civil rights claims as deceptive, it reinforces the imbalance declared by the claim of special rights. As deceptive individuals, morally unfit for democratic society and the benefits of citizenship, this discourse also legitimates exclusion. But it also permits a curious form of misrecognition to go unnoticed on the part of the sovereign majority. One of the arguments for deceitful behavior on the part of gays and lesbians is that they hide behind civil rights rather than talking about marriage. One typical newspaper ad put this copy beside the picture of a smiling elderly local woman who could have been anyone's grandmother: "Spin doctors recommend hiding the same-sex marriage issue from Hawai'i families. People who support the same-sex marriage issue rarely ever talk about same-sex marriage. That's 'cause same-sex marriages make most Hawai'i voters uncomfortable." While it is true that same-sex marriage supporters avoided talking about marriage (a poor strategic choice, I believe), so did opponents who never justified the virtues of opposite-sex marriage, but nowhere is this acknowledged. Arguments about the lack of fitness for citizenship of gays and lesbians instead established a support for traditional marriage on only the narrowest grounds of disidentification.

The creation of rational, ethnic, colonial and classist boundaries through these tactics prevents self-recognition by limiting what Lévinas has noted to be the impertative of "the proximity of the other, origin of all putting into question of self" (Lévinas, 1999, p. 99). As Critchley argues,

> From the standpoint of the self, the ethical relation is a relation with an absolutely singular other whom I can neither include nor exclude from my psyche. The other defies ontological comprehension within intentional consciousness, and yet insinuates him or herself within the psyche in a way that cannot be ignored (1999, p. 179).

These imaginative boundaries are barriers to the other, metaphorical restrictions on proximity. But they also justify a physical distance, a misrecognition and a denial of identity and in this sense ally with Lévinas' concern to move beyond speech to the "sensibility" of the other. One native Hawaiian lesbian noted this in an interview with me after the campaign.

> Gay is constructed as white, and the campaign looked so white. I think the idea [that] gay equals male, equals white, equals middle class . . . is a problem for a lot of our families here. This is the thing that keeps repeating over and over again in my work with gay men of color: our families think that we are white. You know, you can't think you are a lesbian and not be white. So you are either a betrayal to your race or you are an oreo or you are doing something weird. But you are not what we know to be our daughter.[28]

The misrecognition of one's daughter is, as well, a refusal to put the self into question, a process repeated at the social level.

Security and Citizenship

Sovereignty is an important idiom for security, and this is as much an economic concern in the modern world as it is a military one. Special rights were seen to be costly particulars that disabled the whole. "Special rights seem to be some kind of zero-sum game in which granting a civil right to one person somehow takes it away from someone else," as a pro-same-sex marriage state commission concluded.[29] In the words of the state's justice department that argued against same-sex marriage rights, "every dollar spent on a same-sex couple, or a cohabiting couple, of necessity strips a dollar from the State's ability to assist married couples."[30] In this economy of rights, special rights were a slippery slope that would inevitably erode common benefits. As one person calculated this probability,

> Taken to its logical conclusion, if we extend special rights and privileges to homosexuals based on their lifestyle preferences and behaviors, we must give them to all. What about a family of three or four? Where do we and can we stop, anything short of whatever anyone wants to call a family will be discriminating.[31]

If this fear of overreaching reinforced a homogeneous equal rights space, other concerns about the economic consequences of special rights eroded any sense of discrete boundaries. Same-sex marriage was argued to be harmful to Hawai'i's position as a premier tourist destination.

> I object [to same-sex marriage] on economic grounds. Tourism will suffer since 98% are heterosexuals with family values who will not appreciate homosexual 'honeymooners' celebrating their nuptials in public. Family flight will occur. Boycotts will occur. Job loss and many other economic losses will occur.[32]

Proponents countered that if Hawai'i were the first to recognize same-sex marriage, it would reap millions from a new tourist venue. But as the debate increasingly commodified the issue, the ethical imperative of civil rights was progressively more difficult to hear. Instead, the ethical emphasis was placed on the desire for an unnamed and faceless traveler, a relation that reinforced the passivity essential to economic survival within a neoliberal framework of highly mobile capital. This imagery linked the idea of fiscal prudence to legal caution. "How many new schools would not be built, and how many programs for needy women and children would be sacrificed to pay for the increased public costs associated with luring the same-sex traffic to Hawai'i? Who knows what these costs might be?"[33]

To some degree, these neoliberal economic arguments on behalf of democratic sovereignty construct an ethical position. Within a logic of scarcity, they are used to direct political attention to a community bounded by economic necessity and infused with economic rationality. The ideal subjectivity of citizenship projected in this political economy is modeled on the taxpayer, concerned about short-term investment and the implications of economic choice for self and family. Against the background of a global neoliberalism in which higher taxes may lead to competitive disadvantage – the logic that some have called the race to the bottom – expenditures of time, money, and attention designed to improve the fates of society's disadvantaged reap a questionable value. But, it is also clear that such values are rarely questioned, and remain perhaps unquestionable from the perspective of neoliberalism.

Neoliberal economics sets up one version of the political space of post-civil rights sovereignty, both distinct from and interconnected with other economic sovereigns and individuals on the basis of mutual security. Two other forms of marking space are noticeable in the campaign against same-sex marriage in Hawai'i, and deserve brief mention for what they can tell us about the ethical limits of self-recognition. The first concerns the rejection of "queer space." The political logic of social space has been transformed in the Twentieth century from an "immigrant" model based on incorporation into a universal body politic (Rupert, 1995) to an "integrationist" model in which wrongly excluded groups comprised a divided, pluralist space (Brown, 1995). The democratic fiction that pluralist spaces were infinitely flexible and did not materially overlap has been slowly altered by neoliberal arguments of scarcity as well as by right wing and progressive social movements. As Patton sees this,

> New Right and queer activists each, and arguably *together*, began to effect a different logic of social space. In contrast with liberal pluralism, each believes that space is deeply material and non-partitionable, and the presence of any group necessarily presses on every other group .... The New Right views dissident bodies – homosexuals, women who seek abortion, Afrocentric blacks – as intrusions of evil into space, intrusions encouraged by liberal pluralism's mismanagement and fragmentation of space. 'Queer' politics stepped into this gap and attempted to produce a politics of presence that did not rely on the dispossession strategy held in common by lesbian and gay rights and black civil rights groups. In this logic, space is a matrix of surges and flows in which queerness precedes any attempt to balkanize bodies that represent points of density in a continuous, gridlike space. Material queerness has always-already been here, *central*, present: we're here, we're queer, get over it (1997, pp. 10–11).

Queer activists were not "here," playing a subdued if not unnoticeable role in the marriage case in Hawai'i which was defended in mostly liberal civil rights language. Nonetheless, antagonism to queer politics fueled an attempt to recreate popular sovereign social space without the unwanted intrusion of rights. Using a quotation that was widely repeated in the campaign, one detractor noted,

> Chuck Colson, winner of the Templeton Award as founder of Prison Fellowship, states in a recent commentary: 'Queer theory is radical. One proponent says, 'we want to break it all down – heterosexuality, the family, the social order.' Gay rights are not just working for basic human rights for homosexuals. The Normal, the natural, the conventional will be overturned. Like Marxism, queer theory is an aggressive ideology that aims to tear down existing society.' ... Make no mistake, this is a power struggle having nothing to do with puny rights.[34]

Overcoming puny rights means reasserting a powerful absolutist space in which the community can legitimately reject rights intrusions. If civil rights are all about overturning the normal, the natural and the conventional, then it can only be just to refuse to listen to these appeals and to demand silence.

The cited dangers of queer politics and the refusal to just "get used to it" impeded analogies that same-sex marriage supporters tried to draw to previous civil rights groups. This was a strategy implicitly designed to question the basis of the 1993 *Baehr* decision. There, the court cited approvingly *Loving v. Virginia* (1967), the case that struck down antimiscegenation laws while declaring with the exuberance and self-certainty of liberal legalism that "Marriage is one of the 'basic civil rights of man.' "[35] In an effort to sustain this analogy of racism to heterosexist policy, pro-marriage forces began a campaign to compare the amendment plebiscite to Japanese American internment and exclusion during WWII. In one provocative newspaper advertisement, a proud Japanese American family with its gathered belongings stands next to a sign saying "Japs Keep Out You Rats." Below the picture the copy reads "It must not happen again. To anyone ever." This tragic image hearkens back to the founding myth of the state of Hawai'i in which the Democratic Party, propelled by Japanese American veterans who fought in segregated units in WWII and returned as some of the most decorated soldiers of the war, declared a multiethnic basis for citizenship and drove from office the Republican Caucasian oligarchy.

The idea of redemption of citizenship through wartime heroism points to the myths that link liberal rights through analogy to republican virtues, and it built support for same-sex marriage among many elderly Japanese Americans in Hawai'i. But lauding military heroism also conjures up limitations on open gay and lesbian participation in the military – the policy of "don't ask, don't tell" – that adds definition and legitimation to a post-civil rights mentality. Without the open support of Senator Inouye, the most visible icon for the linkage between military heroism and Hawai'i citizenship, and faced with many Japanese American veterans of WWII who advocated against same-sex marriage in television and newspaper ads, the analogy could not stick among the wider population. But the anti-marriage response served as another forum in which to energize a new idea of popular sovereignty. Opponents were like soldiers, heroic to the extent they stood up for traditional marriage in the electoral battlefield, shoulder to shoulder in homosocial propriety, following orders, respecting the social chains of command. As soldiers, they were performing the virtues of citizenship already, and no court-ordered affirmation of civil rights were needed to enhance their equality and their commitments to the sovereign.

An Ethical Flatland

The idea of the sovereign space that emerged in the campaign images and rhetoric that defeated same-sex marriage in Hawai'i positioned civil rights arguments as costly, intrusive, and irrational. Committed to a civil rights strategy and concerned what the first constitutional amendment opposing a declared civil right for gays and lesbians might mean in other venues, the organizations fighting for same-sex marriage nevertheless found themselves debating within the sovereignty idiom, accused of dissembling whenever they argued that courts should have the last word. Nor could they easily escape the special rights argument, even when trying to turn the tables on their detractors as the following quotes illustrate:

> Who gets to decide who is morally entitled to civil rights. We can't allow a special interest group to influence the denial of rights to another group.[36]

> The state gives special rights to married couples.[37]

These reversals failed to explain why marriage for same-sex couples should be valued by others, and the historical record of advertisements and public debate is nearly devoid of the words love, marriage, and family. From the sovereign frame, the lack of a concrete defense for same-sex marriage permitted an overturning of the legal burden of proof. Where courts had ruled that the state must show a compelling interest for denying marriage for same-sex couples – indeed, even after the circuit court ruled that the state had failed utterly in its charge – the argument for popular sovereignty reversed this, convicting gays and lesbians as unfit for the benefits of citizenship due to their silence.

At the same time, the indictment of the plaintiff's silence made it easy to elide the fact that the sovereign majority had not itself defended the privilege of heterosexual marriage. Instead, heterosexual marriage was articulated simply as "traditional" without any accounting for the complexities of tradition in Hawai'i despite the recent history of colonialism, the integrity of non-Western cultural roots,[38] and the memories of sexual openness still celebrated in its commercial appeal as a honeymoon destination. The homogeneity assumed in the idea of a singular tradition had consequence for law and sovereignty. Consider Fig. 3, a newspaper advertisement in which tradition is depicted as three ancient Romans holding the symbols of state and empire. The implication that Western law is nearly timeless and its tradition unbroken, its genealogy entwined with the rise of Christian ethics, seems to explain away the equally common narratives among some conservative activists that Rome fell from within by moral decay and fed its Christians to the lions.

This flattening of tradition builds a counter-memory reinforced by appeal to the future condensed in concerns over the fate of children in a society that recognizes same-sex marriage. The ethical demands of children featured prominently in arguments made by the state in its courtroom defense of heterosexual privilege, as well as in advertisements that predicted confusion from books such as "Daddy's

Fig. 3. *Source*: Honolulu *Advertiser* (30 September 1998), p. A17.

Wedding" taught in the schools; "If you don't think homosexual marriage will affect you, how do you think it will affect your children?," one television ad asked. Burlein has recently argued that images of children "act as affective magnets, attracting fears about sexuality and gender, race, class and nationhood in ways that move people into the Right's orbit without requiring them actually to agree with its philosophical, doctrinal or political positions" (2002, ms). As the audience is invited to view the world as parents concerned about the impact of civil rights for same-sex relationships, citizenship is imagined metonymically through children, what Berlant (1997) has called "fetal citizenship." Within this political subjectivity, children substitute for other civil rights subjects but they also do more, providing the sign in whose defense love can legitimately transmogrify into aggression. The sovereign civilizational timeline from Rome to the child assertively rejects the need for self-recognition and moral discourse.

> By securing concrete embodiment in children's future, the nation is proclaimed *in retrospect* as God-given and God-destined, as innocent as the children we wish we were and in whose name we claim to act. By speaking in the name of children, we represent our exercise of power and our assertion of rights as legitimate – untouched by the uncertainty that characterizes intentionality and untainted by moral ambivalence (Burlein, 2002, ms).

It is only with moral ambivalence, a tugging of the Other on one's sleeve, that the demand for citizenship rights can be recognized as a question of justice. "Justice . . . marks a subordination of me to the other . . .. Jankélévitch worded it well: 'We don't have any right; it is always the other who has rights' " (Lévinas, 1999, p. 102).

NATIVE HAWAIIAN RIGHTS AND KANAKA MAOLI SOVEREIGNTY

> The ethical saying must proceed through an abuse of language (Lévinas).
>
> To hear what is not said, to see what cannot be seen, and to know the unknowable, that is aloha (Hardy Spoer).[39]

The recognition of Kanaka Maoli[40] sovereignty has been simmering since the overthrow of the Hawaiian monarchy by American marines in 1893 and the annexation of Hawai'i to the United States five years later. Unlike American Indians who have some limited forms of constitutional protection, Kanaka Maoli were never acknowledged as a nation within a nation after the conquest. Demands for some type of recognition and even outright sovereign self-determination have been renewed by Kanaka Maoli in the past three decades as a renaissance of Hawaiian culture and language infused a stronger sense of identity and cultural pride within the community and among other Polynesian groups across the Pacific. Numerous nationalist groups have organized and work sometimes in concert and often with diverse goals and means of protest, linking local and international issues.

An embracing of this fluid sense of culture and identity (Osorio, 2001), and the changing dynamics of indigenous struggles throughout the Pacific[41] have made the case of Kanaka Maoli recognition so complex and interesting. Complexity also stems from the ironies of history that have made law a contradictory problem for post-colonial Hawai'i. Sally Merry (1998, 2000) has shown how threats by the United States, France, and Britain to the strategically and economically attractive Hawaiian kingdom in the early nineteenth century were met with attempts by the ali'i [ruling caste] to conform society, culture, and politics to colonial ideas of "civilization." In part, this can be seen as a capitulation to the powers and discourses of colonialism: global mechanisms of imperialism, capitalist expansion, the rise of modernity, and the *mission civilisatrice*. From another angle, however, incorporating and redefining some aspects of this civilizing mission served as a form of resistance, a strategy of survival that could stave off threats to Hawaiian sovereignty. This imparted an ambivalent – and hegemonic – role to law as deference to Western legal norms became both sign of state legitimacy and agent of cultural change and oppression. This ambivalence has endured into the Twenty First Century with a complicated twist as clarifications of international law have raised questions about the propriety of American annexation of Hawai'i in the late 19th Century, and the legality of the wording of the plebiscite that sanctioned Hawai'i statehood in 1959. Whether Western law would countenance the legitimacy of Western rights has become a question animating much of Kanaka Maoli nationalism, and imparting an innovative post-civil rights sensibility to Kanaka Maoli claims for sovereignty.

Demands from Kanaka Maoli and support by Hawai'i's congressional delegation led President Clinton to sign public law 103–150 in 1993, offering an apology[42] to the Hawaiian people for the illegal overthrow of their monarchy. For Kanaka Maoli, this offered one pivot around which to press further recognition claims and renegotiate the ambit of Western law. For those opposed to indigenous sovereignty and the growing legal apparatus recognizing native Hawaiian access and gathering rights on private property,[43] indigenous control over former crown lands, and Democratic Party power supported by Native Hawaiian trusts, Native Hawaiians were the beneficiaries of special rights.

In February 2000, in its *Rice v. Cayetano* decision, the U.S. Supreme Court reset the tone for this special rights debate by refusing to accept the state of Hawai'i's claim that historically and constitutionally Native Hawaiians have a "special trust relationship" with the federal government. The *Rice* case involved a challenge to the Office of Hawaiian Affairs which is empowered by the Hawai'i Constitution to oversee a trust for native Hawaiians endowed by "ceded lands" that once were controlled by the Hawaiian monarchy. OHA's board was elected solely by self-identifying indigenous people and was challenged by a local rancher on both 14th Amendment equal protection grounds (e.g. that benefactors of the trust were restricted by race) as well as on grounds that the restricted electoral eligibility violated the 15th Amendment. Justice Kennedy, writing for a 7–2 majority, accepted only the 15th Amendment argument, striking down the electoral laws. For Kennedy, indigenous people had first to acknowledge the sovereignty of the state of Hawai'i before pressing their claims for justice.

> When the culture and way of life of a people are all but engulfed by a history beyond their control, their sense of loss may extend down through the generations, and their dismay may be shared by many members of the larger community. As the state of Hawai'i attempts to address these realities, it must, as always, seek the political consensus that begins with a sense of a shared purpose. One of the necessary beginning points is this principle: the Constitution of the United States, too, has become the heritage of all citizens of Hawai'i.[44]

This "beginning point" must be how closely Hawai'i, including indigenous citizens, are linked to the broader national community rather than how much they are distinct. This view inverts Kanaka Maoli from victims of colonial violence to oppressors seeking law to weaken the bonds of citizenship; it accuses these Hawaiians of excess, of asking for special rights.

Justice Stevens offers a very different perspective in his dissent. His opinion is premised on the distinctiveness of Hawai'i's history and culture that legitimate a measure of native self-government. According to Stevens, in its "wooden approach"[45] the Court majority ignored the difference between Fifteenth Amendment cases and the "unique history of the state of Hawai'i."

> The former recalls an age of abject discrimination against an insular minority in the old South; the latter at long last yielded to the 'political consensus' the majority claims it seeks . . . – a consensus determined to recognize the special claim to self-determination of the indigenous peoples of Hawai'i.[46]

Stevens does not accept the inversion of the native Hawaiian from victim to oppressor. Hawaiians are not "abject" discriminators against an "insular minority;" they are, quite literally, an insular minority who have historically felt the sting of oppression.

It was clear in the aftermath of the *Rice* decision that the debate over OHA resonated with broader issues of civil rights raised in the same-sex marriage case, affirmative action, and other issues. Four days after the Supreme Court handed down the decision, John Goemans (2000, p. B1), the attorney who had originally recruited Freddy Rice as plaintiff, wrote an op-ed piece that began by quoting

Kennedy's words about the Constitution being the heritage for Hawai'i. Goemans went on to describe Hawai'i as a place full of unconstitutional "special rights" for Hawaiians. He made clear that *Rice* was the first step in not only getting rid of all of these "special" rights for a particular "racial classification" but also "whole universe of other state and federal laws that have been passed during the past two decades."

Justice Stevens' vision is apparent in a newspaper editorial entitled "Rice: How Well does the Court Understand Us?" which appeared one day after the Goemans piece.[47] The editorial argued that the majority opinion did not recognize Hawai'i's particular history and culture. It said that Justice Kennedy's description of Freddy Rice "as a citizen of Hawai'i and thus himself a Hawaiian in a well-accepted sense of the term" is certainly not "well accepted" in Hawai'i. It went on to say that maybe everyone in Iowa and California are Iowans or Californians, but Rice is "not a Hawaiian. Not in Hawai'i." As a result of the decision, "the goal [of compensating indigenous peoples for past wrongs and maintaining a vibrant culture], not to mention the far more challenging pursuit by Hawaiians of self-determination, now becomes more difficult."

Months later, the Hawai'i congressional delegation introduced what was locally known as the Akaka Bill[48] (named for one of Hawai'i's senators) as a direct response to that decision. That bill, which passed the House but died in the Senate and was later reintroduced in the 106th Congress, would begin the process establishing "a special trust relationship to promote the welfare of the native people of the United States, including Native Hawaiians" through the treaty making power of the United States. The Akaka Bill attempts to establish something like a tribal status for Kanaka Maoli so that they become eligible for special constitutional considerations that Indian tribes get. Both the Court opinions and this proposed legislation show the basic differences in visions of Hawaiian rights and the attempts by Kanaka Maoli groups to avoid being caught in the confines of contemporary sovereignty debates and arguments over special rights while at the same time continuing to claim uniqueness.

In the discussion that follows, I examine the testimony taken in the August and September, 2000, Congressional Hearings in Honolulu, over the Akaka Bill. Those hearings which took place before Hawai'i's assembled House and Senate delegation – three out of four who had already declared themselves in favor of the Akaka legislation – were highly acrimonious and involved numerous challenges to the limitations of scope and comportment that Congressional rules required. Some of these challenges are noted in the transcripts, but others, particularly the use of the Hawaiian language by some witnesses and the physical violation of established space and protocol, go unmentioned or are only briefly noted. Their reference here is made to acknowledge the limitations of this primarily textual evidence. Nonetheless, as I show below, there are numerous ways in which the testimony was used to confront the ontological presumptions of sovereignty to which the Akaka Bill's backers are often unconsciously committed, forcing an ethical confrontation with the indigenous other.

This case offers a fractal comparison to the same-sex marriage debates, appearing similar in shape if not in substance. In contrast to the earlier contest – indeed, in many ways, because of it – the supporters of the Akaka Bill saw themselves as picking up the cudgel of pre-1980s civil rights commitments (especially as enshrined in the Hawai'i constitutional amendments of 1978 that conceptualized indigenous rights in the same language as other civil rights that animated the constitutional convention held that year[49]). This commitment made opposition complex. Some arguments against the bill used the idea of special rights to effectuate a post-civil rights sovereignty idiom, sharing with same-sex marriage opponents the argument that rights were excessive. In an important wrinkle, however, opposition by many Kanaka Maoli to the Akaka Bill attempted to point out the ethical deficiencies of law and rights for indigenous people. These activists used an inventive language of sovereignty to repel legal recognition and sidestep the legal debris left in the wake of *Rice*. In style, the sovereignty rhetoric is not unlike that used by anti-same-sex marriage activists. However, by avoiding a commitment to an equal rights space based on the ignorance-power of a legitimated silence about colonial history, the basis for liberal sovereignty itself was thrown into question.

An Apology for Special Rights

The few conservatives – mostly Caucasion – who spoke at the hearings reiterated their opposition to the Akaka Bill in language redolent of Justice Kennedy's. The bill would drive a racial wedge into the heart of Hawai'i multiculturalism. "Senator Inouye, Dan Inouye, please look me in the eye," challenged one. "Do you want the epitome of your distinguished career to be a Federal Bill that makes AJA's [Americans of Japanese Ancestry] in Hawai'i second class citizens?"[50] The reference to the AJA community drew from the founding myth of contemporary Hawai'i history in much the same manner as same-sex marriage supporters, but here the defense of pluralism demanded exclusion of rights, not their recognition. It was not that some forms of reparations were not owed the indigenous peoples of the Islands in these accounts. After all, suggested another conservative opponent, the heritage of Hawai'i must be read through the Hawaiian monarchs' 19th Century acceptance of the policy of universal citizenship and franchise which was the true legacy of the past.[51] It was, rather, that legal reparations based on race violated the very idea of the body politic, threatening to "divide us along racial lines,"[52] "create an environment for conflict – oh-oh – just like on Fiji, whose actions was loudly condemned around the world,"[53] or ensure that "Hawai'i will be either partitioned along racial lines or will secede from the United States."[54] Alternative histories were dangerous. What would happen, cautioned one detractor, if political history were instead measured from the time of Captain Cook's arrival before the unification of the islands?

> Because there were several independent sovereign nations in the island before Kamehameha set out to expand his empire, each island should be recognized as a separate, independent entity .... If you don't restore independent sovereignty to each nation, you will be, in effect, legitimizing the armed aggression of Kamehameha, while invalidating the non-violent transition to democracy by the citizens of the island.[55]

Fragmentation, in this testimony, threatened the logic of Benedict Anderson's oft-quoted argument that the temporal frame of the nation projects sovereignty as "fully, flatly, and evenly operative over each square centimeter of a legally demarcated territory" (1983, p. 25). Pluralism could legitimately be recognized only within a sovereign and spatial whole.

If such testimony reflects a concern for maintaining spatial integrity, its spatial dimensions also reinforce the mythological temporality of a coherent community seen from present vantages to be fragmenting and dissolving. David Campbell, following Derrida (1994),[56] has called this notion an *ontopology* in which "political possibilities have been limited by the alignment between territory and identity, state and nation, all under the sign of 'ethnicity' supported by a particular account of history" (1998, p. 80). In the ontopological account, community is animated by "a desire for presence, a desire that is nostalgic for the time when (it is alleged) community was closely knit, homogeneous, and harmonious" (Ibid., p. 168). Here, the rhetoric of nostalgia smoothes over the colonial wrinkles of history and politics and anchors the opposition to rights in Kennedy's notion of a sovereignty of the local ethnic population overriding political division.

As can be expected, the politics of history suffuse this testimony, and operate in many different fashions to play against this ontopological coherence. For some indigenous peoples who voiced support for the Akaka Bill, history is a product of social conflict which cannot be erased through ethnic appeals nor equated with special rights.

> These lands of the Government of the Kingdom of Hawai'i were illegally seized by the provisional government, and turned over to the Republic of Hawai'i, which ceded those lands to the U.S. Government .... I do not believe that non-Hawaiians have claims and entitlements which equal that of native Hawaiians to the cultural and natural resources of these Hawaiian National Lands. I believe that the perpetuation of Hawaiian language, culture, and spiritual beliefs, the pursuit of subsistence fishing, gathering, and farming, access to health care and education

are entitlements for native Hawaiians [and] must be recognized by the U.S. Government, and acknowledged and respected by those who choose to make Hawai'i their home.[57]

History could also reveal fixed points at which sovereignty could be reimagined and purified of the taint of illegality, such as the 19th century treaties with France, Britain and Japan that gave formal recognition to the Kingdom of Hawai'i.[58] Or, cultural history could provide another form of imagination, one capable of re-working 19th century citizenship from a civic model based on voting rights, to one based on shared ideals such as aloha from which citizenship could be recognized within a sovereignty of affection.

These alternatives work against the taunt of special rights propounded by the Akaka Bill's conservative detractors by undermining the logics of scarcity and insecurity that ontopology is believed to create. Hawaiian culture has the ability to expand beyond legal or racial boundaries (Osorio, 2001, 362ff) and spatial jurisdictions, as any visitor to the islands can appreciate, and yet it still provides a strong rationale for recognition; in an embellishment to Hawai'i license plates that announce the "Aloha State," a common bumper sticker admonishes non-indigenous residents, "No Hawaiians, No Aloha." As one indigenous opponent of the Akaka Bill testified, "Hawaiians never excluded anybody. But if you go to the Mainland, the continent, now you may see a different story there. There is no liberty and justice up there."[59] And a history which respects the old treaties and takes the Apology Bill seriously allows for the transmutation of special rights into unique rights by rejecting the nationalist mapping of peoples to spaces that the *Rice* case promotes. Instead, the invocation of the old kingdom jars the smooth continuity of tradition by suggesting the complex historical and spatial relations that work against a binary of equal rights/special rights.

For some who advanced this position with their testimony, this meant appreciating the ways in which indigenous rights would make a difference to those indigenous peoples living in diaspora, a Lévinasian reminder of those excluded and overlooked in a restrictive ontopology.

Because 40% of the Hawaiian population has been forced to leave Hawai'i for economic reasons, due to the taking of Hawaiian lands, it is important that those Hawaiians who live outside of Hawai'i be included as members of the Hawaiian community, and the new Hawaiian nation, and not be doubly penalized for the modern diaspora suffered by our people. All Hawaiians have family members who live outside of Hawai'i and who are yearning to come home. They would do so if lands were available for their use in Hawai'i.[60]

For others, contemporary migrations exposed the contingent framework of minority and majority relations on which much of the special rights claims rested.

I was hoping that . . . our Tongan brothers might come up, and all the Polynesians from across the isles of the sea, that find Hawai'i to be their home base, and they would come out and support

> us, as native Hawaiians. Because if they do, we will become the majority, and not the minority, in our home lands, because we are all brothers and sisters in the eyes of the sea.[61]

Focused within the fluid eyes of the sea rather than the rigid and fixed categories of Occidental law that floated here accidentally, sovereignty is reimagined as prior to and more extensive than the cartographic boundaries of Hawai'i. It is coterminous with past migrations, and the cultural renaissance of Polynesians begun with the modern recreation of the voyaging canoes that have sailed across the Pacific since 1975.[62]

This testimony also cites the ethical imperative for inclusion of others forgotten in the ontopological imagination, and the consequent transformation of borders and politics. As Ruiz theoretically amplifies these concerns,

> Ethics may not be synonymous with politics; but politics is inescapably ethical. With the constant aggregation, desegregation, and reaggregation of... communities, due in large part to the transformations of space, time and place brought about by (economic and political) migrations, 'border crossings,' 'foot wanderers,' and exiles – in short, of diaspora – the reality of a territorially circumscribed community is no longer self-evident. Thus, the question, 'Which community?' – and, therefore, 'Which ethics?' or 'Whose ethics?' – becomes a profound issue (1999, p. 644).

Perhaps just as profound an issue stems from the question "Whose law?" which seems to have infused this testimony and directed itself to the ethical question of the relevant community.

It is here that I think it important to step back and give a fuller sense of the testimony. While the special rights/equal rights issue framed around the nature of the sovereign community animated the conservative detractors of the Akaka Bill, they were few in number at these hearings. Supporters of the Akaka Bill who were willing to answer these conservative voices were vocal, but were also a numerical minority. A reader of the transcripts is impressed by the vast majority of the testimony from indigenous people who were vehemently and eloquently opposed to the Akaka Bill. These voices were not opposed to rights or to sovereign recognition; contrariwise, most spoke passionately about gaining this recognition. But few trusted the processes and mechanisms of the Akaka Bill, the American government or its representatives to provide what had never been forthcoming from law and rights before. Their appearance at the hearing – indeed their domination throughout the five-day hearing – suggests that this was an important site for legal mobilization. What I argue below is that this upwelling of disagreement was voiced through an engagement with the law in an effort to provoke recognition of indigenous people; in Lévinas' terminology this was a performance to signal the proximity of the Other and the ethical obligations this forced to consciousness. In addition, by arguing that law was incapable of sufficiently providing for indigenous sovereignty, a new ground for imagining what an Apology might look like was promoted.

Identity and Legal Recognition

The ethical problematization of recognition is perhaps most clearly seen in the voiced concern over naming. The Akaka Bill recognized the unique political status of "Native Hawaiians," but this terminology was not mirrored back by indigenous opponents.

> Stop calling us native Hawaiians, it is insulting and shameful.[63]
>
> Let's be clear who we are. We are Kanaka Maoli. Let's lose the native Hawaiian, the Native American, the Indian and tribunal labels.[64]
>
> I have thought about this daily. I do not think, at this point testifying to you today, that I ever want the United States to define who we are.[65]
>
> Hawaiians are not and never will be an indigenous people of the United States. Okay, never have been, never will be.[66]
>
> We are not native Hawaiians, we are not indigenous. However, in America's dreams of technicality we may be, but we are Kanaka Hawai'i in our aspect. We are o'iwi, the bones of this land that our kupuna [elders/ancestors] have passed on to us. We are the rightful caretakers of this land. This bill should contain as much Hawaiian language as possible . . .. If you are drafting a bill that is truly supposed to represent us as a people, then you must use our language.[67]

This refusal to be named, this rejection of "American technicality," is a dismissal of legal sequence and the privileges of naming that underlie it. Law should absorb autonomously-derived social identities, and not substitute for this process. As one opponent put it, "These measures were drafted and submitted to Congress without incorporation of the manao [thoughts, input] of Kanaka Maoli[,] prior to the achievement of that absolutely mandatory 'unity of purpose.' "[68] This unity of purpose need not – indeed likely would not – require mediation by legal language; perhaps importantly it may evade civil rights subjectivity and be agreed to solely in the Hawaiian language, outside the understanding of the American state. Only once this is decided can law properly, and in a limited fashion, recognize Kanaka Maoli sovereignty.

These sentiments also stood as a denial of analogies implied in this power of naming. To be addressed as a "Native Hawaiian" by the Bill, was, for many of these opponents, to be incorporated as American Indians and to be forced to live with the nation-within-a-nation semi-sovereign status that such terminology implied. Against the public insistence of Senator Inouye that "this bill does not make Native Hawaiians part of Indian Country. I can make that flat assertion and guarantee. It does not make them an Indian tribe, nor will they become part of Indian programs,"[69] few were willing to agree.

> The Kingdom remains in place. The Kingdom is there. Why are you trying to find another identity for us? . . . It is not the Kingdom that is lost to us, it's us, we are lost to the Kingdom. And we want to identify ourselves as native Hawaiians of the new Kingdom and now even with that we are going to fall under Indian Affairs. What is that?[70]
>
> This bill claims Hawaiians are Native American tribes. We know that Hawaiians are not Native Americans. They do not have tribes. Hawaiians are Kanaka Maoli. They are descendants of the citizens of the Independent Kingdom of Hawai'i. Let Hawaiians decide what they want and when they want it.[71]

Like the shameful policies against Native Americans, this was another "traitorous document,"[72] a colonial move towards "genocide."[73] While proponents tried to push other analogies – "The closest analogy for our native Hawaiians, of course, is the Maoris in New Zealand . . . they have resources now, and they did this by . . . fighting for their rights and working to . . . set aside their status of being outsiders"[74] – Russell Means and Glen Morris of the Lakota Sioux and Shoshone Nations sent testimony urging another: "Let us share with you what federal recognition translates to: American apartheid."[75]

The refusal of legal labels and the analogy of legal policy to abhorrent and uncivilized relations recalls Levinas' philosophical distinction between the saying and the said. This distinction is for Citchley a "way of explaining how the ethical signifies within ontological language. The Saying is my exposure – corporeal, sensible – to the Other, my inability to refuse the Other's approach. It is the performative stating, proposing, or expressive position of myself facing the Other" (Critchley, 1999, p. 7). Seen from this perspective, the refusal of the "said" of the law is accomplished through a performative self-definition grounded in a yet-to-be-determined Hawaiian community agreement and signified by the otherness of Hawaiian language. It cannot be reduced to legal categories without representing that anarchic other – genocide, apartheid – that always opposes the promises of American sovereign recognition, or dissolving into a sameness contoured to the exigencies of equal rights. As a performance, it is a reminder of the powerlessness of law to recognize, and in so doing, to resolve the problem of indigenous peoples as Other. It is a reminder of the need for a truly ethical encounter, not one that takes the Other as assimilable and as real, for this is the violence of totalization.

This is performative in a second fashion, as well. Embedded within the analogies to genocide and apartheid – and the death and loss of a people that they signify – is also an ethical gesture toward the Other which simultaneously offers the means to reclaim subjectivity and citizenship. These analogies announce the impossibility of presenting an otherness for recognition in such a public event. For Lévinas, the saying opposes the said by invoking a subjectivity in which the Other is present but uncontained, and this is the importance of death that this language captures. "The approach of death indicates that we are in relation with something that is absolutely other, something bearing alterity not as a provisional determination we can assimilate through enjoyment, but as something whose very existence is made of alterity" (Lévinas, 1987, p. 74). To move beyond the ego – here the legal subject – then, is to recollect the Other through loss, to mourn. "The duality evinced in death becomes the relationship with the other and time" (Lévinas, 1987, p. 41). As Cornell captures the significance of this sentiment:

> we run into the limit of our narcissism, however, as we realize that, will what we might, we cannot rewrite the Other back into life, remaking history so that she is still with us. She is gone. In her absence, we feel the pull of otherness.... The inevitable failure of memory to enclose the Other, opens us to the 'beyond' (1992, p. 73).

The testimony of those opposed to the Bill is filled with such mourning for the past. "Why throughout this bill and throughout the Apology Bill, is there no real reference to the loss of a nation? Everything is addressed to the Hawaiian people, which lessens our rights. It's our nation we lost and our nation that we want restored."[76] Levinas writes that "the other is the future" (Lévinas, 1987, p. 77) and the loss associated with federal recognition is mourned as a future loss as well.

> It was instilled in me as a child that the people of old, the wise ones, especially the kupuna, when they think about the lineage of their family, or even their immediate families, or the people as a whole, they thought seven generations down the line. They didn't think about what I can get now.... The thing is, seven generations down the line Hawaiians are not going to exist. We still may have a brown skin, and we still may have the koko [blood] in us, but we are not going to be known as Hawaiians. We are not going to have our identity.... So I think it is a conflict of interest to write this bill and author it in you folks' words. I think we need to discuss along with the people some more. But, decide to stop it for now, just because there is a chance we may be doing damage seven generations down the lane.... Stop, look, the Kingdom is in place. We as a people may not be ready to do what the Kingdom needs, but the path is there for us. But the thing is, we cannot go rushing off trying to identify ourselves as something else. Okay, just stop. Mahalo.[77]

The mourning for generations not yet born in this speech serves as an ethical model for what reactions to the Apology Bill ought to produce.

Progress and Subjectivity

The insistence on altering the temporal perspective via a mourned past or future also served in this public testimony to challenge the framework of subjectivity that a nation-within-a-nation relationship created by the bill would entail. Indigenous supporters agreed with the Congressional sponsors that recognition through the Akaka Bill would facilitate the satisfaction of immediate human needs. In an implicit Maslowian hierarchy, the bill was proposed to "protect native Hawaiian programs, including Hawaiian homes, from court challenges from those who would deny or ignore unique historical circumstances that make these programs legitimate and necessary"[78] and later provide a forum for organization. The political argument to use legal recognition as a means of solving immediate material needs was reinforced by the general climate of Clinton's last few months in office and the risk of a less-friendly administration taking over. While this contributed a pressure that many acknowledged who testified for the bill, it also threatened dependency.

> This bill must not be a final step to permanent wardship for the Kanaka Maoli people. There is no joy in being needy. There is no joy in having to receive support from elsewhere. Kanaka Maoli don't want to be dependent forever. The history of our people is one of centuries of self-sufficiency. Kanaka Maoli long to be self-sufficient again and self-supporting in the future. And we will. Sadly, after 100 years, Kanaka Maoli have become dependent on programs and support systems. Kanaka Maoli needs for health, education, housing and economic support are real and immediate and will not go away overnight.[79]

For many who opposed the bill, the subjectivity of wardship and dependency was not worth the psychic cost, and would itself preclude individual and community growth. Autonomy depended on control of land, and the Akaka Bill would not affect that. " 'If' federal recognition will put our lands in our hands, then I would support it."[80] For many, this was a timeless story of American colonialism. "In the common sense of U.S. hegemony, 'returning Hawaiians to the land' thus effaced the alternative of returning the land to Hawaiians" (Kauanui quoted in Osorio, 2001, p. 363).

Only a sense of reconciliation through recognition could restore the idea of progress, of seeing the Akaka Bill as a step toward sovereignty and self-determination. This was the intended meaning of the Maori analogy cited earlier, and of the testimony of the director of the Department of Hawaiian Home Lands who argued that "this was the next logical step in the cultural evolution of our people."[81] These images are in many ways Hegelian and Homeric, steps along a journey of return. But others rejected this narrative and stressed the timelessness of the struggle in which the bill was a meaningless signpost.

> 104 years and we have made no progress for us, the Kanaka Maoli. We suffer. The provisional government burned my ancestors' homes to the ground in Kalalau chasing the Ko'olau, a Kanaka Maoli and his family who had contracted leprosy and did not want to be deported . . .. Will the bill help us to receive justice, or is it like [the Apology Bill], a ghost, an illusion?[82]
>
> For 20 years, for 100 years, we've been running around in circles . . .. It doesn't matter what you do with this bill, whether you rewrite it or anything, it still leads to what I call the valley of the lost. It still leads there, and all the while the path is on the ridge of the mountain.[83]

For the majority who testified that they, too, remained trapped in the valley of the lost, that they, too, suffered, American law could not efface the theft of the Kingdom or propel a directional, linear narrative of progress. Indeed, the disruptive nature of some testimony and the massive show of indigenous opposition to the bill performed the impossibility of its success as a compass to lead to the ridge-line path. Disrupting progressive and dialectical narratives can be seen as one way in which to signal the ethical imperatives of alterity and to make the call of suffering heard. Lévinas argued as much in his rejection of Hegelian ontological narratives: "It is not a matter of traversing a series of contradictions, or of reconciling them while stopping History. On the contrary, it is toward a pluralism that does not merge into unity that I should like to make my way" (Lévinas, 1987, p. 42).

A similar pluralism can be seen in challenges to progressive narratives by new forms of spatial linking in which Otherness could be expressed as a radical alterity. Foucault has called heterotopia those spaces "which are something like counter-sites, a kind of effectively enacted utopia in which the real sites, all of the other real sites that can be found within the culture, are simultaneously represented, contested, and inverted" (Foucault, 1986 [1967]). Certainly, the proponents of the bill saw the hearing as an opportunity to transmute opposition and acrimony into harmony, to reconcile a hundred years of wrong into a commitment to rights. But opponents likewise used the hearing as a heterotopia in which spaces could be transformed and time reordered in an effort to escape, or at least make others confront the valley of the lost.

One common tactic in the creation of this heterotopia was to refuse the centrality of the American sovereign and to appeal to plural rights recognized throughout the Pacific and the world. For Senator Akaka, this was not necessarily problematic when done in the proper sequence. His bill was the "next step" which did not "impact alternatives sought at the international level[; activists] will be able to continue their efforts."[84] But opponents repeatedly cited international law, natural law, the law of nations, the legal precedent of aboriginal rights in Australia, as well as obscure Latinate rules such as the laws of *post-lininium*,[85] to argue that indigenous claims were situated within a space that subsumed the hearings.

> This bill attempts, once again, to use U.S. domestic laws to try to resolve an international issue, the issue of our independence.[86]
>
> The right for self-determination is enshrined in two United Nations covenants, which the Akaka Bill appears determined to take from us. The wording reads: "All peoples have the right to self-determination. And by virtue of that right, they freely determine their political status and freely pursue their economic, social and cultural development."[87]
>
> The nation worldwide is just waiting out there for the Hawaiian people to decide. They are backing us all the way. These nations of the world will back the Hawaiian Kingdom to the end.[88]

In many respects, sentiments such as these appealed to international respect through the original idiom of sovereignty and the genealogy of Western law in

Hawai'i. But in the creation of a heterotopia, these arguments also served to shake up and invert spatial and temporal meanings and in this way promote a radical alterity in which identity is uncertain (e.g. irreducible to race, ethnicity, place or historical fact) and sovereignty overlapping. This articulation of sovereignty was therefore unlike that propounded by same-sex marriage opponents who envisioned a singular sovereignty based on a timeless moral code within which difference legitimated political exclusion.

The articulation of a radical alterity by these Kanaka Maoli activists was as much designed to constitute the otherness of those the bill was aimed to subject as it was a performance designed to recreate the otherness of those who promoted the legal solution. Consider the claims of one opponent of the bill who is "speaking on behalf of my family from time immemorial to present time . . . *this is foreign soil, not American soil.*"[89] Here perspective is strangely warped to make what is present and other to American sovereignty nonetheless foreign. Could this mean foreign to the speaker as well as the American Senators and Representatives? Why can't the soil be addressed in sovereign terms – "my soil" perhaps, or "our soil"? This speaker inhabits multiple spaces simultaneously: the land is both Kanaka Maoli and yet foreign from the perspective of America. As Lévinas reminds us, to be conscious of alterity, "I posit myself deposed of my sovereignty. Paradoxically it is qua *alienus* – foreigner and other – that man is not alienated" (Lévinas, 1991, p. 59). Or, consider the wonderful inversion in this speaker's imagery:

> The Hawaiian Homes Commission Act [of 1921] qualified a native Hawaiian by a process that proved your ancestors lived here prior to 1778. *That is when the Hawaiian Islands discovered Captain Cook, lost in the Pacific Ocean.*[90]

Here, Western discovery and with it both the naming of the islands and the shaming of Polynesian navigation are reordered. As Shapiro reminds us, "to produce an ethics responsive to contestations over identity and the spatial stories upon which structures of recognition rest, it is necessary to disrupt the dominant practices of intelligibility" (1999, p. 59).

This disruption of intelligibility leaves more than silence in its wake, but what remains cannot be easily revealed. To repeat the epigraph of this section taken from the Akaka Bill testimony, "To hear what is not said, to see what cannot be seen, and to know the unknowable, that is aloha." In an echo of Psalm 115,[91] this recitation constructs the face of the false idol in the ontology of all that appears evident to ears and eyes. It is only by acknowledging what is unknowable by these senses that aloha – the indigenous ethical relation – is reconstructed within, and only by a reminder of the true face of the other that it can lead to justice.

CONCLUSION

> All the excess of generosity that I must have toward the other [must be] subordinated to a question of justice (Lévinas).[92]

The appeal to justice through civil rights is much harder to hear in Hawai'i today, and certainly elsewhere. The resurgence of sovereignty language with its ontopological emphasis on spatial unity, timeless history, and appropriate rationality has subordinated legal arguments for equal treatment to democratic social interests in security and economy. Arguments about civil rights as special rights have leveraged this sovereign framework to invert the nature of harm and redefine majorities as victims of anarchic demands and as authentic rights subjects. As counter-memories, these frameworks for rethinking the place of civil rights produce an excoriated remainder: an idea of legal and social excess that serves as the reason against rights and impedes authentic justice.

Lévinas suggests that this construction must be inverted in order to realize an ethics that escapes the vicissitudes of this ontological imagination; the excess claimed by those deploying special rights discourse is really sign of an ethical vacuum. Excess, for Lévinas, is instead intrinsic to the ethical relationship of ego to other and limited by the *insufficiencies* of law whose necessary overcoming is a belated journey to citizenship. "I move from the order of responsibility, in which even what isn't my business is my business, from mercy, to justice, which limits that initial priority of the other that we started out from" (Lévinas, 1999, p. 103). For Lévinas, this journey from responsibility to justice involves a recognition of the third: "with the arrival of the third party, the problem of fundamental justice is posed, the problem of the right, which initially is always that of the other" (Ibid., p. 102). In some sovereign arguments about civil rights – e.g. where same-sex marriage violates the rights of majorities, and where indigenous rights must be packed within Kennedy's command of "the political consensus that begins with a sense of a shared purpose" – the abstract "third" is mistaken for the other, and the limits of citizenship bounded by self-consciousness. This closure, for Lévinas, is an ontology that confuses the conditions of the self for the Good.

> To reduce men to self-consciousness and self-consciousness to the concept, that is, to history, to deduce from the concept and from history the subjectivity and the 'I' in order to find meaning for the very singularity of 'that one' in function of the concept, by neglecting, as contingent, what may be left irreducible after this reduction, what residue there may be after this deduction, is, under the pretext of not caring about the inefficacity of 'good intentions' and 'fine souls' and preferring 'the effort of concepts' to the facilities of psychological naturalism, humanist rhetoric and existentialist pathetics, to forget what is better than being, that is, the Good (Lévinas, 1991, pp. 18–19).

Indigenous activists opposing the mechanisms of legal recognition of the Akaka Bill argued that the ethical spirit of the Apology Bill could not be realized within the context of an ontopologically fixed idea of sovereignty since the Good resided in the excesses of history and space that were forgotten or ignored by its supporters. Refusing to be named; demanding an accounting of historical dislocations, violence and death; calling upon a trans-Pacific set of rights that could not be constitutionally located; rejecting the legal identity of a racial group and invoking a pan-Pacific and cultural subjectivity; and insisting on an opportunity to develop a community voice prior to its fixation in the law; these activists tried to force an accounting for the other through a reminder that "the other is invisible" (Lévinas, 1969, p. 6) escaping "representation and diagnosis" (Burggreaeve, 1999, p. 30), and revealing that "the limit of the state is the sign of the existence of nonrepresented people" (Herzog, 2002, p. 219).

Little of the public discourse supporting same-sex marriage tried anything similar. Civil rights and claims for equality were promoted by analogy and unspecified common interests of gay and straight couples, by appeals to increasing economic benefit through "rights tourism," through judo-like attempts to engage sovereignty rhetoric to raise suspicions of legislative action and hence preserve court precedent, and even through special rights language. In retrospect, none seem to have been successful tactics in preventing a supermajority of 69% from voting for the Amendment that killed same-sex marriage in Hawai'i in 1998. And yet, the engagement of indigenous activists with the Akaka Bill suggests the potential of a powerful alternative worth considering for what it can tell us about the progressive possibilities within post-civil rights politics.

Speculation by many disappointed activists in the years since the passage of the Amendment has focused on the untried alternative of thematizing the family and making a more direct appeal to the good of same-sex marriage. Rather than simply appealing to the logic of the law or the advancement of the common good, the campaign to support same-sex marriage could have been waged on the basis of an invitation to a public rethinking of the family on a local model. Hawai'i families are famously diverse for many reasons reflecting Hawai'i's history and economic circumstances: families are often multigenerational and informal, of mixed ethnicity, constituted by marriage and traditional hanai (informal adoption), and sexually tolerant (reflecting Kanaka Maoli tradition). In these extended families, many have relatives who are openly gay.[93] Acknowledgment of these concrete relationships would have introduced a reference point into the debate not easily homogenized into an anonymous "third." Making family diversity the centerpiece of the campaign could have highlighted the centrality of love and desire for the familiar and most-proximate Other, the relations of mutual dependence that constitute family. It could have also exposed the historical underpinnings of diversity, questioning the unbroken linearity of a singular tradition from which to know the certainty of the marriage form. And it could have named already-ethical relations as a primary basis for understanding family. Lévinas has written that "I am called upon in my uniqueness as someone for whom no one else can substitute himself. One can ask if anything in the world is less conditioned than man, in whom the ultimate security a foundation would offer is absent" (Lévinas, 1991, p. 59). Stripped of one's sovereignty, the appeal to equal marriage rights can become a reminder of the responsibility toward another, and a commitment to her choices and freedoms.

These tactics might still be tested in civil rights struggles over same-sex marriage around the United States. More generally, the Hawai'i struggles over civil rights – particularly struggles over indigenous rights – suggest that an ethical appeal may rest upon deconstructing many of the sovereign binaries around which civil rights have been confronted by popular politics. Invocations of the pluralism of overlapping social spaces, narratives that can disrupt a linear temporality and weaken the justification for a "post-rights" position, appeals to a multiplicity of rights sources, and images that invoke the face-to-face encounter with real people might together provide a tactical menu. It is not the case, I think, that these tactics would guarantee a different outcome as much as they might subtly nourish a transformation in the way civil rights is now thought and argued.

One prominent and persistent danger of any attempt at codifying rights or arguing for universal ideals is that ontological arguments will intrude into discussions of justice, silencing debate and freezing ideas of one's duty to others around stable conceptions of the self. Certainly, family and nation are two prominent contemporary examples around which subjectivity has ossified because of fixed and largely unexamined ideas of what makes a family or can secure a nation. Just as certainly, the strategic choice presented above to allow the familiar and the loved person to expand ideas of family and nation, and then expand the civic calculus outward to be disrupted by overlooked faces, carries its own risks and ironies. In addition, whether reimagination of the sovereignty of the state will also expose the heterosexist ontologies of colonialism and nationalism remains an important question not easily solved;[94] Derrida and others have shown how a reversion to the ontological is found even within Lévinas' thought.[95]

Nonetheless, Lévinas points us in an important political direction: the mobilization of rights discourse to challenge conventional understandings and arrangements of self and other. This direction will not necessarily take us beyond sovereignty, especially where new sovereign notions are used to resist certain formulations of rights (e.g. the Akaka Bill). Nonetheless, it will help eliminate what is most pernicious in the sovereignty discourse. In particular, it will encourage us to make the "third" less abstract and homogenized, more individual and diverse. The complexities of representation that result might work to lessen the ability to maintain a divide between special and equal rights, muting the tendency for two (unequally weighted) models of social justice. Far from ending civil rights discourse, this new direction will instead tend to delaminate it from its ontopological confines, encouraging its rearticulation with culture, human rights, and alternative ideas of what sovereignty can mean.

NOTES

1. Gamble (1997). Gamble's research spans the years 1959–1993. See also the concerns of Bell (1978).

2. The term is from Schacter (1997).

3. Studies of legal mobilization critically examine the reproduction and successes of rights advocacy with the understanding that "legal norms and discourses derive their meaning primarily through the practical forms of activity in which they are developed and expressed" (McCann, 1994, pp. 261–262), a contemporary echo of Marx's (1977) argument that law is one of the "forms in which men become conscious of . . . conflict and fight it out" (see also the arguments of Bourdieu, 1987; Ewick & Silbey, 1992; Fantasia, 1988; Marshall, 1983; Marx, 1977; Restated by Thompson, 1975, p. 267). Mobilization theory suggests that rights are conducive to social alliance, and hence, facilitative of group conflict (McCann, 1994; Milner, 1986; Scheingold, 1974; Silverstein, 1996; Stychin, 1998; Zemans, 1983). Legal meaning is therefore not precise and definitive, but rather contingently mapped onto wider social textures and dependent on divergent experiences with and beliefs about rights (Herman, 1994; Milner, 1986) as well as the "inclinations, tactical skills, and resources of the contending parties who mobilize judicial endowments" (McCann, 1994, p. 170). This diversity of belief and engagement with the law reveals legal consciousness to be "variable, volatile, complex and contradictory" (McCann, 1994, p. 8).

4. See also Cooper (1998), Darian-Smith (1999), Darian-Smith and Fitzpatrick (1999), Stychin (1998).

5. See Ashley (1988), Campbell (1992, 1998), Campbell and Shapiro (1999), Ferguson and Turnbull (1999), Krishna (1999), Shapiro (1997), Soguk (1999), Walker (1993).

6. This sketch is more fully developed in Goldberg-Hiller (2002).

7. The overused terminology is from Justice Stone who wondered in *United States v. Carolene Products*, "whether prejudice against discrete and insular minorities may be a special condition, which tends seriously to curtail the operation of those political processes ordinarily to be relied upon to protect minorities, and which may call for a correspondingly more searching judicial inquiry" (304 U.S. 144, 152 [1938]). The determination of discrete and insular minorities has occupied scholars [e.g. Ely (1980)], the Court, and public opponents of civil rights since.

8. David Campbell, quoting Foucault liberally, writes that a problematization "is something that has made it possible to think in terms of problems and solutions; it is something that 'has made possible the transformations of the difficulties and obstacles of a practice into a general problem for which one proposes diverse practical solutions.' A problematization 'develops the conditions in which possible responses can be given; it defines the elements that will constitute what the different solutions attempt to respond to.' In seeking to show how different solutions to a problem have been constructed and made possible by the way

the problem is posed in the first place, it demonstrates how different solutions result from a specific form of problematization (Campbell, 1998, p. x).

9. These binaries are catalogued in Walker (1993). Walker's interest is in the relationship of sovereignty to international relations. I broaden that concern to issues of civil rights here, but see our projects as ultimately intertwined.

10. See Crenshaw (1991), Kwan (1997).

11. *Baehr v. Miike* Haw. Civ. No. 91-1394-05 (1996).

12. Constable (1993), Fitzpatrick (1999), Dillon (1995), and others have shown that Foucault was strikingly ambivalent about law and sovereignty. Although he is famously noted for suggesting that sovereignty is an inadequate basis for theory ("in political thought and analysis, we still have not cut off the head of the king" (Foucault, 1980, pp. 88–89)), at the same time he saw that with governmentality "the problem of sovereignty is made more acute than ever" (Foucault, 1991, p. 101). However much sovereignty is distinguished from law, Fitzpatrick has argued that there remains a theoretical interconnection. "Law as state law and law as governmentality are simply [not] the same. There is, rather, a relation of apposition between them. The constituent limits of each come from their mutual inviolability, from a certain mutual opposition in the face of their similarity to each other. The element of alterity between them is set in the opposed character of each being a condition for the distinct identity and operation of the other. Each takes on that which operatively remains of the other but is incompatible with the other's self-presentation as pervasive.... In their alternation, the relation between state law and governmentality becomes one of mutual dependence in which they are integral to each other yet necessarily opposed. One constituently limits the other to a distinct space yet sustains a claim of that other to be unlimited" (1999, p. 27).

13. This is Derrida's conclusion (1978, 96ff). Lévinas writes, "To reduce the good to being, to its calculations and its history, is to nullify goodness" (1991, p. 18). Shapiro (1999, p. 63) argues that Lévinas' refusal of the Western ethical tradition from which he has obviously sprung is a reminder of the need to encounter the other in new grammars.

14. "If man were only a saying correlative with the logos, subjectivity could as well be understood as a function or as an argument of being. But the signification of saying goes beyond the said. It is not ontology that raises up the speaking subject; it is the signifyingness of saying going beyond essence that can justify the exposedness of being, ontology" (Lévinas, 1991, pp. 37–38). This was Lévinas' response to Derrida who saw metaphysical violence in any reliance on ontology. Critchley nicely explains the distinction between the Saying and the Said as "how the ethical signifies within ontological language. The Saying is my exposure – corporeal, sensible – to the Other, my inability to refuse the Other's approach. It is the performative stating, proposing, or expressive position of myself facing the Other. It is a verbal or non-verbal ethical performance, whose essence cannot be caught in constative propositions. It is a performative *doing* that cannot be reduced to a constative description. By contrast, the Said is a statement, assertion or proposition, concerning which the truth or falsity can be ascertained. To employ another model, one might say that the content of my words, their identifiable meaning, is the Said, while the Saying consists in the fact that these words are being addressed to an interlocutor. *The Saying is the sheer radicality of human speaking, of the event of being in relation with an Other; it is the non-thematizable ethical residue of language that escapes comprehension, interrupts philosophy, and is the very enactment of the ethical movement from the Same to the Other*" (Critchley, 1999, p. 7, emphasis mine).

15. As Critchley notes, "Lévinas's critique of politics and his insistence on the primacy of ethical difference does not result in an a-politicism, in a quietism or a "spirituality of angels" – that is the source of his critique of Buber's I-Thou relation. Rather, ethics leads back to politics, responsibility to questioning, to the interrogative demand for a just polity. I would go further and claim that, for Lévinas, ethics is ethical for the sake of politics – that is, for the sake of a new conception of the organization of political space." (1999, pp. 222–223). I return to this theme of reorganizing political space later in this paper.

16. See the works of Burggreaeve (1981), Cornell (1992), Critchley (1999), Herzog (2002), Peperzak and Lévinas (1993), Ruiz (1999), and Simmons (1999) who all approach Lévinas as a political theorist as well as a normative philosopher. Central to most of these accounts is Lévinas' treatment of the Third.

17. "Only justice can wipe it [ethical responsibility] away by bringing this giving-oneself to my neighbor under measure, or moderating it by thinking in relation to the third and fourth, who are also my 'others,' but justice is already the first violence" (Levinas quoted in Simmons, 1999, p. 94).

18. Lévinas (1991, p. 117).

19. Jasmine Sarns, written testimony submitted to the House Judiciary Committee hearings, 20 January 1997.

20. Pastor Stephen Kirk, written testimony submitted to the House Judiciary Committee 27 October 1993.

21. Mike Gabbard, President, Alliance for Traditional Marriage, speaking at a public forum on same-sex marriage, 20 October 1998, Honolulu, Hawai'i. Transcript by the author.

22. Wattie Mae Hedemann, written testimony submitted to the House Judiciary Committee hearings, 13 October, 1993.

23. Jim Hochberg, written testimony submitted to the House Judiciary Committee, 27 October 1993.

24. Rosemary Garciduenas, State Director of the Christian Coalition of Hawai'i, written testimony submitted to the House Judiciary Committee hearings, 25 October 1993.

25. See quotation and discussion at page [between note 10 and note 11].

26. Justice Scalia's dissent in *Romer* upholding the *Bowers* standard used this very phrase. The various arguments in *Bowers v. Hardwick* for democratic antipathy to homosexuality outlined in the text can be found in the opinions of J. White and C. J. Burger.

27. Mike Gabbard, Director of Common Sense Now!, written testimony submitted to the House Judiciary Committee, 16 September 1993.

28. Author's interview with Val Kanuha, 10 November 1999.

29. Commission on Same-sex Marriage and the Law, State of Hawai'i, 1995, p. 24.

30. State's legal brief, *Baehr v. Miike*, 1996, p. 34.

31. Name illegible, testimony before the Commission on Same-sex Marriage and the Law, Minutes of 6 December, 1995. University of Hawai'i library.

32. Gerald Wright, written testimony submitted to the House Judiciary Committee, 29 September 1993.

33. State of Hawai'i Report of the Commission on Sexual Orientation and the law, 1995, Minority Report, p. 55.

34. Janice Judd, written testimony submitted to the House Judiciary Committee, October 1993.

35. Warren, C. J., 388 U.S. 1, 12 (1967).

36. Cheryl Donahue, written testimony submitted to the House Judiciary Committee, 20 October 1993.

37. Bill Potter, written testimony submitted to the House Judiciary Committee, 26 October 1993.

38. One of the original plaintiffs, Ninia Baehr, testified that "People like Genora [Dancel] and me are not the enemy of those who support the family values of love, commitment, and mutual care. We don't look like the Waltons, but families come in many varieties, particularly here in Hawai'i, where the practice of loving people of one's own sex was accepted for years and years before the white missionaries came. For this reason, we believe it is especially fitting that Hawai'i be the first state to stop discriminating against same-sex couples who seek to marry." Testimony submitted to Hawai'i House Judiciary Committee, 29 October 1993, O'ahu. I explore the politics among indigenous activists to break through the Western notions of tradition in Goldberg-Hiller (2002, Ch. 5).

39. Testimony of Hardy Spoehr, presented by Myron Thompson, Joint Hearing before the Committee on Indian Affairs United States Senate and the Committee on Resources United States House of Representatives, September 1, 2000, Honolulu, Hawai'i. Serial No. 106–98, Part 5, p. 104. Spoehr, as others in the hearings, is recalling the words attributed to Queen Liliu'okalani when she capitulated to American forces in 1893. She is remembered to have said then, "You must remember never to cease to act because you fear you may fail. The way to lose any earthly kingdom is to be inflexible, intolerant, and prejudicial. Another way is to be too flexible, tolerant of too many wrongs, and without judgement at all. It is a razors edge. It is the width of a blade of pili grass. To gain the kingdom of heaven is to hear what is not said, to see what cannot be seen, and to know the unknowable, that is Aloha."

40. Kanaka Maoli is the name most often used by the indigenous peoples of the islands of Hawai'i. As the issue of naming is frequently at stake in contests over legal recognition, I choose to use this term as a sign of respect and as a reminder of alterity involved in these contests over indigenous civil rights. The terms Hawaiian and Native Hawaiian have legal significance, and I use these terms to indicate accordingly. "Native Hawaiians" are "those who are descendants of the races inhabiting the Hawaiian Islands previous to 1778 [the arrival of Captain Cook] with at least a 50% Hawaiian blood quantum" (Haw. Rev. Stat. @ 10–2). "Hawaiians" or "native Hawaiians" are defined as "those who are descendants of the races inhabiting the Hawaiian Islands previous to 1778 without reference to blood quantum (Haw. Rev. Stat. @ 10 2).

41. Most notable here are the *Mabo* decision in Australia (1992) repudiating the doctrine of terra nullius by which the presence of indigenous peoples was legally erased; the New Zealand Waikato Raupatu Bill (1995) recognizing Maori land titles; and the Canadian establishment of Nunavut as a semi-sovereign territory (1993).

42. That apology reads in part, "The Congress –

(1) on the occasion of the 100th anniversary of the illegal overthrow of the Kingdom of Hawai'i on January 17, 1893, acknowledges the historical significance of this event which resulted in the suppression of the inherent sovereignty of the Native Hawaiian people;
(2) recognizes and commends efforts of reconciliation initiated by the State of Hawai'i and the United Church of Christ with Native Hawaiians;
(3) apologizes to Native Hawaiians on behalf of the people of the United States for the overthrow of the Kingdom of Hawai'i on January 17, 1893 with the participation of

agents and citizens of the United States, and the deprivation of the rights of Native Hawaiians to self-determination;

(4) expresses its commitment to acknowledge the ramifications of the overthrow of the Kingdom of Hawai'i, in order to provide a proper foundation for reconciliation between the United States and the Native Hawaiian people; and

(5) urges the President of the United States to also acknowledge the ramifications of the overthrow of the Kingdom of Hawai'i and to support reconciliation efforts between the United States and the Native Hawaiian people."

43. Hawai'i's dual legal system recognizing distinct civil rights for Kanaka Maoli was judicially constructed soon after statehood. In 1968 in what was the first of a long line of cases acknowledging indigenous land tenure, the Supreme Court unanimously ruled that a landowner could not assert clear title to a fishing pond that lay within an ancient Hawaiian district (ahupua'a) whose modern-day inhabitants were entitled to enjoy ancient rights to access (*Palama v. Sheehan* 50 Haw 298, 440 P.2d 94 (1968)). See also *McBride Sugar Co. v. Robinson* 54 Haw. 174, 504 P.2d 1330, aff'd on rehearing, 55 Haw. 260, 517 P.2d 26 (1973), appeal dismissed for want of jurisdiction and cert. denied, 417 U.S. 962 (1974) (accepting ancient water rights in the determination of modern access and use); *In re Ashford*, 50 Haw. 314, 440 P.2d 76 (1968) (holding that shoreline property had to conform to ancient notions that presumed rights to beach access for all). In an important opinion delivered in 1995, the Hawai'i Supreme Court ruled that a group of Native Hawaiians had the right to intervene in a private developer's application for a use permit to construct a resort hotel on the island of Hawai'i. After an extensive review of the legal, constitutional, and diplomatic history of the Hawaiian islands, the court generalized the principle to the law of private property: "the western concept of exclusivity is not universally applicable in Hawai'i" *Public Access Shoreline Hawai'i v. Hawai'i County Planning Commission* 79 Hawai'i 425, 903 P.2d 1246 (1995).

44. 528 US 495, 524 (2000).

45. Ibid., @ 547.

46. Ibid., @ 546.

47. *Honolulu Advertiser*, February 28, 2000:A-8.

48. S. 2899, H. R. 4904, 106th Congress 2d Session, 2000.

49. Article XII, Section 7 of the Hawai'i Constitution heralds this commitment: "The State reaffirms and shall protect all rights, customarily and traditionally exercised for subsistence, cultural and religious purposes and possessed by ahupua'a tenants who are descendants of native Hawaiians who inhabited the Hawaiian Islands prior to 1778, subject to the right of the State to regulate such rights. [Add Const Con 1978 and election Nov 7, 1978.]

50. Testimony of H. William Burgess, Joint Hearing before the Committee on Indian Affairs United States Senate and the Committee on Resources United States House of Representatives, September 1, 2000, Honolulu, Hawai'i. Serial No. 106–98, Part 5, p. 107.

51. Testimony of Kenneth Conklin, Joint Hearing before the Committee on Indian Affairs United States Senate and the Committee on Resources United States House of Representatives, August 30, 2000, Honolulu, Hawai'i. Serial No. 106–98, Part 3, p. 95.

52. Ibid., p. 94.

53. Testimony of George Theis, Joint Hearing before the Committee on Indian Affairs United States Senate and the Committee on Resources United States House of Representatives, August 30, 2000, Honolulu, Hawai'i. Serial No. 106–98, Part 3, p. 133.

54. Testimony of H. William Burgess, Joint Hearing before the Committee on Indian Affairs United States Senate and the Committee on Resources United States House of Representatives, September 1, 2000, Honolulu, Hawai'i. Serial No. 106–98, Part 5, p. 108.

55. Testimony of George Theis, Joint Hearing before the Committee on Indian Affairs United States Senate and the Committee on Resources United States House of Representatives, September 1, 2000, Honolulu, Hawai'i. Serial No. 106–98, Part 3, p. 135.

56. Derrida writes that ontopology is an "axiomatics linking indissociably the ontological value of present-being [*on*] to its *situation*, to the stable and presentable determination of a locality, the *topos* of territory, native soil, city" (1994: p. 82).

57. Testimony of Daviana McGregor, Joint Hearing before the Committee on Indian Affairs United States Senate and the Committee on Resources United States House of Representatives, August 29, 2000, Honolulu, Hawai'i. Serial No. 106–98, Part 2, p. 94.

58. Testimony of Lilikala Kame'eleihiwa, Joint Hearing before the Committee on Indian Affairs United States Senate and the Committee on Resources United States House of Representatives, August 30, 2000, Honolulu, Hawai'i. Serial No. 106–98, Part 3, p. 126. This argument also led some to reject the Akaka Bill because it would not restore recognition of these treaties.

59. Testimony of James Manaku, Sr., Joint Hearing before the Committee on Indian Affairs United States Senate and the Committee on Resources United States House of Representatives, August 29, 2000, Honolulu, Hawai'i. Serial No. 106–98, Part 2, p. 102.

60. Testimony of Lilikala Kame'eleihiwa, Joint Hearing before the Committee on Indian Affairs United States Senate and the Committee on Resources United States House of Representatives, August 30, 2000, Honolulu, Hawai'i. Serial No. 106–98, Part 3, p. 129.

61. Testimony of Ululani Beirne, Joint Hearing before the Committee on Indian Affairs United States Senate and the Committee on Resources United States House of Representatives, August 31, 2000, Honolulu, Hawai'i. Serial No. 106–98, Part 4, p. 94.

62. The voyaging canoes which now number about a dozen throughout the Pacific are often credited with sparking the resurgence of Polynesian identity. They have been accurately sailed without the aid of modern navigation instruments across thousands of miles of open ocean and have proved that Polynesians historically possessed the skills to travel at will within a triangle bordered by Aotearoa (New Zealand), Rapa Nui (Easter Island), and Hawai'i. Contrary to Missionary stories that Polynesians accidentally washed up on Pacific islands, these recent voyages have demonstrated that Polynesians were likely the most accomplished sailors in the world, and certainly the equal of Captain Cook at the time of his (accidental) arrival.

63. Testimony of Leiliwin Mahuiki-Denson, Joint Hearing before the Committee on Indian Affairs United States Senate and the Committee on Resources United States House of Representatives, August 28, 2000, Honolulu, Hawai'i. Serial No. 106–98, Part 1, p. 118.

64. Testimony of Beadie Kanahele Dawson, Joint Hearing before the Committee on Indian Affairs United States Senate and the Committee on Resources United States House of Representatives, August 30, 2000, Honolulu, Hawai'i. Serial No. 106–98, Part 3, p. 89.

65. Testimony of Na'unanikina'u Kamali'i, Joint Hearing before the Committee on Indian Affairs United States Senate and the Committee on Resources United States House of Representatives, August 29, 2000, Honolulu, Hawai'i. Serial No. 106–98, Part 2, p. 109.

66. Testimony of Randy Rego, Joint Hearing before the Committee on Indian Affairs United States Senate and the Committee on Resources United States House of Representatives, September 1, 2000, Honolulu, Hawai'i. Serial No. 106–98, Part 5, p. 134.

67. Testimony of Adrian Kamali'i, Joint Hearing before the Committee on Indian Affairs United States Senate and the Committee on Resources United States House of Representatives, September 1, 2000, Honolulu, Hawai'i. Serial No. 106–98, Part 5, p. 90.

68. Testimony of Kai'opua Fyfe, Joint Hearing before the Committee on Indian Affairs United States Senate and the Committee on Resources United States House of Representatives, August 28, 2000, Honolulu, Hawai'i. Serial No. 106–98, Part 1, p. 109.

69. Statement of Senator Inouye, Hearing before the Committee on Indian Affairs, United States Senate, September 14, 2000, Washington, D.C., p. 42.

70. Testimony of Jeff Kapele, Joint Hearing before the Committee on Indian Affairs United States Senate and the Committee on Resources United States House of Representatives, September 1, 2000, Honolulu, Hawai'i. Serial No. 106–98, Part 5, p. 129.

71. Testimony of Marion Kelly, Joint Hearing before the Committee on Indian Affairs United States Senate and the Committee on Resources United States House of Representatives, August 29, 2000, Honolulu, Hawai'i. Serial No. 106–98, Part 2, p. 108.

72. Ibid., p. 107.

73. The analogy of the Akaka Bill to "genocide" is repeated at least 20 times in the testimony.

74. Testimony of Jon Van Dyke, Joint Hearing before the Committee on Indian Affairs United States Senate and the Committee on Resources United States House of Representatives, September 1, 2000, Honolulu, Hawai'i. Serial No. 106–98, Part 5, p. 118.

75. Testimony of Russell Means and Glen Morris read by Roy Dahlin, Joint Hearing before the Committee on Indian Affairs United States Senate and the Committee on Resources United States House of Representatives, August 31, 2000, Honolulu, Hawai'i. Serial No. 106–98, Part 4, p. 115.

76. Testimony of Lela Hubbard, Joint Hearing before the Committee on Indian Affairs United States Senate and the Committee on Resources United States House of Representatives, August 30, 2000, Honolulu, Hawai'i. Serial No. 106–98, Part 3, p. 142.

77. Testimony of Jeff Kapele, Joint Hearing before the Committee on Indian Affairs United States Senate and the Committee on Resources United States House of Representatives, September 1, 2000, Honolulu, Hawai'i. Serial No. 106–98, Part 5, p. 130.

78. Statement of Rep. Neil Abercrombie, Joint Hearing before the Committee on Indian Affairs United States Senate and the Committee on Resources United States House of Representatives, August 28, 2000, Honolulu, Hawai'i. Serial No. 106–98, Part 1, p. 74.

79. Testimony of Beadie Kanahele Dawson, Joint Hearing before the Committee on Indian Affairs United States Senate and the Committee on Resources United States House of Representatives, August 30, 2000, Honolulu, Hawai'i. Serial No. 106–98, Part 3, p. 88.

80. Testimony of Kawika Cutcher, Joint Hearing before the Committee on Indian Affairs United States Senate and the Committee on Resources United States House of Representatives, August 28, 2000, Honolulu, Hawai'i. Serial No. 106–98, Part 1, p. 111.

81. Testimony of Raynard Soon, Joint Hearing before the Committee on Indian Affairs United States Senate and the Committee on Resources United States House of Representatives, August 30, 2000, Honolulu, Hawai'i. Serial No. 106–98, Part 3, p. 83.

82. Testimony of Leiliwin Mahuiki-Denson, Joint Hearing before the Committee on Indian Affairs United States Senate and the Committee on Resources United States House of Representatives, August 28, 2000, Honolulu, Hawai'i. Serial No. 106–98, Part 1, p. 119.

83. Testimony of Jeff Kapele, Joint Hearing before the Committee on Indian Affairs United States Senate and the Committee on Resources United States House of Representatives, September 1, 2000, Honolulu, Hawai'i. Serial No. 106–98, Part 5, p. 127.

84. Statement of Senator Akaka, Joint Hearing before the Committee on Indian Affairs United States Senate and the Committee on Resources United States House of Representatives, August 28, 2000, Honolulu, Hawai'i. Serial No. 106–98, Part 1, p. 76.

85. "That law is called post-lininium. It states that the conqueror must restore the conqueree to its full potential and enforce that country's law, not the conqueror's law. It is page 313 in the Law of Nations." Testimony of Sam Kaleiliki, Joint Hearing before the Committee on Indian Affairs United States Senate and the Committee on Resources United States House of Representatives, August 31, 2000, Honolulu, Hawai'i. Serial No. 106–98, Part 4, p. 103. This rule of international law can be found in (de Vattel & Chitty 1839: Book III, Ch. 14 Sec. 204).

86. Testimony of Solomon Naluai, M. D., Joint Hearing before the Committee on Indian Affairs United States Senate and the Committee on Resources United States House of Representatives, August 31, 2000, Honolulu, Hawai'i. Serial No. 106–98, Part 4, p. 78.

87. Testimony of Kekuni Blaisdell, Joint Hearing before the Committee on Indian Affairs United States Senate and the Committee on Resources United States House of Representatives, August 30, 2000, Honolulu, Hawai'i. Serial No. 106–98, Part 3, p. 123.

88. Testimony of Harold Mehuela, Joint Hearing before the Committee on Indian Affairs United States Senate and the Committee on Resources United States House of Representatives, September 1, 2000, Honolulu, Hawai'i. Serial No. 106–98, Part 5, p. 111.

89. Testimony of Kekane Pa, Joint Hearing before the Committee on Indian Affairs United States Senate and the Committee on Resources United States House of Representatives, August 28, 2000, Honolulu, Hawai'i. Serial No. 106–98, Part 1, p. 103. emphasis added.

90. Testimony of Michael Kahikina, Joint Hearing before the Committee on Indian Affairs United States Senate and the Committee on Resources United States House of Representatives, August 29, 2000, Honolulu, Hawai'i. Serial No. 106–98, Part 2, p. 98. emphasis added

91. Their idols are silver and gold, the work of human hands.
They have mouths but do not speak, eyes but do not see.
They have ears but do not hear, noses but do not smell.
They have hands but do not feel, feet but do not walk, and no sound rises from their throats.
Their makers shall be like them, all who trust in them. (Verses 4–8).

92. Lévinas (1999, p. 102).

93. Lesbian is a term rarely used colloquially among local people in Hawai'i. Same-sex relationships were commonly acknowledged in pre-contact Hawai'i, and continue today under many diverse forms. See Kame'eleihiwa (1992), Morris (1996).

94. There is some interesting evidence that this is happening within some quarters of the indigenous sovereignty movement. See the discussion in Goldberg-Hiller (2002, Ch. 5).

95. See Campbell (1998, 176ff), Campbell and Shapiro (1999), Derrida (1978), Shapiro (1999).

ACKNOWLEDGMENTS

I gratefully acknowledge Neal Milner whose discussions with me about this project, and whose joint writing with me on related issues of Hawai'i rights politics have been instrumental in my thinking. A special thanks goes to my colleague Noenoe Silva whose commentary and perspectives on indigenous politics have been invaluable. I also wish to thank Austin Sarat and the faculty and study participants at a seminar at Amherst College for their engaging discussion, suggestions, and criticism in May, 2002, where an earlier draft of this article was presented. Finally, I thank the anonymous reviewers for *Studies in Law Politics* for their generosity in sharing their insights and reactions to this piece. I have benefited immensely from these scholarly exchanges, but my conclusions, of course, remain my own. This paper is dedicated to my godfather, Mayer Zald.

REFERENCES

Anderson, B. (1983). *Imagined communities: reflections on the origin and spread of nationalism*. London: Verso Press.

Ashley, R. (1988). Untying the sovereign state: A double reading of the anarchy problematique. *Millenium: Journal of International Studies, 17*(2), 227–262.

Bell, D. (1978). The referendum: democracy's barrier to racial equality. *Washington Law Review, 54*, 1–29.

Berlant, L. G. (1997). *The queen of America goes to Washington city: essays on sex and citizenship, Series Q*. Durham, NC: Duke University Press.

Blasius, M. (1992). An ethos of lesbian and gay existence. *Political Theory, 20*, 642.

Bordo, S. (1993). *Unbearable weight: feminism, western culture, and the body*. Berkeley: University of California Press.

Bourdieu, P. (1987). The force of law. *Hastings Law Journal, 38*, 201.

Bravmann, S. (1997). *Queer fictions of the past: history, culture, and difference, Cambridge cultural social studies*. Cambridge, U.K.; New York, NY: Cambridge University Press.

Brown, W. (1995). Wounded attachments: Late modern oppositional political formations. In: J. Rajchman (Ed.), *The Identity in Question*. New York: Routledge.

Burggreaeve, R. (1981). The ethical basis for a humane society according to Emmanuel Lévinas. *Ephemerides Theologicae Lovanienses, 57*, 5–57.

Burggreaeve, R. (1999). Violence and the vulnerable face of the other: The vision of Emmanuel Lévinas on moral evil and our responsibility. *Journal of Social Philosophy, 30*, 29–45.

Burlein, A. (2002). *Lift high the cross: Where white supremacy and the christian right converge*. Durham, NC: Duke University Press.

Butler, J. P. (1990). *Gender trouble*. New York: Routledge.

Butler, J. P. (1996). *Excitable speech*. New York: Routledge.

Campbell, D. (1992). *Writing security: United States foreign policy and the politics of identity*. Minneapolis: University of Minnesota Press.

Campbell, D. (1998). *National deconstruction: violence, identity, and justice in Bosnia*. Minneapolis: University of Minnesota Press.
Campbell, D., & Shapiro, M. J. (1999). *Moral spaces: rethinking ethics and world politics*. Minneapolis: University of Minnesota Press.
Clarke, E. O. (2000). *Virtuous vice: homoeroticism and the public sphere, Series Q*. Durham [NC]: Duke University Press.
Connolly, W. E. (1991). *Identity/difference: democratic negotiations of political paradox*. Ithaca, NY: Cornell University Press.
Constable, M. (1993). Sovereignty and governmentality in Modern American immigration law. *Studies in Law, Politics, and Society, 13*, 249–271.
Cooper, D. (1998). *Governing out of order: space, law, and the politics of belonging*. London; New York: Rivers Oram Press; Distributed in the USA by New York University Press.
Cornell, D. (1992). *The philosophy of the limit*. New York: Routledge, Chapman and Hall, Inc.
Crenshaw, K. (1991). Mapping the margins: Intersectionality, identity politics, and violence against women of color. *Stanford Law Review, 43*(6), 1241.
Critchley, S. (1999). *The ethics of deconstruction: Derrida and Lévinas* (2nd ed.). West Lafayette, IN: Purdue University Press.
Darian-Smith, E. (1999). *Bridging divides: the Channel Tunnel and English legal identity in the new Europe*. Berkeley: University of California Press.
Darian-Smith, E., & Fitzpatrick, P. (1999). *Laws of the postcolonial, law, meaning, and violence*. Ann Arbor: University of Michigan Press.
Davies, M. (1999). Queer property, queer persons: Self-ownership and beyond. *Social & Legal Studies, 8*(3), 327–352.
Derrida, J. (1978). *Writing and difference*. Chicago: University of Chicago Press.
Derrida, J. (1994). *Specters of Marx: The state of the debt, the work of mourning, and the new international*. New York: Routledge.
Dillon, M. (1995). Sovereignty and governmentality: From the problematics of the "New World Order" to the ethical problematic of the world order. *Alternatives, 20*, 323–368.
Ely, J. H. (1980). *Democracy and distrust: A theory of judicial review*. Cambridge, MA: Harvard University Press.
Evans, D. (1993). *Sexual citizenship: The material construction of sexualities*. London: Routledge.
Ewick, P., & Silbey, S. (1992). Conformity, contestation, and resistance: An account of legal consciousness. *New England Law Review, 26*, 731–749.
Fantasia, R. (1988). *Cultures of solidarity: Consciousness, action and contemporary American workers*. Berkeley: University of California Press.
Ferguson, K., & Turnbull, P. (1999). *Oh say can you see: The semiotics of the military in Hawai'i*. Minneapolis: University of Minnesota Press.
Fitzpatrick, P. (1999). Law's pervasion. Chicago: Law & Society Association Annual Meeting.
Foucault, M. (1977). *Language, counter-memory, practice: Selected essays and interviews*. Ithaca: Cornell University Press.
Foucault, M. (1980). *The history of sexuality, An introduction*. In: R. T. Hurley (Ed.), Vol. 1. New York: Random House [imprint: Vintage].
Foucault, M. (1986 [1967]). Of other spaces. *Diacritics, 16*, 22–27.
Foucault, M. (1991). Governmentality. In: G. Burchell, C. Gordon & P. Miller (Eds), *The Foucault Effect: Studies in Governmentality*. Chicago: University of Chicago Press.
Gamble, B. (1997). Putting civil rights to a popular vote. *American Journal of Political Science, 41*(1), 245–269.

Gamson, J. (1996). Must identity movements self-destruct? A queer dilemma. In: S. Seidman (Ed.), *Queer Theory/Sociology*. Cambridge, MA: Blackwell Publishers.

Gerstmann, E. (1999). *The constitutional underclass: Gays, lesbians, and the failure of class-based equal protection*. Chicago: University of Chicago Press.

Goemans, J. (2000). Rice decision will help return Hawai'i to all of its citizens. *Honolulu Advertiser* (27 February), B-1.

Goldberg, S. (1994). Gay rights through the looking glass: Politics, morality and the trial of Colorado's Amendment 2. *Fordham Urban Law Journal*, *XXI*, 1057.

Goldberg-Hiller, J. (2002). *The limits to union: Same-sex marriage and the politics of civil rights*. Ann Arbor: University of Michigan Press.

Goldberg-Hiller, J., & Milner, N. (2001). Rights as excess: Understanding special rights. Paper read at Law and Society Association Annual Meeting, at Budapest, Hungary.

Herman, D. (1994). *Rights of passage*. Toronto: University of Toronto Press.

Herman, D. (1997). *The anti-gay agenda: Orthodox vision and the Christian right*. Chicago: University of Chicago Press.

Herzog, A. (2002). Is liberalism "All we Need"? Lévinas's politics of surplus. *Political Theory*, *30*(2), 204–227.

Hobbes, T. (1968 [1651]). *Leviathan*. Baltimore, MD: Penguin.

Kame'eleihiwa, L. (1992). *Native land and foreign desires – Ko Hawai'i 'Aina a me na koi puumake a ka Po'e Haole*. Honolulu: Bishop Museum Press.

Keen, L., & Goldberg, S. (1998). *Strangers to the law*. Ann Arbor: University of Michigan Press.

Krishna, S. (1999). *Postcolonial insecurities: India, Sri Lanka, and the question of nationhood, Borderlines*, Vol. 15. Minneapolis, MN: University of Minnesota Press.

Kwan, P. (1997). Intersections of race, ethnicity, class, gender and sexual orientation: Jeffrey Dahmer and the cosynthesis of categories. *Hastings Law Journal*, *48*, 1257–1292.

Lévinas, E. (1969). *Totality and infinity: an essay on exteriority*. Pittsburgh: Duquesne University Press.

Lévinas, E. (1987). *Time and the other*. Pittsburgh, PA: Duquesne University Press.

Lévinas, E. (1991). *Otherwise than being, or, beyond essence*. Dordrecht: Kluwer Academic.

Lévinas, E. (1999). *Alterity and transcendence, European perspectives*. New York: Columbia University Press.

Marshall, G. (1983). Some remarks on the study of working-class consciousness. *Politics & Society*, *12*, 263.

Marx, K. (1977). Preface to a critique of political economy. In: D. McLellan (Ed.), *Karl Marx: Selected Writings*. Oxford: Oxford University Press.

Marx, K. (1977 [1844]). On the Jewish question. In: D. McLellan (Ed.), *Karl Marx Selected Writings* Oxford: Oxford University Press.

Massaro, T. M. (1996). Gay rights, thick and thin. *Stanford Law Review*, *49*, 45.

McCann, M. (1994). *Rights at work: Pay equity reform and the politics of legal mobilization*. Chicago: University of Chicago Press.

Merry, S. (1998). Law, culture, and cultural appropriation. *Yale Journal of Law and The Humanities*, *10*, 575–603.

Merry, S. (2000). *Colonizing Hawai'i: The cultural power of law*. Princeton: Princeton University Press.

Milner, N. (1986). The dilemmas of legal mobilization: Ideologies and strategies of mental patient liberation. *Law & Policy*, *8*, 105–129.

Morris, R. (1996). Configuring the bo(u)nds of marriage: The implications of Hawaiian culture and values for the debate about homogamy. *Yale Journal of Law the Humanities*, *8*, 105–159.

Osorio, J. K. (2001). What kine Hawaiian are you? A Mo'olelo about nationhood, race, history, and the contemporary sovereignty movement in Hawai'i. *The Contemporary Pacific*, *13*(2), 359–379.

Patton, C. (1993). Tremble, Hetero Swine! In: M. Warner (Ed.), *Fear of a Queer Planet: Queer Politics and Social Theory*. Minneapolis: University of Minnesota Press.

Patton, C. (1995). Refiguring social space. In: L. Nicholson & S. Seidman (Eds), *Social Postmodernism: Beyond Identity Politics*. Cambridge: Cambridge University Press.

Patton, C. (1997). Queer space/God's space: Counting down to the apocalypse. *Rethinking Marxism*, *9*(2), 1–23.

Peperzak, A. T., & Lévinas, E. (1993). *To the other: an introduction to the philosophy of Emmanuel Lévinas, Purdue University series in the history of philosophy*. West Lafayette, IN: Purdue University Press.

Phelan, S. (1999). Bodies, passions and citizenship. *Critical Review of International Social and Political Philosophy*, *2*(1), 56–79.

Ruiz, E. (1999). In pursuit of the "Body Politic": Ethics, spirituality, and diaspora. *Transnational Law and Contemporary Problems*, *9*, 633–652.

Rupert, M. (1995). *Producing hegemony*. Cambridge: Cambridge University Press.

Schacter, J. (1994). The gay civil rights debate in the States: Decoding the discourse of equivalents. *Harvard Civil Rights – Civil Liberties Law Review*, *29*, 283.

Schacter, J. (1997). Skepticism, culture and the gay civil rights debate in a post-civil-rights era. *Harvard Law Review*, *110*, 684.

Scheingold, S. (1974). *The politics of rights*. New Haven: Yale University Press.

Seidman, S. (1997). *Difference troubles: queering social theory and sexual politics, Cambridge cultural social studies*. Cambridge; New York: Cambridge University Press.

Shapiro, M. (1997). *Violent cartographies: Mapping cultures of war*. Minneapolis: University of Minnesota Press.

Shapiro, M. (1999). The ethics of encounter: Unreading, unmapping the Imperium. In: D. Campbell & M. Shapiro (Eds), *Moral Spaces: Rethinking Ethics and World Politics*. Minneapolis: University of Minnesota Press.

Silverstein, H. (1996). *Unleashing rights: law, meaning, and the animal rights movement, Law, meaning, and violence*. Ann Arbor: University of Michigan Press.

Simmons, W. P. (1999). The third: Lévinas' theoretical move from an-archical ethics to the realm of justice and politics. *Philosophy & Social Criticism*, *25*(6), 83–104.

Soguk, N. (1999). *States and strangers: refugees and displacements of statecraft, Borderlines*, Vol. 11. Minneapolis: University of Minnesota Press.

Stychin, C. (1995). *Law's desire: Sexuality and the limits of justice*. London: Routledge.

Stychin, C. (1998). *A nation by rights: national cultures, sexual identity politics, and the discourse of rights, queer politics, queer theories*. Philadelphia, PA: Temple University Press.

Stychin, C. (1999). Dis-integrating sexuality: Citizenship, space and the European Union. Paper read at Law & Society Association Annual Meeting, at Chicago.

Thompson, E. P. (1975). *Whigs and hunters: the origin of the Black Act*. London: Allen Lane.

Turner, B. (1984). *The body and society: Explorations in social theory*. Oxford: Basil Blackwell.

de Vattel, E., & Chitty, J. (1839). *The law of nations; or, Principles of the law of nature, applied to the conduct and affairs of nations and sovereigns* (5th American ed.). Philadelphia: T. & J. W. Johnson.

Walker, R. B. J. (1993). *Inside/Outside: International relations as political theory*. Cambridge: Cambridge University Press.

Warner, M. (1992). The mass public and the mass subject. In: C. Calhoun (Ed.), *Habermas and the Public Sphere*. Cambridge, MA: MIT Press.

Wildman, S. (1995). Language and silence: Making systems of privilege visible. *University of Santa Clara Law Review*, *35*, 881–906.

Zemans, F. (1983). Legal mobilization: The neglected role of the law in the political system. *American Political Science Review*, *77*, 690–703.

www.ingramcontent.com/pod-product-compliance
Ingram Content Group UK Ltd.
Pitfield, Milton Keynes, MK11 3LW, UK
UKHW020843290926
15470UKWH00004B/1524

9 780762 310159